The Word Within the Word

2

STUDENT MANUAL

Revised Third Edition

August 2012

Michael Clay Thompson

Royal Fireworks Press
Unionville, New York

For my mom,
Mary Murphy.

Royal Fireworks Press
First Avenue, PO Box 399
Unionville, NY 10988-0399
TEL: (845) 726-4444
FAX: (845) 726-3824
website: rfwp.com; email: mail@rfwp.com

ISBN: 978-0-88092-692-8

Printed and bound in the United States of America on acid-free, recycled
paper using soy-based inks and environmentally friendly cover coating
by the Royal Fireworks Printing Company of Unionville, New York.

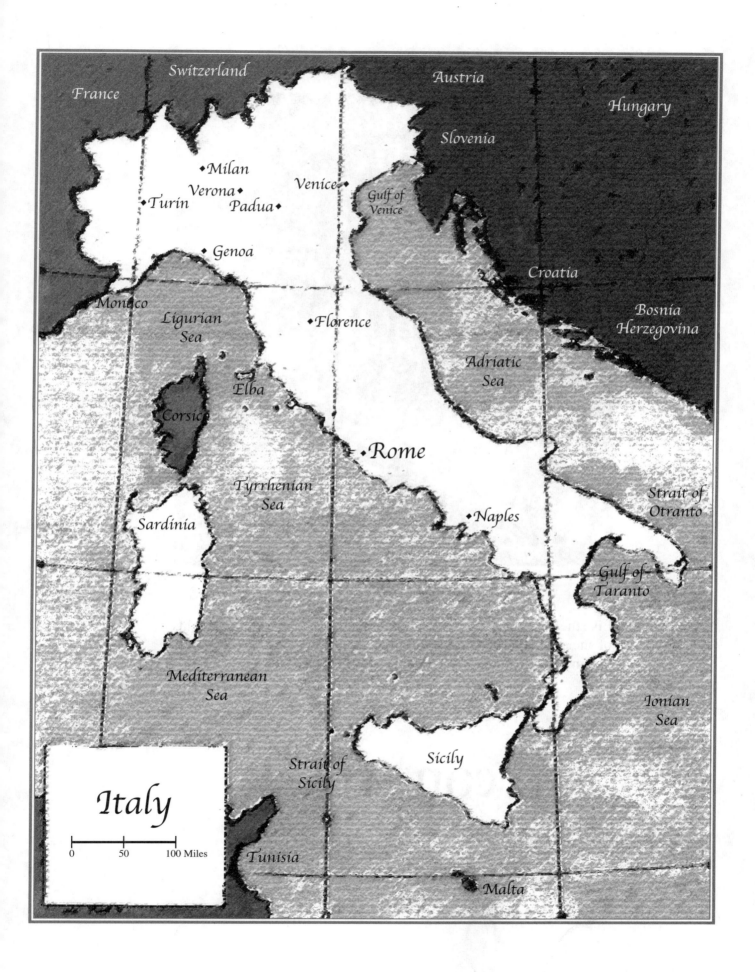

France
Switzerland
Austria
Hungary
Slovenia
Milan
Verona
Padua
Venice
Gulf of
Venice
Turin
Croatia
Genoa
Bosnia
Herzegovina
Monaco
Ligurian
Sea
Florence
Elba
Adriatic
Sea
Corsica
Rome
Strait of
Otranto
Tyrrhenian
Sea
Naples
Sardinia
Gulf of
Taranto
Mediterranean
Sea
Ionian
Sea
Sicily
Strait of
Sicily
Italy
Tunisia
Malta

0   50   100 Miles

Like the rocky rubble of ancient Rome and Athens, the word fragments of ancient Latin and Greece are still here, and we use these fragments to **construct** the words of modern English.

construct

• mal	(bad)	malapropism	• non	(not)	nonplussed
• post	(after)	postlude	• *archy*	(government)	hierarchy
• *port*	(carry)	portly	• inter	(between)	interdiction
• dict	(say)	benediction	• vid	(look)	vide
• omni	(all)	omnibus	• *mono*	(one)	monolithic
• *lith*	(rock)	monolithic	• pond	(weight)	imponderable
• bene	(good)	benediction	• in	(not)	incredulous
• cred	(believe)	incredulous	• sci	(know)	omniscient
• *neo*	(new)	neophyte	• *phyte*	(plant)	neophyte
• uni	(one)	unilateral	• lat	(side)	unilateral

malapropism (ludicrous misuse of a word) His malapropisms amused us.

nonplussed (perplexed) He was nonplussed by the unexpected question.

postlude (concluding section) It was a tragic postlude to her long life.

hierarchy (ranking) There must be a hierarchy of values.

portly (stout) The portly doorman carried himself gracefully.

interdiction (prohibition) The judge's interdiction stopped the construction.

vide (see) Vide Johnson's definition of politics on page 35.

omnibus (covering many things) The omnibus legislative bill passed.

monolithic (massive and uniform) The monolithic totalitarian society revolted.

imponderable (difficult to ponder) He tried to weigh the imponderable issue.

•   •   •

benediction (blessing) The grandfather's benediction made them happy.

incredulous (not believing)   Her incredulous face revealed her mistrust.

omniscient (all-knowing) The story was told from an omniscient point of view.

neophyte (beginner) The graduate was a neophyte in the business world.

unilateral (one-sided) The unilateral decision required no conference.

As Used by Sir Walter Scott in *Ivanhoe*

	After	these	**neophytes**	came	a	guard	of	warders.
Parts of Speech:	prep.	adj.	**n.**	v.	adj.	n.	prep.	n.
Parts of Sentence:				AVP		subject		
Phrases:	-----prepositional phrase-----					--prep. phrase--		
Clauses:	--------------------------------independent clause----------------------------------							
	one independent clause, a simple declarative sentence							

Here Sir Walter Scott uses the plural common noun *neophytes* as the object of a preposition, where the prepositional phrase modifies the verb. Notice how the subject and verb are reversed! The word *these* is a demonstrative adjective here. *AVP* means action verb predicate.

Pronunciation

malapropism	mal a PRO pism	**monolithic**	mono LITH ic
nonplussed	non PLUST	**imponderable**	im POND er ah ble
postlude	POST lood	**benediction**	beneh DICT shun
hierarchy	HI er arky	**incredulous**	in KRED ju luss
portly	PORT lee	**omniscient**	om NIH shunt
interdiction	in ter DICT shun	**neophyte**	NEE oh fite
vide	VIE dee	**unilateral**	yoo nih LAT eral
omnibus	OM nih buss		

Spanish Cognates

English and Spanish are very close relatives, as we see in these cognates:

incredulous	incrédulo	**omniscient**	omnisciente
interdiction	interdicción	**omnibus**	ómnibus
neophyte	neófito	**benediction**	bendición
monolithic	monolítico	**hierarchy**	jerarquía
unilateral	unilateral	**imponderable**	imponderable

6

1. A **Micropoem**: When we say that a beginner is a **neophyte**, we are comparing the beginner to a new (neo) plant (phyte) that has just pushed through the surface of the ground. In other words, to call a person a neophyte is to use a metaphor—only we often become so accustomed to using a word in its metaphorical sense that we forget that we are even doing so. The word **neophyte** is also a good example of the way we borrow words from various fields (in this case botany) for more general usage.

2. Why does the adjective **nonplussed** mean perplexed? In the Latin it literally means no (non) more (plus). It is a plea for mercy! Please, no more, I am confused enough already! By the way, **nonplussed** is also sometimes spelled **nonplused**.

3. The adjective **monolithic** can refer to something made of stone, such as a large column formed from a single **stone**—as are some of the stones at Stonehenge. But we also use the word **monolithic** to refer to human societies. In 1989 Chinese students, massed in Tiananmen Square to protest for democratic reform, learned through bloodshed that their government intended to keep China monolithic: massively, totally uniform.

4. The noun **malapropism** is based on the character Mrs. Malaprop, created by Richard Brinsley Sheridan in his 1775 comedy, *The Rivals*. It was Mrs. Malaprop's habit to misuse words in ridiculous fashion, usually confusing two words that sounded similar. Sheridan no doubt formed Mrs. Malaprop's name from the French *malapropos* meaning "badly suited to the purpose."

5. The verb **vide** is sometimes pronounced *weeday,* and sometimes *vyedee*, the latter being probably more common. It is rare in speech but is often used in formal academic writing to direct the reader's attention to a specific passage.

6. Please do not confuse the adjectives **incredible** (unbelievable) and **incredulous** (full of disbelief). If you witness an incredible phenomenon, such as a tornado, you will have an incredulous expression on your face.

7. A **Classic Word**: the adjective **portly** is often seen in the classics. In 1596 Shakespeare used it in *Romeo and Juliet*: "'A bears him like a portly gentleman." (The *A* in Shakespeare's sentence is not a typo; it was shorthand for he.) Almost three hundred years later, in 1876, Mark Twain used portly to modify the same noun: "a fine, portly, middle-aged gentleman." Barrie described "two **portly** figures" in *Peter Pan*. In *Lord Jim* (1900), Joseph Conrad described a man "well set up, portly, and of conquering mien." But the most fun to be had with portly was by that American genius, Herman Melville, who used portly to describe—what else—the whale! "The Fin-back," said Melville with his distinguished tongue in cheek, "resembles the right whale, but is of a less portly girth." The sperm whale, according to Melville, was also portly. Even the words themselves that Melville applied to the whale seemed to him to be necessarily portly: "Applied to any other creature than the Leviathan—to an ant or a flea—such portly terms might justly be deemed unwarrantably grandiloquent."

In each case below, one of the choices was really the word used by the author in the sentence provided. All of the choices can be found in the example words on the first page of this lesson. Your challenge is to decide which word the author used. This is not a test; it is more like a game, because more than one word choice may work perfectly well. See if you can use your sensitivity and intuition to guess correctly which word the author used. You may need a dictionary.

1. **From Herman Melville's *Billy Budd***

    He was _____, evincing a confusion.
    a. omnibus
    b. monolithic
    c. nonplussed
    d. omniscient

2. **From Herman Melville's *Moby Dick***

    What things real are there, but _____ thoughts?
    a. omnibus
    b. imponderable
    c. incredulous
    d. unilateral

3. **From Joseph Heller's *Catch-22***

    His ruddy _____ face softened with amusement.
    a. incredulous
    b. portly
    c. nonplussed
    d. monolithic

4. **From E.L. Doctorow's *Ragtime***

    He talked incessantly in his European accent, with _____ he himself ... laughed over.
    a. malapropisms
    b. imponderables
    c. neophytes
    d. benedictions

5. **From John Milton's *Paradise Lost***

    Sternly he pronounced the rigid _____.
    a. hierarchy
    b. postlude
    c. interdiction
    d. benediction

Though it is a good thing to have an expansive vocabulary, it is not a good thing to abuse that vocabulary by writing abstruse, verbose, sesquipedalian sentences. Those who overuse their vocabularies often do so at the expense of clarity.   Translate the following showy, verbose, ponderous passage into graceful, direct English. Do not use slang, but do use words that seem familiar and comfortable.

UPON   HEARING   the   omniscient   judge   issue   his imponderable interdiction against omnibus legislation and monolithic government, the nonplussed, portly neophyte unilaterally pronounced a benediction, which included the following malapropism: "I have not begun to postlude remarks about such matters." This sentence formed a condign postlude to the day's events.

monolithic

Reading Comprehension

1. In Translation 31, which of the following best expresses the main idea?
    A. Most judges do not know what they are talking about.
    B. Powerful governments need to be restrained by the people.
    C. A beginner was pleased that the judge stood up to big government.
    D. It is important to choose your words precisely.

2. The author's attitude in Translation 31 is best described as:
    A. The day's events had been ridiculous.
    B. Judges deserve more respect than they get.
    C. The neophyte should have kept quiet.
    D. The day's events had been important and meaningful.

Analogies

3. **BENEDICTION : INTERDICTION ::**
    A. order : command
    B. blessing : judge
    C. Pope : judge
    D. church : prohibition

4. **IMPONDERABLE : NONPLUSSED ::**
    A. confusing : confused
    B. heavy : more
    C. impressive : noncombatant
    D. perplexed : difficult to ponder

Antonyms

5. **INCREDULOUS :**
    A. incredible
    B. credulity
    C. omniscient
    D. gullible

6. **OMNIBUS :**
    A. taxicab
    B. narrow
    C. monolithic
    D. unilateral

benediction

synthesis

With which other word in List 31 do you think the adjective **nonplussed** has the most in common? Explain why you think the two words have something in common. Remember that your connection can be in any category at all.

analysis

Imagine that you decided to organize your own values into a **hierarchy** so that you knew what was really important to you. To begin, you would sort your values into categories in order to make better sense of them. What would be some of the main categories of values you would use?

divergence

List as many things as you can that might be described as **imponderable**. Remember to keep listing after the easy answers are exhausted so that you find some original and creative answers.

convergence

If you had to live in a **monolithic** society in which a tyrannical government demanded mass, uniform adherence to its ideas, which society would you choose? You may select any society you can think of, ancient or modern, fictional or historical. Explain your choice.

application

Use five or more of the words in List 31 to describe something or to make a statement.

evaluation

What criteria might a judge use to determine whether or not to issue an **interdiction** against building a toxic waste site in a populated area? List at least five criteria and then rank them in order of importance.

ethics

Imagine that a strange virus was slowly giving you the power of **omniscience**, but that you could still choose not to know certain things if you wished. What things, other than some of the obvious private matters in individuals' lives, would you choose not to know because you think it would not be ethical for you to know them?

intuition

You have just written a short story in which the character wakes with a start, a completely **incredulous** expression on his face. Why is he incredulous?

emotion

Is being **nonplussed** an emotion? Or is it not an emotion but simply a perception, more intellectual than affective? Explain.

Neologist's Lexicon

Use the stems in this list to create a new word (neologism). Give the word, the pronunciation, the part of speech, the etymology, and the definition(s). Keep a record of the neologisms you create from list to list. Here are some examples:

monoscient (mo no' se ent) adj. [mono (one), sci (know)] 1. being fixed and obsessed with a single idea 2. so specialized as to know only one thing, while being ignorant of all else

lithovidesis (lith o vid' e sis) n. [lith (rock), vid (look)] 1. a look that turns one to stone, as the look of the Gorgon   2. the look of one whose name you have mispronounced

Sesquipedalian Theater

Using at least one word from this week's list in every sentence, write a small one-act play. If circumstances allow, it would be good to perform the Sesquipedalian Play in class. Having a witty prop is a good idea. Use a pseudonym, or *nom de plume*, if you like. Emphasis should be on creativity and fun; feel free to be silly or absurd. As an example:

Unidentified Flying Monoliths
by Michael Skellig

Scene: A small group of people are walking in the park. One is pulling a stuffed animal on a leash. One is bouncing a basketball and never stops, speaks, or looks up throughout the play. One is chewing gum animatedly and stares wide-eyed at the audience the whole time.

One: Look, in the imponderable sky! It's a bird, a plane, an unidentified flying monolith!

Two: Monolith?? Oh no! I see, but I'm incredulous, but I see, but I'm incredulous!

One: Be not nonplussed! Trust to the verification of your own eyes!

Three (looking up, agape): Oh my omnibus mind, my neophyte eyes! Can this vision be unilateral, or does all the world see what I see?

One and Two: Vide, VIDE, VIDE!! (They pronounce the word differently each time.)

One: Oh hierarchy of truths! Oh benediction and postlude to nonplussed day! Oh omniscient visitors from afar! What interdictions have we broken, that you visit us??

Two: Wait!

One: Oh, my earthbound portliness! Oh, my . . .

Two: Wait!

One: Oh, OMNIBUS OMNISCIENT BENEDICTIONS AND INTERDICTIONS AND...

Two: WAIT! Did you say "unidentified flying monolith?" That's no monolith! That's a monoPLANE, you neophyte! MONOPLANE! Ha!! What a malapropism!

One: Monoplane? . . .

One: Plane? . . .

One: Malapropism? . . .

All (muttering): Ooohh nooo . . .

All stare blankly at audience.

finis

• *hypo*	(under)	hypothecate	• *hetero*	(different)	heterodox
• *dox*	(opinion)	heterodox	• pater	(father)	paterfamilias
• put	(think)	putative	• ver	(true)	aver
• *mega*	(large)	megaton	• sangui	(blood)	sangfroid
• alter	(other)	altercation	• ego	(I)	alter ego
• contra	(against)	contravene	• ven	(come)	contravene
• con	(together)	confluence	• flu	(flow)	confluence
• circum	(around)	circumlocute	• loqu	(talk)	circumlocution
• sol	(alone)	soliloquy	• moll	(soft)	mollify
• fy	(make)	mollify	• greg	(group)	gregarious
• ous	(full of)	gregarious	• tion	(act or state)	altercation

hypothecate (pledge as security) Hypothecate the land as security.

heterodox (unorthodox)   He was criticized for his heterodox opinions.

paterfamilias (male head of family) Please consult with the paterfamilias.

putative (thought-to-be) He was the putative leader of the mafia.

aver (affirm or declare) He had seen nothing; he averred to the prosecutor.

megaton (force of a million tons of dynamite) A ten-megaton bomb exploded in the desert.

sangfroid (cold-blooded composure) She performs with cool sangfroid in emergencies.

alter ego (second self) She was not just a friend but an alter ego to me.

altercation (heated dispute) Talleyrand heard the noisy altercation in the streets.

contravene (go against) Do not contravene a command intentionally.

•　　•　　•

confluence (a flowing together) The U.S. is a confluence of many peoples and cultures.

circumlocution (talking in circles) His circumlocution of the issue rankled the audience.

soliloquy (speech to oneself) He roamed the kitchen in humorous soliloquy.

mollify (make soft) We need to mollify the client's resentment.

gregarious (sociable) The warm host had a gregarious personality.

As Used by Henry James in *The American*

	His	unconscious	sangfroid	was	boundless.
Parts of Speech:	adj.	adj.	**n.**	v.	adj.
Parts of Sentence:			subject	LVP	subject complement
Phrases:	-----no prepositional, appositive, or verbal phrases-----				
Clauses:	--------------------------------independent clause-------------------------------- one independent clause, a simple declarative sentence				

Here Henry James uses the singular common noun *sangfroid* as the subject of the verb *was*; *was* is a linking verb that connects the subject *sangfroid* to the subject complement *boundless*. In this sentence the word *his* is being used as a possessive adjective. LVP means linking verb predicate.

Pronunciation

hypothecate	hi POTH uh kate	**altercation**	alter KAY shun
heterodox	HETT er o dox	**contravene**	contra VEEN
paterfamilias	PAH ter fa ME lee us	**confluence**	KONN flu ence
putative	PYOO tah tiv	**circumlocution**	SIR cum lo KYOO shun
aver	ah VUR	**soliloquy**	so LIL o kwee
megaton	MEG a tun	**mollify**	MOLL ih fye
sangfroid	sahn FRWAH	**gregarious**	greh GAR ee us
alter ego	alter EE go		

Spanish Cognates

heterodox	heterodoxo	**putative**	putativo
contravene	contravención	**confluence**	confluencia
soliloquy	soliloquio	**gregarious**	gregario
circumlocution	circunlocución	**altercation**	altercado

1.   The verb **mollify** does mean to make soft, but it does not apply to physical objects; we do not say that we mollify hard clay by kneading it. We mollify hard minds, hard feelings, anger. To mollify is to appease, to make soft the hard attitude of an intractable opinion.

2.   It is interesting to contrast the noun **circumlocution** with the verb **equivocate** and the noun **subterfuge**. Each of these words refers to a way of avoiding a straight answer, but each is different. Circumlocuting is talking (locu) in circles (circum), equivocating is giving equal (equi) voice (voc) to both sides of an issue while taking neither side, and a subterfuge is a trick or dodge that lets the speaker duck (fug: flee, sub: under) the question.

3.   If the adjective **putative** seems strange or alien at first, think of other words that also have the **put** (think) stem, such as **computer**, **reputation**, and **dispute**. A computer is a thinking machine (sort of), a reputation is what you have when they know you again, and a dispute is what happens when people don't think alike.

4.   The adjective **heterodox** can mean "of many opinions": the United States is a heterodox nation, consisting of many different subcultures. The word can also mean simply "not orthodox": a person's heterodox views can land him or her in trouble in a rigid society or group that does not approve of divergent opinions.

5.   A **Classic Word**: We think of the word **soliloquy** as a technical term to use in describing famous scenes from Shakespearean plays. The phrases spill from one's memory: to be or not to be; tomorrow and tomorrow and tomorrow; here's yet some liquor left; I have no cause to spurn at Caesar but for the general, he would be crowned. And yet **soliloquy** has been a popular word for many modern novelists, especially in the Nineteenth Century. Hardy, Twain, Thoreau, Melville, Stowe, and the Brontës all used soliloquy in their works. In *Tom Sawyer*, Sid soliloquizes just audibly. At Walden Pond, Thoreau finds himself soliloquizing and talking to all the universe at the same time. Melville's Stubb soliloquizes at the try-works in *Moby Dick*. Harriet Beecher Stowe and Emily Brontë used soliloquy over and over. In *Uncle Tom's Cabin* we find Andy cutting short Tom's soliloquy, Cassy stealing up on a soliloquy, and people in reveries soliloquizing to themselves as if by music. In *Wuthering Heights* we find characters murmuring in soliloquy, half soliloquizing, indulging in a soliloquy of execrations, soliloquizing in an undertone of peevish displeasure, and soliloquizing on the length of the night as they look at their watches.

6.   The noun **sangfroid** is the French word for cold-bloodedness. It refers to not getting rattled, to keeping your cool, to being self-possessed, poised, in control of yourself, despite conditions that would leave some people shook up. Elvis Presley was all shook up and lacked sangfroid. In other words, this word is fun. Pronounce this word sän frwa'. (Yes, Elvis and I should have said "shaken up," but then the wink of the line would have been lost!)

7.   A **Micropoem**: The noun **confluence** contains a beautiful image of liquids streaming together, as when two rivers meet. This metaphorical word is often used to depict the flowing together of minds or the confluence of cultures.

In each case below, one of the choices was really the word used by the author in the sentence provided. All of the choices can be found in the example words on the first page of this lesson. Your challenge is to decide which word the author used. This is not a test; it is more like a game, because more than one word choice may work perfectly well. See if you can use your sensitivity and intuition to guess correctly which word the author used. You may need a dictionary.

1.   **From Henry James's *The American***

He was not embarrassed, for his unconscious _____ was boundless.
a. alter ego
b. sangfroid
c. confluence
d. soliloquy

2.   **From George Orwell's *1984***

Suddenly the group broke up, and two of the men were in violent _____.
a. paterfamilias
b. confluence
c. circumlocution
d. altercation

3.   **From Robert Penn Warren's *All the King's Men***

"Pressure is a prettier word," I _____.
a. averred
b. hypothecated
c. contravened
d. mollified

4.   **From Emily Brontë's *Wuthering Heights***

I declined answering Mrs. Dean's question, which struck me as something _____.
a. gregarious
b. putative
c. heterodox
d. mollified

5.   **From Jonathan Swift's *Gulliver's Travels***

It put me to the pains of many _____ to give my master a right idea of what I spoke.
a. circumlocutions
b. altercations
c. confluences
d. soliloquies

16

Though it is a good thing to have a rich vocabulary, it is not a good thing to abuse that vocabulary by writing verbose, abstruse, sesquipedalian sentences. Those who overuse their vocabularies often do so at the expense of clarity. Translate the following showy, ponderous passage into graceful, direct English. Do not use slang, but do use words that seem familiar and comfortable.

WITH ADMIRABLE SANGFROID and without circumlocution, the omniscient paterfamilias, in order to achieve a confluence of heterodox viewpoints, and to avoid the need for mollifying the disputants, urged all present to avoid further altercations over warheads, megatons, and putative future doom. "Gregarious though you be," he averred, "confine your assertions to soliloquy or to your *alter egos*; do not contravene my unilateral interdiction against altercation. If you are nonplussed or incredulous, then please respect the hierarchy of family authority."

Reading Comprehension

1. The author does all of the following EXCEPT:
   A. describe a male head of household's interdiction
   B. describe a violent altercation
   C. describe someone speaking very directly to others
   D. describe an interfamilial mollification

2. The author's attitude is best described as:
   A. it is good to be even-tempered and candid
   B. a father should rule the household
   C. disagreement should be kept to oneself
   D. global dangers should not be discussed openly

Analogies

3. MOLLIFY : ALTERCATION ::
   A. mollusk : alternator
   B. soften : endurance
   C. soothe : dispute
   D. peace : violence

4. SOLILOQUY : CIRCUMLOCUTION ::
   A. orbit : sun
   B. solo : symphony
   C. mumble : periphrasis
   D. evasion : speech

Antonyms

soliloquy

5. HETERODOX :
   A. doxology
   B. dogmatic
   C. heteromorphic
   D. unorthodox

6. SANGFROID :
   A. hot-tempered
   B. bloody
   C. acerbic
   D. cool

synthesis

What character in literature or mythology can you recall who behaves with **sangfroid** at a time of danger? Can you think of more than one character?

divergence

Think of the **soliloquies** you have with yourself, in which you scold yourself, remind yourself, encourage yourself. How many soliloquy topics can you think of that are common in your life? List as many soliloquy topics as you can.

convergence

Our planet is a **heterodox** place, containing many cultures with many customs. If you had to write a 50-page typed research paper on one culture other than your own, what other culture would you choose, purely on the basis of interest? Why?

ethics and evaluation

Many people believe that it is usually right to behave lawfully, in accordance with legally constituted authority, but that sometimes, as Thoreau and Gandhi indicated, it is right to **contravene** even legally constituted authority if that authority requires you to engage in a crime against humanity. An obvious example of this idea is the war crimes trials held to prosecute Nazi war criminals, who often argued that they were simply obeying the commands of their superiors. The question is, where do you draw the line between when it is wrong to disobey authority and wrong to obey authority? In creating an answer to this difficult but important question, remember that you must always create and employ intelligent criteria when you are trying to evaluate a difficult question.

analysis

Altercations do not normally erupt instantaneously, but evolve from pleasant conversations into heated disputes. Think about this process, and list the stages of interaction that often lead from discussion to altercation.

intuition, emotion, and imagination

You are watching a play, and the gregarious protagonist is in the midst of a **soliloquy** characterized by an extreme emotion. What is the emotion, and what is the subject of the soliloquy? Use your intuition and imagination to form an elaborate version of the scene, and then describe it in detail.

aesthetics and application

If you were going to develop a poster to depict the effects of a twenty-**megaton** nuclear weapon, what colors would you use, and what would the primary image be?

Neologist's Lexicon

Use the stems in this list to create a new word (neologism). Give the word, the pronunciation, the part of speech, the etymology, and the definition(s). Keep a record of the neologisms you create from list to list. Here are some examples:

sanguiloquacious (san gwe lo kwa' shus) adj. [sangui (blood), loqu (talk)] 1. excessive use of the adjective *bloody* 2. speaking in coarse, offensively explicit language

heteromollidoxical (het er o moll i dox' i cal) adj. [hetero (different), moll (soft) dox (opinion)] 1. having many soft-headed or ill-founded opinions 2. pertaining to a society in which such views have wide acceptance

Sesquipedalian Poetry

Using at least one word from this week's list in every line, write a short poem. You may use regular meter, internal or end rhyme, or other poetic devices, or not! Here is a sample:

Cool Kid

megaton, megaton
anthropodynamo
cool kid, cool—if you ask me
confluent talent
my young alter ego
halt not your ego
go, go, contravene limits
unorthodox and gregarious (precarious)
you mollify my putative spirit of various altercations
with your soliloquies and
   c
    i
     r
    c
   u
  m
     locutions/talktome/talktome
willowtree will you grow
small spirit with your cool sangfroid
you cool kid
cool

• de	(down)	declaim	• clam	(cry out)	declaim
• voc	(voice)	sotto voce	• trans	(across)	translucent
• luc	(light)	translucent	• fort	(strong)	forte, fortissimo
• acr	(sharp)	acerbity	• per	(through)	perambulate
• ambul	(walk)	perambulate	• fid	(faith)	perfidy
• pugn	(fight)	impugn	• non	(not)	non sequitur
• sequ	(follow)	non sequitur	• ego	(I)	egocentric
• **centri**	(center)	egocentric	• loqu	(talk)	loquacious
• ous	(full of)	loquacious	• sacro	(holy)	sacrosanct
• sanct	(holy)	sacrosanct	• **caco**	(bad)	cacophony
• **phon**	(sound)	cacophony	• tang	(touch)	tangible

declaim (speak rhetorically) The pompous opponents declaimed rhetorically.

sotto voce (in a low voice) He tried to inform her, *sotto voce*, of the problem.

translucent (semitransparent) The glass was translucent, not completely transparent.

forte (strong point) Spelling is not his forte. (Pronounced *fort*; *fortay* is for music.)

fortissimo (very loudly) The orchestra played a thunderous *fortissimo* passage.

acerbity (sharpness of temper) His constant acerbity was demoralizing.

perambulate (wander through) The boy perambulated through the park.

perfidy (breach of faith) We deplored the scoundrel's perfidious act.

impugn (attack as false) Another witness impugned his testimony.

non sequitur (an idea that does not follow) The idea was a ludicrous *non sequitur*.

• • •

egocentric (self-centered) His egocentric conversation became boring.

loquacious (talkative) We avoided the loquacious chatterbox.

sacrosanct (sacred) The second rule is sacrosanct and inviolable.

cacophony (bad noise) We heard the cacophonous blaring of the horns in the street below.

tangible (touchable) The nice office is a tangible benefit of the job.

As Used by Charles Dickens in *David Copperfield*

	I	stood	amazed	at	the	revelation	of	all	this	**perfidy.**
Parts of Speech:	pron.	v.	adv.	prep.	adj.	n.	prep.	adj.	adj.	**n.**

Parts of Sentence:	subj.	AVP

Phrases: -------prep. phrase------- -------prep. phrase------

Clauses: ----------------------------------independent clause----------------------------------
one independent clause, a simple declarative sentence

Here Charles Dickens uses the singular common noun *perfidy* as the object of the preposition *of*. This sentence is a good reminder of how much we use prepositional phrases.

Pronunciation

declaim	dee KLAIM	**impugn**	im PYOON
sotto voce	sotto VO chay	*non sequitur*	non SEK wih tur
translucent	trans LOO sent	**egocentric**	ego SEN trik
forte	FORT	**loquacious**	lo KWAY shus
fortissimo	for TEE see mo	**sacrosanct**	SACK ro sankt
acerbity	ah SIR bih tee	**cacophony**	kah KOFF uh nee
perambulate	per AM byoo late	**tangible**	TANJ ih bul
perfidy	PURR fid ee		

Spanish Cognates

translucent	translúcido	**acerbity**	acerbidad
perambulate	perambulación	**perfidy**	perfidia
loquacious	loquaz	**sacrosanct**	sacrosanto
cacophony	cacofonía	**tangible**	tangible

1. The noun **forte**, when used to mean "strong point," should be pronounced *FORT*. The pronunciation *FORTAY* is used for the musical term that means to play a musical passage with great strength. The *FORTAY* passage is the *FORT* of some orchestras. Since this is very widely misunderstood, you may have to use the correct pronunciation with extra confidence.

2. We often use the adjective **sacrosanct** in a sincere sense, as to describe the sacrosanct values of a religious faith. But we also use the word in an ironic sense, for the purpose of pointed humor, as when we tell a selfish person, "Excuse ME for touching your sacrosanct typewriter."

3. A **non sequitur** is a pseudo-logical conclusion that a speaker draws, but that actually does not follow from what has been said previously. In Eugene Ionesco's play *Rhinoceros*, characters completely misunderstand the relationships in logic and wind up with the following reasoning: All cats are mortal, and Socrates was mortal; therefore, Socrates was a cat. This, we will note, is a **non sequitur**. The correct relationship of a **syllogism** (for that is what the characters were trying to demonstrate) is as follows: All cats are mortal, and Schmerz is a cat; therefore, Schmerz is mortal.

   > WRONG: All A is C, B is C, therefore B is A.
   > RIGHT: All A is C, B is A, therefore B is C.

4. The verb **declaim** is an interesting word. It combines the stems of *de* (down) and *clam* (cry out), and the crying down to which it refers is pompous, dramatic, or highly emphatic rhetorical speech. In *A Separate Peace*, the students declaim their threats to enlist in the war, with a grinding of teeth and a flashing of eyes. One of my favorite sentences using declaim is this one from Wilder's *The Bridge of San Luis Rey*: "and often until dawn they would remain there declaiming to one another the lordly conversation of Calderón."

5. A **Classic Word**: Authors from Jonathan Swift in the early 1700s to John Knowles in the 1950s have found it helpful to distinguish between the **tangible** phenomena that we can touch and the intangible phenomena that we cannot touch but nevertheless recognize. In one of his voyages, Swift's Gulliver finds inhabitants condensing air into a dry, tangible substance. Melville describes Moby Dick's intangible malignity. Dickens, in *A Tale of Two Cities*, describes the intangible impurities of poverty and deprivation. Conrad explains that some facts are visible, tangible, and open to the senses. In *Ethan Frome*, Edith Wharton notes signs of Zeena's disfavor as intangible but disquieting. Classic authors have described tangible proofs of convalescence (Emily Brontë), the remoteness and intangibility of a minister (Hawthorne), the tangible, separate existence of a people (Stowe), the intangible tints of morning or evening (Thoreau), swinging and clawing at the intangible air (Twain), and looking for the call of the wild as though it were an intangible thing (London).

6. A **Micropoem**: The adjective **egocentric** contains a striking geometric image of the self (ego) at the center (centri) of all other phenomena, which are revolving around it.

In each case below, one of the choices was really the word used by the author in the sentence provided. All of the choices can be found in the example words on the first page of this lesson. Your challenge is to decide which word the author used. This is not a test; it is more like a game, because more than one word choice may work perfectly well. See if you can use your sensitivity and intuition to guess correctly which word the author used. You may need a dictionary.

1.   **From Harriet Beecher Stowe's *Uncle Tom's Cabin***

        His life is a logical result of his opinions, and mine is a complete _____.
        a. *fortissimo*
        b. perfidy
        c. cacophony
        d. *non sequitur*

2.   **From Nathaniel Hawthorne's *The House of the Seven Gables***

        The judge's smile seemed to operate on her _____ of heart like sunshine upon vinegar.
        a. acerbity
        b. perfidy
        c. *non sequitur*
        d. translucence

3.   **From Aldous Huxley's *Brave New World***

        With closed eyes...John was softly _____ to vacancy.
        a. impugning
        b. perambulating
        c. declaiming
        d. *sotto voce*

4.   **From James M. Barrie's *Peter Pan***

        They suddenly saw the _____ pirates bearing down upon them.
        a. perfidious
        b. translucent
        c. tangible
        d. egocentric

5.   **From Jack London's *The Call of the Wild***

        They were _____ skeletons.
        a. *fortissimo*
        b. *sotto voce*
        c. perambulating
        d. loquacious

Though it is a good thing to have a rich vocabulary, it is not a good thing to abuse that vocabulary by writing verbose, abstruse, sesquipedalian sentences. Those who overuse their vocabularies often do so at the expense of clarity. Translate the following showy, ponderous passage into graceful, direct English. Do not use slang, but do use words that seem familiar and comfortable.

STANDING BEFORE the translucent stained glass window, the loquacious conductor, knowing that *sotto voce* remarks were not his forte, declaimed with acerbity against the cacophony of the orchestra's *fortissimo* passage, impugning the musicians' integrity, accusing them of egocentric perfidy because of their performance of the sacrosanct Fifth Symphony. With ironic *sangfroid*, the neophyte bassoon player noted that this was a *non sequitur* and that the players had not wished to contravene the omniscient conductor's directions. She also remarked that musicians do not play for the tangible rewards, but for the imponderable glories of the musical experience. Unilaterally, the incredulous bassoon player decided to resign and, rising from her stool, began to perambulate through the orchestra on her way to the exit.

translucent

Reading Comprehension

1. Which of the following best expresses the main idea of Translation 33?
   A. A conductor suffered the insolence of a musician.
   B. A musician defended her dignity from an abusive conductor.
   C. An orchestra played Beethoven in lackluster fashion.
   D. Beginners often make serious mistakes.

2. With which statement would the author likely agree?
   A. You are obligated to accept the instructions of your superior.
   B. You must not be disruptive when your team depends on you.
   C. You are an individual, free to participate voluntarily in events or not.
   D. Sometimes discipline requires sacrifice.

Analogies

3. **CACOPHONOUS : SOTTO VOCE ::**
   A. bad : good
   B. ululation : voice
   C. racket : whisper
   D. pandemonium : wine

4. **PERFIDY : SACROSANCT ::**
   A. break : rule
   B. faith : holy
   C. declaim : *fortissimo*
   D. treachery : sacred

Antonyms

5. **TANGIBLE :**
   A. translucent
   B. solid
   C. ineffable
   D. incorporeal

6. **TRANSLUCENT :**
   A. black
   B. opaque
   C. dense
   D. intransitive

cacophonous

synthesis

We can use **perambulate** in its physical sense, as to perambulate through a park. But we can also use **perambulate** in a metaphorical sense. How many different experiences can you think of that might be metaphorically described by the verb **perambulate**?

divergence and convergence

Make a list of acts of **perfidy**, either fictitious or historical. One example from literature is Iago's deliberate destruction of Othello and Desdemona in Shakespeare's *Othello*. After you have made your list, choose the one you personally deplore most, and explain the reasons for your choice.

evaluation

Think of something that you have spent a lot of time doing and/or learning to do and that you regard as beneficial. Then make a list of two **tangible** benefits and two intangible benefits of this experience. Then rank the four benefits in order of importance. Is the chief benefit tangible or intangible? What criteria did you use to make your **hierarchy** of benefits?

emotion

After a very unusual event happens, you tell your best friend about it, but your friend **impugns** your veracity. You sincerely aver that you are telling the truth, but your friend again impugns your veracity. How does this make you feel?

aesthetics

Are there any forms of **cacophony** that routinely detract from the quality of your life? Do they keep you awake, or keep you from studying, or keep you from thinking or talking? What are the sources of these noises?

imagination and intuition

In a dream, you suddenly find yourself in a monochrome world, where everything is one color. There you meet a unique being whose **forte** is a talent completely unknown to you previously. What color is the world, what is the being like, and what is his forte? Remember that forte is pronounced *fort* unless it refers to music.

Neologist's Lexicon

Use the stems in this list to create a new word (neologism). Give the word, the pronunciation, the part of speech, the etymology, and the definition(s). Keep a record of the neologisms you create from list to list. Here are some examples:

sacrophonous (sak raw' fun us) adj. [sacro (holy), phon (sound) ous (full of)] 1. sacred in sound, as the wind in the Grand Canyon 2. high-toned in language, as the speaking tone adopted for religious ceremonies

egopugnant (eego pug' nant) adj. [ego (I), pugn (fight) 1. being repulsive to others in one's essential personality 2. being repulsive to others as a result of one's inherent hostility or pugnacity

Sesquipedalian Fiction

Using at least one word from this week's list in every sentence, write a short play, scene, or story. You may also use words from previous lists if you like. Feel free to be imaginative, silly, or absurd. Do not let your critical or judgmental faculties interfere with your creative ideas.

Sesquipedalian Caption

Using words from this week's list, make up a phrase or sentence that you can use as the caption of a cartoon or drawing. For example, can you think of funny cartoons to draw for the following captions: Mort declaimed with acerbity against the cacophonous video game. Or: Perambulation, she learned, was not her forte. Write some captions of your own, and draw the cartoons or drawings.

Sesquipedalian Poetry

Using at least one word from this week's list in every line, write a short poem. You may use regular meter, or end rhyme, or other poetic devices, or not! Here is a sample:

Storm

translucent, blue scent, cloudless sky
    horizon high *sotto voce* intimation
ok, (loudless), here I come, sensation
    distant cacophonous rumbling cumulus
impugning this transitory serenity
    approaching *fortissimo*
lightning its forte like a short *non sequitur*
    perfidiously striking like Hecate our
sacrosanct evening, leaving
    only the tangible tangible:
    wet grass
    and puddles

• dict	(say)	obiter dictum	• sequ	(follow)	obsequious
• bas	(low)	abase	• path	(feeling)	pathetic fallacy
• nihil	(nothing)	nihilism	• ism	(doctrine)	nihilism
• muta	(change)	mutatis mutandis	• inter	(between)	interstices
• terr	(land)	terra incognita	• in	(in or not)	inanimate (not)
• cogn	(know)	terra incognita	• sed	(sit)	sedate
• re	(again)	retort	• tort	(twist)	retort
• super	(over)	supersede	• anim	(mind)	inanimate
• de	(down)	declaim	• epi	(on)	epigram
• gram	(writing)	epigram	• ob	(against)	obsequious
• obit	(death)	obiter dictum			

obiter dictum (passing remark) I liked the judge's *obiter dictum* on politics.

obsequious (servilely following) He's an obsequious, fawning flatterer; he is a toady.

abase (to lower) You abase yourself when you always agree.

pathetic fallacy (ascribing feelings to things) Example: It is a lonely sea tonight.

ratiocination (methodical thinking) Her ratiocinations won the point.

mutatis mutandis (with necessary changes) Type this letter, *mutatis mutandis*.

interstice (small space) Wind blew through the wall's interstices, and the candle flickered.

terra incognita (unknown land) He knew not the *terra incognita* of his own emotions.

sedate (calm) The Count's sedate good manners charmed us all, alas.

retort (swift reply) She was famous for her devastatingly witty retorts.

• • •

nihilism (belief in nothing) The new convert forsook his former nihilism.

supersede (replace) This procedure supersedes our former process.

inanimate (lifeless) Inanimate objects tell no tales, but many animate objects have tails.

condescend (lower oneself) His condescending remarks insulted the guest.

epigram (witty comment) She enjoyed his spontaneously brilliant epigram on the topic.

As Used by Joseph Heller in *Catch-22*

	On	the	landing	below	lived	the	**obsequious**	owners.
Parts of Speech:	prep.	adj.	n.	adj.	v.	adj.	**adj.**	n.

Parts of Sentence:	AVP	subj.

Phrases: -----------prep. phrase---------

Clauses: ----------------------------------independent clause----------------------------------
one independent clause, a simple declarative sentence

Here Joseph Heller uses the adjective *obsequious* to modify the singular common noun *owners*, which is the subject of the sentence, even though it is the last word.

Pronunciation

obiter dictum	oh bih ter DICT um	sedate	suh DATE
obsequious	ob SEE kwee us	retort	re TORT
abase	ah BASE	nihilism	NIE ill izm
pathetic fallacy	pah THET ik FAL a see	supersede	super SEED
ratiocination	rah shee ah sin AY shun	inanimate	in AN ih mut
mutatis mutandis	myoo TAH tiss myoo TAND iss	condescend	kon duh SEND
interstice	in TURR stiss	epigram	EPP ih gram
terra incognita	terr ah in kog NEE tah		

Spanish Cognates

obsequious	obsequioso	**interstice**	intersticio
condescension	condescendencia	**nihilism**	nihilismo
epigram	epigrama	**inanimate**	inanimado
retort	retorta	**ratiocination**	raciocinación

1. The verb **supersede** is a rarity; it is the only word I know of that ends in -**sede**. That is because it is not a combination of *super* (over) and *cede* (go), but of *super* and *sed* (sit). That which supersedes something else replaces it, and the image is of the new sitting above the old.

2. An **obsequious** person is a servile, fawning flatterer, such as Lex Luthor's toady in the Superman films. Yes sir, no sir, whatever you say sir. The obsequious toady follows (sequ) his master wherever the master leads.

3. In the age of satellites, it is less common than it once was to speak literally of a **terra incognita**, an unknown land. Today, we more commonly use the term metaphorically, as to describe someone who does not know himself. Of course, the planets stand as a new *terra incognita* for humanity, and the next few centuries should be great and exciting ages of discovery.

4. A **Micropoem**: A **retort** is a reply so swift and effective that it can be thought of as a twisting (tort) back (re) of the other person's remark. In a retort, you do not even give the poor opponent's remark time to land before you twist it back on him. Whack. Some of the loveliest retorts in English literature appear in the sonnet that Shakespeare writes to describe the meeting between Romeo and Juliet; clearly, part of the reason they fall in love is the matching of their minds in this brilliant volley of retorts. It must have been apparent to each of them that they had met someone unusual, capable of wit and quick thinking.

5. The verbs **condescend** and **abase** both suggest a lowering of the self, but the words are very different in meaning. To condescend to someone is an insult to that person, suggesting that you regard yourself as above him or her, but that you are lowering yourself to speak to someone in a low status, as though it were **infra dig** even to speak to someone so below you. To abase yourself is to actually degrade or humble yourself, leaving yourself in a lower status.

6. The **pathetic fallacy** does not acquire its name from the idea of something being pathetic— filled with **pathos**. Instead, the word refers to feelings (path) attributed to things that do not have feelings. And since things can not both have and not have feelings, this is a logical contradiction. As human beings, we are full of feelings, and we often project our own feelings onto the world. We see a mournful sea, a hopeful dawn, or a wrathful storm. In Shakespeare's *Julius Caesar*, Calpurnia implores Caesar not to go to the senate, because it has been a tempestuous night, filled with inexplicable wonders, and she is afraid of these omens. "When beggars die," Calpurnia tells Caesar, "there are no comets seen." To the Romans, such omens and warnings seemed a natural part of the interrelationship between human beings and the cosmos, but to us, they just seem to be examples of the pathetic fallacy. Of course, when we read a play, we don't think that way; instead, we practice what Coleridge called the "suspension of disbelief," imagining that everything we read is true.

In each case below, one of the choices was really the word used by the author in the sentence provided. All of the choices can be found in the example words on the first page of this lesson. Your challenge is to decide which word the author used. This is not a test; it is more like a game, because more than one word choice may work perfectly well. See if you can use your sensitivity and intuition to guess correctly which word the author used. You may need a dictionary.

1. **From Thornton Wilder's *The Bridge of San Luis Rey***

   The frightened mother became meek and _____.
   a. sedate
   b. inanimate
   c. obsequious
   d. nihilistic

2. **From H.G. Wells's *The Invisible Man***

   I went and peered out through their _____.
   a. interstices
   b. ratiocinations
   c. epigrams
   d. *terra incognita*

3. **From Herman Melville's *Moby Dick***

   The plebeian herds crouch _____ before the tremendous centralization.
   a. obsequious
   b. inanimate
   c. abased
   d. superseded

4. **From Herman Melville's *Moby Dick***

   We know the sea to be an everlasting _____.
   a. *obiter dictum*
   b. *mutatis mutandis*
   c. pathetic fallacy
   d. *terra incognita*

5. **From Thomas Hardy's *The Mayor of Casterbridge***

   The usually _____ Farfrae was in the midst of the other dancers.
   a. inanimate
   b. sedate
   c. abased
   d. condescending

Though it is a good thing to have a rich vocabulary, it is not a good thing to abuse that vocabulary by writing verbose, abstruse, sesquipedalian sentences. Those who overuse their vocabularies often do so at the expense of clarity. Translate the following showy, ponderous passage into graceful, direct English. Do not use slang, but do use words that seem familiar and comfortable.

THE SEDATE, condescending villain glared at his loquacious, obsequious toady, who began to wish he could hide in one of the interstices in the wall. "My ratiocinations inform me," the nihilistic villain began, "that I must supersede my recent *obiter dictum* on your merits with a new epigram." The nonplussed toady could not retort. "Your inanimate brain," the villain averred, "is only one sign of your abased condition. The other is your continual use of the pathetic fallacy. Such logic I cannot abide. If your own intelligence is such *terra incognita* to you, then I will have to send notice of your dismissal, *mutatis mutandis*, to my scribe." The toady was heard to reply, *sotto voce*, that the villain would never declaim so to him again.

Reading Comprehension

1. It can be inferred from Translation 34 that:
    A. Condescension is effective in controlling people.
    B. Speaking harshly to others is sometimes necessary.
    C. Being illogical is a good way to get into trouble.
    D. Loyalty must be earned.

2. Translation 34 could be best described as:
    A. two villains forming a plot
    B. an evil boss excoriates his employee
    C. a toady is criticized for not doing what he was told
    D. a rebellion against an unjust command

Analogies

3. CONDESCEND : OBSEQUIOUS ::
    A. stoop : grovel
    B. land : ascend
    C. beg : command
    D. contact : obstruct

4. EPIGRAM : RETORT ::
    A. letter : reply
    B. telegram : answer
    C. epithet : remove
    D. remark : rejoinder

Antonyms

epigram

5. NIHILISM :
    A. credulity
    B. obedience
    C. ratiocination
    D. disbelief

6. ABASE :
    A. condescend
    B. elevate
    C. debase
    D. retort

synthesis

List at least three characters from different novels who have in common the fact that they are either **condescending** or **obsequious**.

application

What might be a real-life situation in which the phrase **mutatis mutandis** would be appropriate? Obviously, the term is erudite enough that in many situations it would not be appropriate, so what do you imagine its appropriate use would be?

imagination and intuition

In a chapter of a science fiction novel, the protagonist, a Galactic Survey surgeon, is slipping silently and carefully through the purple mist of a planet with very low gravity. Suddenly, she stumbles over an inanimate object that proves to be a discovery that revolutionizes human life on the planet. Describe the object, and explain its value.

emotion

What emotions do you associate with the word **sedate**? It might help to think of events that would leave you feeling calm and sedate. If you were writing screenplays, what would be the likely emotions associated with characters who could be described as sedate?

aesthetics

Pretend that you are going to make a film about a **nihilistic** villain, such as one of the exaggerated villains in the Superman or Batman cartoons. What symbolic colors, objects, and sounds will you include in your film to enhance the audience's abhorrence of the nihilism that the character possesses? Thinking about these artistic decisions will give you some insight into the careful planning that film directors and artistic crews go through. Sometimes, directors spend millions of dollars solely on design elements, getting every color, shadow, item of furniture, and so forth, right. In fact, in addition to writing a script, before filming they draw story boards in which the angles and details of every shot are determined and graphically depicted in advance; in other words, they *draw* the movie before they film it! That's planning.

Neologist's Lexicon

Use the stems in this list to create a new word (neologism). Give the word, the pronunciation, the part of speech, the etymology, and the definition(s). Keep a record of the neologisms you create from list to list. Here are some examples:

resequious (ree seek' we ous) adj. [re (again), sequ (follow), ous (full of)] 1. following someone around, even after being asked not to 2. following someone as he or she performs a duty that requires him or her to move back and forth

epitort (eh' pih tort) n. [epi (on), tort (twist) 1. a mechanical object that twists on, such as a soda bottle cap 2. an idea that is difficult for a person to accept, requiring great effort for those who would persuade

Sesquipedalian Advertising

Using the words from this week's list, write a short advertisement. Feel free to make it silly or satirical. You might like to write a spoof on an ad you have heard. A sample:

Alumiwipes, the Metal Towel of Tomorrow, Today!

Friends! Why abase yourself any longer by using old fashioned paper towels? Now, you too can have new, improved ALUMIWIPES, the aluminum towel that lasts forever! Are you tired of paper towel salesmen condescending to you? Are you tired of having the pathetic fallacy used on you as a sales ploy? Have you had enough of obsequious phone calls from towel representatives? Has your cleaning closet become a *terra incognita* of antiquated supplies and materials? Have you lost your sedate equanimity from the acerbic retorts of nihilistic towel salesmen? Do you anguish over the trees that lose their lives in the paper towel manufacturing process? Well your happy day is here! Alumiwipes are made of inanimate metal! Alumiwipes have micro-interstices built in to catch all of the water, grime, and toxic substances, leaving your household surfaces CLEANER THAN THE DAY THEY WERE NEW! No need for ratiocination; buy Alumiwipes today. Buy one: that's all you'll ever need! How much would you pay for such an exciting home improvement product??

But wait! If you buy your Alumiwipe today, you also get *Mutatis Mutandis*, the pestogen that turns all of your household pests into benevolent creatures! Tired of having fleas in your carpet? Turn them into parakeets with *Mutatis Mutandis*! Tired of ants and silverfish in your kitchen cabinets? Turn them into plants and goldfish! It's easy, with *Mutatis Mutandis*! Now, how much would you pay for the AMAZING benefits you get from Alumiwipes and *Mutatis Mutandis*? Five hundred dollars? A thousand? Believe it or not, you get both of these incredible products for only NINETEEN NINETY-FIVE! That's NINETEEN NINETY-FIVE! Order today. Use your Command Card or VITA credit card number!

• *anthropo*	(man)	lycanthrope		• *centri*	(center)	anthropocentric
• *gastro*	(stomach)	gastronome		• medi	(middle)	in media res
• *auto*	(self)	autodidact		• ambi	(both)	circumambient
• contra	(against)	au contraire		• *ism*	(doctrine)	monism
• *viv*	(life)	vivacious		• trans	(across)	transmogrify
• *helio*	(sun)	heliotropic		• ex	(out)	exculpate
• culp	(blame)	exculpate		• intro	(into)	introspective
• spec	(look)	introspective		• trop	(turn)	heliotropic
• *mono*	(one)	monism		• **lykos**	(wolf)	lycanthrope

anthropocentric (man-centered)   We believed in an anthropocentric cosmos.

gastronome (a gourmet or epicure)   Try the gastronome's recipe for squid *a la mode*.

autodidact (self-taught person)   His writing contains the tell-tale errors of the autodidact.

monism (doctrine that reality is one)   Einstein's space-time is a scientific monism.

in medias res (in the middle of things)   *The Odyssey,* by Homer, begins *in medias res*.

lycanthrope (werewolf)   Jove's anger turned Lycaon into a howling lycanthrope.

circumambient (surrounding)   Enjoy the circumambient breezes that waft over the deck.

transmogrify (change form)   The hecklers were transmogrified into obsequious admirers.

reify (treat as real)   To believe in THE DARK FORCE is to reify the concept of evil.

au contraire (to the contrary)   *"Au contraire!"* he exclaimed in protest.

•   •   •

vivacious (lively)   His vivacious conversation entertained the group long into the night.

circumvent (get around)   To circumvent this surgical procedure is dangerous.

heliotropic (sun-following)   The sun-seeking tourists reminded him of heliotropic plants.

exculpate (free from blame)   Fortunately, the jury exculpated the innocent girl.

introspective (inward looking)   His introspective thoughts were too personal to share.

As Used by L.M. Montgomery in *Anne of Green Gables*

	The	big	eyes	were	full	of	spirit	and	**vivacity.**
Parts of Speech:	adj.	adj.	n.	v.	adj.	prep.	n.	conj.	**n.**

						subject	
Parts of Sentence:			subj.	LVP	complement		

Phrases: --------prepositional phrase--------

Clauses: ---------------------------------independent clause---------------------------------
one independent clause, a simple declarative sentence

Here L.M. Montgomery uses the noun *vivacity* as one side of a compound object of preposition. This word appears in its adjective form, *vivacious*, on our list.

Pronunciation

anthropocentric	an thro po SENT rik	**reify**	REE if fy
gastronome	GAS tro nome	*au contraire*	OH kon TRAIR
autodidact	auto DIE dakt	**vivacious**	vie VAY shus
monism	MOAN ism	**circumvent**	sir come VENT
in medias res	in MAY dee as RACE	**heliotropic**	hee lee oh TRO pik
lycanthrope	LIE can thrope	**exculpate**	EX kul pate
circumambient	sir come AM bee ent	**introspective**	intro SPEK tiv
transmogrify	trans MOG ri fie		

Spanish Cognates

vivacious	vivaz	**introspective**	instrospectivo
heliotrope	heliotropo	**monist**	monista
exculpation	exculpación	**anthropocentric**	antropocéntrico
gastronome	gastrónomo		

1. A **monism** is a metaphysical doctrine that holds that ultimate reality is one thing; an example would be Einstein's space-time, the concept that all of reality is a single continuum of four-dimensional space-time, that nothing is really separate from or different in substance from anything else, and that the entire cosmos is actually a single huge geometrical structure of four-dimensional space-time. This monism might be contrasted with a **dualism**, such as Descartes's idea that the universe contains both matter and mind, and that the two are different. Descartes's dualism has been called the *mind/body dichotomy*. If you believed that everything in the universe was actually an idea in the mind of God, that would be a monism.

2. Homer begins *The Odyssey* **in medias res**: Odysseus has left Troy after the events described in *The Iliad* and has not yet reached home.

3. A **Micropoem**: The adjective **heliotropic** is a botanical term, usually applied to plants that turn (tropo) to follow the sun (helio) on its daily path across the sky. We might occasionally use the word metaphorically and humorously to describe vacationing tourists flocking to the beaches, but the primary use of this word is scientific.

4. The adjective **anthropocentric** means centered (centri) around man (anthropo). We could say that human beings have believed in an anthropocentric cosmos, meaning that we often have the theological idea that we are special to the purpose of the universe, not just insignificant dots on a shrimpy planet around a commonplace star. We can also apply the word **anthropocentric** to the unfortunate man-centered ideas with which we rationalize our destruction of other species, such as the wholesale extinctions of species in the Amazon. We might also note that Western art seems more anthropocentric than Oriental art. Compare, for instance, the *Mona Lisa* to a Chinese landscape: the *Mona Lisa* shows us the big person and the little world, but the Chinese landscape shows us a balanced environment in which everything is in scale and harmony, each thing contributing to the whole.

5. A **Classic Word**: Authors from Daniel Defoe in 1719 to George Orwell in 1945 have found **vivacious** [filled with (ous) life (viv)] to be a good word for describing a bright, animated, and lively character. We see this word in *Robinson Crusoe, Gulliver's Travels, Wuthering Heights, Jane Eyre, The Scarlet Letter, Uncle Tom's Cabin, Moby Dick, Walden, A Tale of Two Cities, Tom Sawyer, The Return of the Native, The Mayor of Casterbridge, The Red Badge of Courage,* and *Animal Farm*. In these books we find vivacity and sparkling sharpness in the eye, an exuberance of vivacity, the vivacity excited by rapid motion, an uncommon vivacity of intelligence, sham vivacity, and vivacity rebuked. Characters vivaciously cry, vivaciously wake, and vivaciously accost people. We see vivacious suffering, vivacious features, ordinary vivacious chat, vivacious fish and other vivacious denizens of the waters (Melville, of course), vivacious lilacs, vivacious voices, vivacious fun, and a vivacious Bacchanalian flame (Dickens). Orwell's Snowball "was a more vivacious pig than Napoleon." Melville's Flask is truly vivacious, tumultuous, and ostentatious. One of the most profound uses of **vivacious** is from Harriet Beecher Stowe: "when the bodily eyes are thus out of the lists, the spiritual eyes are uncommonly vivacious and perspicuous."

In each case below, one of the choices was really the word used by the author in the sentence provided. All of the choices can be found in the example words on the first page of this lesson. Your challenge is to decide which word the author used. This is not a test; it is more like a game, because more than one word choice may work perfectly well. See if you can use your sensitivity and intuition to guess correctly which word the author used. You may need a dictionary.

1. **From Herman Melville's** *Billy Budd*

   The _____ air in the clearness of its serenity was like smooth white marble.
   a. heliotropic
   b. anthropocentric
   c. circumambient
   d. vivacious

2. **From John Gardner's** *Grendel*

   The civilization he meant to build has _____ to a forest thick with traps.
   a. reified
   b. exculpated
   c. circumvented
   d. transmogrified

3. **From John Gardner's** *Grendel*

   Importance is primarily _____ in its reference to the universe.
   a. anthropocentric
   b. *in medias res*
   c. monistic
   d. introspective

4. **From Walter Scott's** *Ivanhoe*

   Gurth, knowing his master's irritable temper, attempted no _____ .
   a. exculpation
   b. introspection
   c. circumvention
   d. transmogrification

5. **From Thornton Wilder's** *The Bridge of San Luis Rey*

   Her daughter scolded her for an _____ and for making a cult of sorrow.
   a. introspective
   b. lycanthrope
   c. monist
   d. gastronome

Though it is a good thing to have a rich vocabulary, it is not a good thing to abuse that vocabulary by writing verbose, abstruse, sesquipedalian sentences. Those who overuse their vocabularies often do so at the expense of clarity. Translate the following showy, ponderous passage into graceful, direct English. Do not use slang, but do use words that seem familiar and comfortable.

AMIDST THE HELIOTROPIC VINES, the vivacious lycanthrope (a neophyte of the species and an autodidact in metamorphosis) was caught *in medias res* as she transmogrified cacophonously. An introspective, perambulating gastronome happened to look through the window—open to the circumambient breeze—but his anthropocentric world view (unlike Einstein's abstract monism) interfered with his ratiocinations and prevented him from realizing what he was seeing. We may exculpate the gastronome, however, for he did not circumvent the expected courtesies; *au contraire*: "Good day," he averred. The *sotto voce* growl of her retort left him incredulous.

introspective

Reading Comprehension

1. In Translation 35, the author does all of the following EXCEPT:
   A. explain how the lycanthrope met the gastronome
   B. explain what the lycanthrope was doing when they met
   C. explain how the gastronome felt about the lycanthrope's response
   D. explain how the lycanthrope felt during transmogrification

2. It can be inferred from the passage that:
   A. Anthropocentrism can interfere with clear thinking.
   B. All lycanthropes are vivacious.
   C. Gastronomes are rarely courteous.
   D. Introspective people do more perambulating.

Analogies

3. TRANSMOGRIFY : LYCANTHROPE ::
   A. alter : modify
   B. evolve : chrysalis
   C. metamorphose : insect
   D. transpose : music

4. CIRCUMVENT : CIRCUMAMBIENT ::
   A. evade : surrounding
   B. circumference : circumnavigate
   C. anthropocentrism : *mise-en-scène*
   D. introspection : autodidact

Antonyms

5. EXCULPATE :

exculpate

   A. accuse
   B. convict
   C. impeach
   D. imprison

6. INTROSPECTIVE :
   A. extroverted
   B. thoughtful
   C. meditative
   D. provident

synthesis

Use any five words from List 35 in a single sentence.

divergence and convergence

People often **circumvent** rules, regulations, and traditions that they do not wish to observe or perhaps do not believe in. For example, people who organized the underground railroad in the early Nineteenth Century bravely circumvented the slavery laws, and did so at considerable personal risk. But we often see people circumvent rules solely for personal convenience or gain, as in the case of people who fail to declare portions of their income at tax time. First (divergent question), how many things can you think of that people do or could circumvent? List as many as you can. Second (convergent question), what is one example of a situation in which you would never circumvent the rules? Explain.

intuition and imagination

In a dream you find yourself a research botanist on a distant and little-explored planet. You can breathe the air. The planet is densely covered with **heliotropic** plants and vines. Unlike earth, this planet rotates once a minute, and all of the tall heliotropic vegetation around you leans far east every sixty seconds for the new sunrise, rises straight up as the sun reaches its zenith in fifteen seconds, and leans far west as the sun sets thirty seconds after it rose, only to rise again thirty seconds later. Tell us more about life on this planet. Aesthetic challenge: describe the most beautiful scene on the planet.

emotion

You are talking to your friend, who suddenly breaks into a hideous laugh, her face **transmogrified** into a frightful, twisted, glaring grin. She will not explain and will not stop laughing. How does this make you feel, as you stare into her transmogrified face?

analysis

Using a dictionary, carefully explain the differences between the etymology, the grammar, and the best usage of the words **transmogrify** and **metamorphosis**.

Neologist's Lexicon

Use the stems in this list to create a new word (neologism). Give the word, the pronunciation, the part of speech, the etymology, and the definition(s). Keep a record of the neologisms you create from list to list. Here are some examples:

exism (ecks' ism) n. [ex (out), ism (doctrine)] 1. the pathological addiction to the phrase, "I'm outa here." 2. chronic and habitual staring at the doors and windows during conversation.

lykospection (lie' ko spek shun) n. [lykos (wolf), spect (look), tion (act)] 1. girl-watching, especially at a beach or other holiday area 2. adopting the appearance and mannerisms of a ladies' man.

Sesquipedalian Poetry

Use the words from this week's list to write a poem. This time, try to intensify your poem with sound, even at the expense of meaning. In fact, you might enjoy writing a pure sound poem, that has no intelligible meaning at all. If you don't worry about meaning at all, you can have lots of fun with the euphony and cacophony of the sounds of the vowels and consonants. You can even do creative, experimental things with punctuation! For example:

Autodidact

O, monism, moan, is he? No
gastronome; spent tricks and intricate
anthropocentrics, yes sir. Come
circumambient am being into
vivacious . . . shucks lace life lazy fly
reify wholly transmogrify
au contraire! Circumvent. Specks exculpate
rarely *in medias res*, and so
race to your auto you autodidact!
Did you act it out totally, Lycanthrope?
Hohoho, hopelessly circumvent helioptropes, sir.
Autodidact, invent
Yourself yourself yourself yrslf;:,.
NOW.

sacrosanct   egocentric

perfidy   non sequitur   inanimate

loquacious   obsequious

perambulate   translucent   nihilism   tangible

malapropism   omnibus   epigram

interdiction   unilateral   exculpate

omniscient   incredulous   postlude

neophyte   benediction   retort   impugn

monolithic   imponderable   autodidact

heterodox   supersede   gregarious

altercation   soliloquy   cacophony

sangfroid   contravene   circumlocution

confluence   paterfamilias   heliotropic

pathetic   interstices   transmogrify

anthropocentric

Focus on the central concept of our learning:
the stems are our prize content.
The stems provide us with a vocabulary construction set.
The words are just examples and variations
to show us how the stem system works.
By knowing the stems, we can learn
the words in this book and thousands more.

Adriatic
Sea

ROME

Ionian
Sea

GREECE

Aegean
Sea

Mediterranean Sea

Keep
reinforcing
the origins of
English and
Spanish.

• pre	(before)	a priori	• post	(after)	a posteriori
• *gen*	(origin)	parthenogenesis	• son	(sound)	assonance
• jur	(swear)	objurgation	• *demo*	(people)	demotic
• sopor	(sleep)	soporific	• inter	(between)	internecine
• ped	(foot)	sesquipedalian	• *cracy*	(government)	plutocracy
• lin	(line)	delineate	• *phan*	(appearance)	epiphany
• *tomy*	(cut)	dichotomy	• *dicho*	(in two parts)	dichotomy
• tort	(twist)	tortuous	• **sui**	(self)	sui generis
• ob	(against)	objurgation	• *partheno*	(virgin)	parthenogenesis
• **sesqui**	(one and a half)	sesquipedalian	• *pluto*	(wealth)	plutocracy
• **nec**	(kill)	internecine			

a priori (from theory) The theory was developed through deduction from principle, *a priori*.

a posteriori (from observation) The idea was reached inductively from evidence, *a posteriori*.

parthenogenesis (unfertilized birth) Athena was born by parthenogenesis from Zeus's forehead.

assonance (vowel repetition) Notice the assonance of the words *croon*, *duel*, and *tube*.

objurgation (rebuke) We read the teacher's red-penned objurgations on the term paper.

demotic (of the common people) We studied the demotic alleyway slang.

soporific (sleep-inducing) His soporific platitudes bored everyone in the audience.

internecine (mutually destructive) Their internecine wars doomed the barbarian tribes.

sesquipedalian (very long (words)) Having a sesquipedalian vocabulary is fun.

sui generis (unique) Her self-originated style was boldly *sui generis*.

• • •

plutocracy (government of wealthy) The democracy degenerated into a plutocracy.

delineate (to outline) Please quickly delineate the features of your plan.

dichotomy (two-part division) Is there a clear dichotomy between the two choices?

epiphany (revelation) In a sudden epiphany, he saw the solution!

tortuous (twisting) The tortuous highway winds through the hills of West Virginia.

As Used by Alfred Lansing in *Endurance*

	To reach	them	involved	a	**tortuous**	crawl.
Parts of Speech:	n.	pron.	v.	adj.	**adj.**	n.
Parts of Sentence:	--------subject ------		AVP			direct object
Phrases:	----infinitive phrase----					
Clauses:	----------------------------------independent clause-----------------------------------					
	one independent clause, a simple declarative sentence					

Here Alfred Lansing uses the adjective *tortuous* to modify the singular common noun *crawl*. Of course, *crawl* can also be a verb, but here it is a noun modified by an adjective, and serving as the direct object of the action verb.

Pronunciation

a priori	AY pry OR eye	**sesquipedalian**	SESS kwi pe DAY lian
a posteriori	AY post ear ee OR eye	*sui generis*	swee JEN er iss
parthenogenesis	PAR then oh GEN eh sis	**plutocracy**	ploo TOCK ra see
assonance	AH son ance	**delineate**	de LIN ee ate
objurgation	ob jur GAY shun	**dichotomy**	die KOHT o me
demotic	deh MOHT ic	**epiphany**	ee PIFF a nee
soporific	soh pore IF ic	**tortuous**	TOR tyoo us
internecine	inter NEE seen		

Spanish Cognates

soporific	soporífico	**introspective**	instrospectivo
plutocracy	plutocracia	**epiphany**	epifanía
assonance	asonancia	**tortuous**	tortuoso
delineation	delineación	**parthenogenesis**	partenogénesis

1. Philosophers often use the terms **a priori** (from before) and **a posteriori** (from afterward) when they discuss epistemology, the question of how we know things. *A priori* (pre: before) knowledge is knowledge that can be deduced from principles; it can be known prior to empirical verification. *A posteriori* (post: after) knowledge is knowledge that is dependent upon induction, reasoning after experience, and empirical verification. Some would say human freedom of mind is an *a priori* truth. The scientific method gives us many *a posteriori* truths. *A posteriori* is pronounced ay-posteriOR-eye, and *a priori* is pronounce ay-priOR-eye.

2. A **Micropoem**: The adjective **sesquipedalian** is a humorous word that refers to words that are a foot and a half long! **Sesqui** means one and a half, and **ped** means foot! If you master the vocabulary in this course, you will have a sesquipedalian vocabulary.

3. Poets and novelists make frequent use of **assonance**, the repetition of vowel sounds. When Sandburg wrote "The voice of the last cricket/Across the first frost/Is one kind of goodbye," he used assonance on across/frost and kind/bye (*o* sound and *i* sound). Assonance is different from consonance, the repetition of consonant sounds. To make the cricket chirp, Sandburg used consonance on *voice/last/first/frost* (*s* sound). Both assonance and consonance are different from alliteration, the repetition of initial word sounds, which Sandburg used on *first/frost* (*f* sound).

4. The term **sui generis**, like the word **unique**, is best used for things that are truly one of a kind. Something can not be very unique: it either is unique or it is not. Similarly, to be *sui generis* is to form a kind (generis) all by your self (sui).

5. The adjective **internecine** is pronounced inter-NIECE-een, and refers to mutual slaughter, as in a civil war. It comes from the Latin *inter* (between) and *necare* (to kill).

6. Some insects and algae are able to reproduce from an UNfertilized egg or spore. This ability is known as **parthenogenesis**, after Athena, the Greek goddess of wisdom who was born from Zeus's forehead! Athena's temple in Athens is, of course, the Parthenon.

7. To **delineate** is to outline, but it is not to outline in the complete, systematic manner of a formal outline. Rather, to delineate is to sketch out in words the basic outline of something (de: down, lin: line). Delineation is brief analysis, rather than full formal analysis.

8. A **Classic Word**: The adjective **tortuous** is more commonly found in the classics than you might imagine. Harriet Beecher Stowe described how the red, muddy, turbid current flowed through the abrupt, tortuous windings of the Red River. In Dickens's *A Tale of Two Cities* there is a tortuous, uphill thoroughfare. In Hardy's *The Mayor of Casterbridge* there is a tortuous defile for carriages down the centre of the street. H.G. Wells's Martians are unearthly in their tortuous forms. In *Lord Jim*, Joseph Conrad even described policies as tortuous! Kipling's Kim found a tortuous and indirect person playing a hidden game. Fitzgerald, in *The Great Gatsby*, described superior couples holding each other tortuously.

In each case below, one of the choices was really the word used by the author in the sentence provided. All of the choices can be found in the example words on the first page of this lesson. Your challenge is to decide which word the author used. This is not a test; it is more like a game, because more than one word choice may work perfectly well. See if you can use your sensitivity and intuition to guess correctly which word the author used. You may need a dictionary.

1. **From Charlotte Brontë's** *Jane Eyre*

    The heavy supper she had eaten produced a _____ effect.
    a. soporific
    b. demotic
    c. internecine
    d. sesquipedalian

2. **From Sylvia Plath's** *The Bell Jar*

    His breath shaped _____ smoke signals in the gray air.
    a. demotic
    b. soporific
    c. tortuous
    d. *a priori*

3. **From Mary Shelley's** *Frankenstein*

    How ___ the wretch whom with such infinite pains and care I had endeavoured to form?
    a. dichotomize
    b. internecine
    c. delineate
    d. objurgate

4. **From Rachel Carson's** *Silent Spring*

    The greatest single factor in preventing insects from overwhelming the rest of the world is the _____ warfare which they carry out among themselves.
    a. internecine
    b. dichotomous
    c. tortuous
    d. *sui generis*

5. **From Jack London's** *White Fang*

    His arms [were] raised in _____.
    a. dichotomy
    b. assonance
    c. parthenogenesis
    d. objurgation

Though it is good to have a rich vocabulary, it is not good to abuse that vocabulary by writing verbose, abstruse, sesquipedalian sentences (such as this one). Those who overuse their vocabularies often do so at the expense of clarity. Translate the following showy, ponderous passage into graceful, direct English. Do not use slang, but do use words that seem familiar and comfortable.

AFTER TWENTY YEARS of perfidious, internecine civil conflict over language customs, the victorious, monolithic plutocracy formally rejected the demotic, heterodox slang (an assonant jargon known as *lunorap*) spoken on the lunar colony, and issued an objurgation to the obsequious colonists, insisting on formal use of its own soporific, sesquipedalian language and tortuous logic in all official documents. Putative *a posteriori* knowledge, the omniscient government averred, would no longer be allowed to contradict official *a priori* truth. This unilateral interdiction (actually, it was an omnibus document that in a brief *obiter dictum* outlawed parthenogenesis) superseded all previous language edicts, delineated a dichotomy between sedate GOVSPEAK and loquacious COLSPEAK, and left the nonplussed colonists incredulous; but no cacophonous, acerbic altercation or nihilistic retort followed, and the gregarious colonists did not contravene the condescending edict, even though no effort was made by the government to mollify the colonists.

heterodox

Reading Comprehension

1. In Translation 36 it can be inferred that:
    A. GOVSPEAK is soporific and sesquipedalian.
    B. GOVSPEAK is demotic, heterodox slang.
    C. GOVSPEAK is the dialect spoken by most colonists.
    D. GOVSPEAK is very similar to COLSPEAK.

2. The author does all of the following EXCEPT:
    A. describe the colonists' reaction to the government edict
    B. describe the difference between the official and popular languages
    C. describe the three types of colonists
    D. describe the cause of the civil conflict

Analogies

3. **A PRIORI : A POSTERIORI ::**
    A. microscope : telescope
    B. history : science fiction
    C. theology : science
    D. dreaming : exploration

4. **PLUTOCRACY : DEMOTIC ::**
    A. aristocracy : popular
    B. meritocracy : labor
    C. oligarchy : monarchy
    D. autocracy : heptarchy

Antonyms

dichtotomy

5. **ASSONANCE :**
    A. alliteration
    B. end rhyme
    C. consonance
    D. internal rhyme

6. **DICHOTOMY :**
    A. unity
    B. continuity
    C. ambiguity
    D. contiguity

synthesis

Think of three examples of **internecine** conflict, and explain why you would describe them as internecine. Of course, all wars are to some extent mutually destructive, and yet we do not describe all wars as internecine. What is the difference between internecine wars and non-internecine wars?

analysis

Can you form a **dichotomy** between *a priori* truths and *a posteriori* truths? Consider various ideas, facts, or principles that you consider to be true, and decide whether each one is an *a priori* truth or an *a posteriori* truth. As an example, Jefferson began the *Declaration of Independence* with an *a priori* statement: "We hold these truths to be self-evident . . . ." Find at least five truths of each kind.

intuition

In a dream, you are on a difficult, **tortuous** path leading upwards through steep, rocky, evergreen wilderness. Finally, you climb through a layer of misty clouds into blue mountain summits, and you are completely surprised at what you find in front of you on the mossy boulders. What do you find?

ethics

Consider the implications of living in a **plutocracy**. Then consider that a government could be an official plutocracy, officially requiring a high financial status of all officeholders, or it could be an unofficial plutocracy that does not officially require great wealth but through *de facto* means makes it impossible for anyone without great wealth to successfully seek office. Main question: What do you think are the most important ethical issues in plutocratic rule? Side question: From your study of history, what examples of plutocracy can you think of?

divergence

The word **soporific** means sleep-inducing. Used literally, it can refer to a drug, but used with more humor, it can refer to something that is so boring (such as a bad lecture or program) that it puts people to sleep. Make a long, humorous list of soporifics you have endured.

Neologist's Lexicon

Use the stems in this list to create a new word (neologism). Give the word, the pronunciation, the part of speech, the etymology, and the definition(s). Here are some examples:

sesquinecinary (sess kwee nees' ih nary) adj. [sesqui (one and a half), nec (kill)] 1. killing in a manner far beyond what is necessary (killing and a half) to terminate life, as Achilles's killing of Hector and dragging his body around the walls of Troy 2. obsessive use of the phrase "That kills me"; derived from J.D. Salinger's character, Holden Caulfield, in *The Catcher in the Rye*.

soporocracy (sah pore ah' cracy) n. [sopor (sleep), cracy (government) 1. a government that is asleep to dangers and threats to the nation 2. a government led by individuals who are indifferent to, uninterested in, or uninformed about, national affairs

Sesquipedalian Dialogue

Use the words from List 36 to construct a short philosophical dialogue between two characters. Feel free to be playful or satirical. If you would like a paradigm for a philosophical dialogue, you might like to read one of the shorter Dialogues of Plato. As an example, here is a spoof of a Platonic dialogue. In the real dialogue, the conversation is between Socrates and Meno:

Meanie

Sogreat and Meanie walk down a path and sit on a bench, looking out over a grove called *Countryday*.

Sogreat: Well, Meanie, this beautiful grove reminds me of your sesquipedalian speech yesterday. I must admit that I was quite impressed with your command of ideas. In fact, sometimes it seemed that your complexities became too intricate for me to understand.

Meanie: Oh, Sogreat, you don't fool me with your *sui generis* ironies. I sense your silent objurgations lurking under the surface of your sentences.

Sogreat: No, Meanie, your ideas seemed to emerge fully grown, without the need for logical development, like Athena's parthenogenesis from the head of Zeus.

Meanie: Well, Sogreat, in a demotic society such as ours, we must lead people to epiphanies quickly, without the soporific details that make arguments (such as yours) so tortuous.

Sogreat: I see that you can delineate my faults succinctly, Meanie. I must agree that there is a sharp dichotomy between my tedious logic and your exciting insights. Tell me, Meanie, would you say that *a priori* thinking or *a posteriori* thinking is more likely to lead to knowledge of the truth?

Meanie: Oh, Sogreat, you can't catch me in one of your famous traps.

Sogreat: Meanie, you clever plutocrat, I see that our internecine arguments are accomplishing nothing. In fact, I seem to understand you less now than I did when we sat down!

finis

• thanatos	(death)	thanatopsis		• spir	(breathe)	suspiration
• opia	(sight)	thanatopsis		• syn	(together)	synoptic
• vac	(empty)	vacuous		• man	(hand)	legerdemain
• luc	(light)	lucubration		• ex	(out)	ex cathedra
• ize	(make)	lionize		• ism	(system)	nepotism
• sed	(sit)	assiduous, sedentary		• sub	(under)	subterfuge
• fug	(flee)	subterfuge		• ine	(nature of)	saturnine
• pusill	(small)	pusillanimous		• anim	(mind)	pusillanimous
• nepo	(nephew)	nepotism		• bon	(good)	bon vivant
• viv	(life)	bon vivant		• ous	(full of)	sedulous, vacuous

thanatopsis (view of death) We thoughtfully read the introvert's poetic thanatopsis.

vacuous (stupidly empty of ideas) See the vacuous expression on his uninformed face.

lucubration (late studying) His midnight lucubrations by candlelight tired him.

ex cathedra (from the throne) The king pronounced, *ex cathedra*, his opinion.

legerdemain (sleight of hand) His verbal legerdemain confused those who didn't listen.

suspiration (deep sigh) We endured his mournful suspirations over Lulu.

nepotism (favoritism to relatives) Graft and nepotism weakened the government.

synoptic (general in view) Read the synoptic gospels; view a synoptic chart.

lionize (treat as a celebrity) Upon her return to the city, she was lionized by the joyful crowd.

assiduous (persevering) His assiduous efforts to balance the budget finally paid off.

• • •

subterfuge (evasive dodge) He ducked a question with a clever subterfuge.

bon vivant (indulger in luxury) The wealthy *bon vivant* lived the good life in Hawaii.

saturnine (gloomy and remote) Her saturnine personality caused her to lose friends.

sedentary (sitting) Flagpole sitting is a notably sedentary occupation.

pusillanimous (small-minded) The snub at the losing team was a low, pusillanimous act.

As Used by Bram Stoker in *Dracula*

	I	have	been	practicing	shorthand	very	**assiduously.**
Parts of Speech:	pron.	v.	v.	v.	n.	adv.	adv.
Parts of Sentence:	subject	------------AVP-------------			direct object		

Phrases: ----no prepositional, appositive, or verbal phrase----

Clauses: ----------------------------------independent clause----------------------------------
one independent clause, a simple declarative sentence

Bram Stoker uses the adverb *assiduously* to modify the present perfect action verb *have been practicing*. Notice that the adverb is modified by its own adverb, *very*.

Pronunciation

thanatopsis	thah na TOP siss	**lionize**	LIE on ize
vacuous	VACK yoo us	**assiduous**	ah SID yoo us
lucubration	loo kyoo BRAY shun	**subterfuge**	SUB tur fyooj
ex cathedra	ex cah THEE dra	*bon vivant*	bohn vee VAHN
legerdemain	LEJ ur de MAIN	**saturnine**	SAT ur nine
suspiration	suss pih RAY shun	**sedentary**	SED en tary
nepotism	NEH po tiz um	**pusillanimous**	pyoo si LAN ih muss
synoptic	sin OP tick		

Spanish Cognates

vacuous	vacuo	**nepotism**	nepotismo
subterfuge	suberfugio	**pusillanimous**	pusilánime
assiduous	asiduo	**lucubration**	lucubración
sedentary	sedentario	**synoptic**	sinóptico

56

1. The adjective **assiduous** has more in common with the word **sedentary** than first meets the eye. **Assiduous** traces back to the Latin *ad*: to and *sedere*: to sit. In other words, being assiduous suggests that you are persevering because you sit there until the job is done! A sedentary job is one in which you are sitting down most of the day. One could have a sedentary job without necessarily being assiduous.

    Assiduous is a good **Classic Word**. In the writings of Brontës, Stowe, Thoreau, Dickens, Wells, Conrad, and Wilder, we find characters proceeding assiduously with their occupations, assiduously giving reading lessons, knitting away assiduously, gnawing assiduously at the near foreleg of an enemy, being too assiduously engaged to talk, chewing betel assiduously, and cultivating the city assiduously for material. There are assiduous pupils, those who arrange cups and spoons with assiduous celerity, and those who are equally assiduous in every duty.

2. Named after the Roman god Saturn, who is identified with the Greek god Cronus, the giant ringed planet is the second largest planet in our solar system and the sixth from the Sun. When we describe a person as **saturnine**, however, we suggest none of the beauty that is identified with the great ringed planet. Rather, we mean that, like Saturn, the person is remote, gloomy, and silent.

3. The adjective **pusillanimous** is best regarded in light of its opposite, **magnanimous**. To be magnanimous is to be generous, brave, large, or great (magn) in spirit (anim). To be pusillanimous is to be small-minded, timid, or even cowardly.

4. Popes and kings can make pronouncements **ex cathedra**, literally from their thrones. We can still use this term, however, even when we are not actually describing magnates or potentates. If we wish to satirize someone who is behaving in a self-important, puffed up manner, we can use **ex cathedra** to enhance the sense of irony: The little boy straddled the hobby horse and issued his instructions to his nursemaid, **ex cathedra**.

5. The noun **lucubration** refers to laborious studying, especially writing done late at night. A poetic word, **lucubration** gives us the image of the writer leaning over his or her desk in the early hours of the morning, the soft light (luc) of the candle casting its glow on the newly written ideas. The Latin *lucubrare* meant to work by artificial light.

6. A **Micropoem**: **Subterfuge** is an especially descriptive noun. It refers to the evasions we use to avoid being pinned down. You can evade a question with a subterfuge, as by distracting the questioner with an unrelated counter-question. The word contains a metaphorical image of what is really happening: to use a subterfuge is to duck, to flee (fug) underneath (sub).

7. The noun **thanatopsis** was coined by William Cullen Bryant for a poem musing on death. The word literally means a view (opsis, opia) of death (thanatos). There are some other interesting words that come to mind in light of Bryant's contribution. One is **thanatology**, the study of death, and another is **thanatophobia**, an abnormally great fear of death.

In each case below, one of the choices was really the word used by the author in the sentence provided. All of the choices can be found in the example words on the first page of this lesson. Your challenge is to decide which word the author used. This is not a test; it is more like a game, because more than one word choice may work perfectly well. See if you can use your sensitivity and intuition to guess correctly which word the author used. You may need a dictionary.

1.   **From Dava Sobel's** *Longitude*

And this was done through the application of some mathematical _____ called the Equation of Time.
a. subterfuge
b. legerdemain
c. *bon vivant*
d. thanatopsis

2.   **From Alfred Lansing's** *Endurance*

He was _____ wherever he went...knighted by his king.
a. synoptic
b. vacuous
c. lionized
d. sedentary

3.   **From Joseph Conrad's** *Lord Jim*

She chewed betel _____.
a. assiduously
b. *ex cathedra*
c. synoptically
d. pusillanimously

4.   **From William Shakespeare's** *Hamlet*

Hamlet described the "windy _____ of forced breath."
a. legerdemain
b. subterfuge
c. lucubration
d. suspiration

5.   **From Joseph Heller's** *Catch-22*

Now she sat resting in _____ indolence.
a. saturnine
b. vacuous
c. pusillanimous
d. assiduous

Though is is a good thing to have a rich vocabulary, it is not good to abuse that vocabulary by writing verbose, abstruse, sesquipedalian sentences (such as this one). Those who overuse their vocabularies often do so at the expense both of clarity and of others' patience. Translate the following ostentatious, ponderous passage into graceful, direct English. Do not use slang, but do use words that seem familiar and comfortable.

FIRST OBSEQUIOUSLY LIONIZED by the public and then accused of perfidious nepotism and egocentrism, the nonplussed plutocrat—with assiduous lucubration, frequent suspirations, and *sotto voce* epigrams—devoted himself to an introspective and saturnine thanatopsis. Without verbal legerdemain, circumlocution, or subterfuge, he delineated the pusillanimous and vacuous character of the sedentary *bon vivants*, portly gastronomes, putative autodidacts, and heterodox neophytes who had dared to impugn his *ex cathedra* synoptic ratiocinations. Condescendingly and with sedate sangfroid, he noted that he need not mollify the acerbity of the incredulous or exculpate himself from the specious charges of abased nihilists who, with their constant internecine cacophonous altercations contravened every reasonable interdiction and declaimed with loquacious retorts and tortuous *non sequiturs* against every *obiter dictum*. "*Au contraire*," he averred in his postlude, "the soporific objurgations and demotic malapropisms of the gregarious masses trouble me not. As paterfamilias of the nation, I must allow nothing to supersede my *sui generis* sacrosanct *a priori* responsibilities. These matters are an imponderable *terra incognita* to those whose hierarchy of values begins and ends with the tangible." Then, in a sudden epiphany, he added, "One cannot expect lycanthropes to appreciate heliotropes; it isn't their forte."

circumlocution

Reading Comprehension

1. For Translation 37, which of the following does the passage suggest:
    A. Corrupt rulers manipulate the people.
    B. An educated populace is essential in a democracy.
    C. Public favor is an ephemeral phenomenon.
    D. Intellectuals make poor government officials.

2. The passage could be best described as:
    A. A thoughtful ruler stands by his principles.
    B. A plutocrat enriches himself from the public coffers.
    C. A tyrant ignores the voice of the people.
    D. Power corrupts, and absolute power corrupts absolutely.

Analogies

3. LUCUBRATION : ASSIDUOUS ::
    A. sedentary : sedate
    B. thanatopsis : mordant
    C. synopsis : verbose
    D. application : sedulous

4. BON VIVANT : SATURNINE ::
    A. legerdemain : confusing
    B. thanatopsis : subterfuge
    C. sedentary : flagpole
    D. monograph : synoptic

Antonyms

saturnine

5. VACUOUS :
    A. cognizant
    B. fecund
    C. ignorant
    D. effusive

6. BON VIVANT :
    A. stoic
    B. epicurean
    C. ascetic
    D. eremite

ethics

Nepotism, the corrupt practice of showing favoritism to friends and relatives, is almost universally regarded as unethical. For example, if a high governmental official appoints a close friend or family member to a desirable or lucrative position, the governmental official could be condemned and accused of nepotism (literally, nephew-ism). Specifically, what are the reasons why nepotism is unethical? Try to list several very precise reasons why widespread nepotism could be harmful to a nation's well-being. It might help to remember that nepotism actually is widespread in many countries.

imagination and intuition

You are a research scientist in a biological research station in a rain forest. For years, you have worked on the solution to a problem, and now you have it. For this solution, you will be **lionized** by the public, esteemed by the scientific community, and might very well receive the Nobel Prize. Describe your work in the rain forest, and explain your problem and its solution.

synthesis

Use any ten of the words from List 37 in a single coherent paragraph. Humor is acceptable.

emotion and analysis

In *Leaves of Grass*, Walt Whitman gives a new angle to the term **thanatopsis**. The smallest blade of grass, Whitman explains, shows that there is really no death. Whitman notes that many feel it is lucky to be born, but he says that it is just as lucky to die. Whitman claims to know this. Find a copy of *Leaves of Grass* and examine these passages and others; then analyze Whitman's concept of no-death, and discuss your emotional response to Whitman's ideas. You might enjoy comparing Whitman's poem to Bryant's famous poem, "Thanatopsis."

Neologist's Lexicon

Use the stems in this list to create a new word (neologism). Give the word, the pronunciation, the part of speech, the etymology, and the definition(s). Keep a record of the neologisms you create from list to list. Here are some examples:

pusillopia (pyoo sill opia) n. [pusill (small), opia (sight)] 1. a form of egocentrism in which the victim sees all other persons as smaller and less important than himself 2. chronic, pathological condescension

fuganimism (fyooj anim ism) n. [fug (flee), anim (mind), ism (doctrine) 1. the tendency to avoid experiences that contain, or require the comprehension of, ideas 2. reflexive switching of the radio channel when the news comes on

Sesquipedalian Pet Commands

Using words from List 37 or previous lists, construct a series of commands useful for training a pet, such as a dog, raccoon, or chimpanzee. A few examples:

1. BE SEDENTARY! The pet will instantly sit down and look silently into your eyes, waiting for the next instruction.

2. ESCHEW NEPOTISM! The pet will promptly ignore his or her brothers and sisters, and will come to you.

3. SUSPIRATE! The pet will look at you in a longing way and then emit a deep sigh, as of adoration. This command is best issued when the pet is hungry, just prior to feeding.

4. LIONIZE! At this command, the pet will effusively manifest joy in your presence, running back and forth, jumping up and down, and whining with glee.

Sesquipedalian Poetry

Use the words from List 37 to create a poem. This time, work to establish interesting rhythms or metrical patterns. The whole poem does not have to be iambic, trochaic, dactylic, or anapestic, but try to control the fall of the syllables so that the rhythm is consonant with the meaning of the poem.

• log	(reason)	syllogism	• nym	(name)	metonymy
• phor	(carry)	anaphora	• ize	(make)	bowdlerize
• loco	(place)	locus classicus	• re	(again)	reiterate
• de	(down)	desultory	• ambul	(walk)	funambulist
• phobia	(fear)	lyssophobia	• ideo	(idea)	idée fixe
• schizo	(divide)	schism	• apo	(up)	apotheosis
• theo	(god)	apotheosis	• pre	(before)	precursor
• curs	(run)	precursor	• cosmo	(universe)	cosmology
• eu	(good)	euphony	• phon	(sound)	euphony
• funi	(cord)	funambulist	• meta	(change)	metonymy

syllogism (three-part deduction) Ex.: All A is B; C is A; therefore, C is B.

metonymy (association name) Ex.: The White House has announced a new policy.

anaphora (repetition in successive phrases) Dr. King used anaphora, repeating, "I have a dream."

bowdlerize (censor prudishly) We deplore the bowdlerization of great literature.

locus classicus (classical example) *The Iliad* is a *locus classicus* for the heroic ideal.

reiterate (repeat) It is needless to reiterate one's objections.

desultory (rambling) He gave a desultory, soporific lecture.

funambulist (tightrope walker) The speech was an act of political funambulism.

lyssophobia (fear of insanity) It was a family of schizophrenics and lyssophobiacs.

idée fixe (obsession) For Ahab, the whale was an *idée fixe*.

•   •   •

schism (division) A schism developed in the Democratic party. (pronounced SIZZum not skizm)

apotheosis (raising to god status) We noted the public's apotheosis of the new champ.

precursor (forerunner) This unfortunate event was the precursor of the tragedy to come.

cosmology (study of the universe) The existence of the Big Bang is a cosmological question.

euphony (beautiful sound) Hear the soft euphony of the wind in the trees.

As Used by Herman Melville in *Moby Dick*

	Straight	up,	leaps	thy	apotheosis!
Parts of Speech:	adv.	adv.	v.	adj.	**n.**

Parts of Sentence:			AVP	subject

Phrases: ----no prepositional, appositive, or verbal phrase----

Clauses: ----------------------------------independent clause----------------------------------

one independent clause, a simple exclamatory sentence

Here Herman Melville uses the noun *apotheosis* as the subject of the sentence. Notice that the subject comes after the verb, for effect.

Pronunciation

syllogism	SILL oh jiz um	**lyssophobia**	LISS oh FO bee ah
metonymy	meh TAHN o mee	***idee fixe***	EE day FEEKS
anaphora	ah NAFF o rah	**schism**	SIZZ um
bowdlerize	BOW dler ize	**apotheosis**	a POTH ee O siss
locus classicus	LO kuss KLASS ikuss	**precursor**	pre KURR sor
reiterate	ree IT er ate	**cosmology**	kozz MAH lo jee
desultory	DESS ul tory	**euphony**	YOO fo nee
funambulist	foo NAM byoo list		

Spanish Cognates

reiteration	reiteración	**anaphora**	anáfora
schism	cisma	**euphony**	eufonía
syllogism	silogismo	**precursor**	precursor
apotheosis	apoteosis	**metonomy**	metonimia

1. In 1818 an English editor, Thomas Bowdler, published an expurgated edition of Shakespeare, removing passages that he found to be offensive. Today, we say a work has been **bowdlerized** when it has been prudishly censored.

2. The noun **metonymy** is actually composed of the Greek stems *meta*, which in this case means other, and *nym*, which means name. **Metonymy** is another name, a name exchanged for the usual name. When we say that the White House has announced a new policy, we don't really mean that the building spoke; instead of saying that the President announced the policy, we say that the White House announced the policy, since the White House is an image that everyone associates with the President.

3. A **Micropoem**: A **desultory** speech or conversation is one that is not coherent or connected; it is random and aimless, wandering. It is lacking in structure, sequence, purpose. The word desultory—pronounced DESultory—comes from *de* (down) and *salire* (leap), the idea being that in speaking so aimlessly, you are jumping off the subject. One common reason for losing the theme is that one really has no purpose or theme to care about.

   Desultory is also a good **Classic Word**. It is a word that Thomas Hardy especially loved and used in many of his novels in the 1870s and 1880s because it captured the aimlessness and lack of purpose that he found in the effete and decadent *fin de siecle*. Hardy described his characters' desultory ramblings, desultory chats, and desultory conversations. In *The Mayor of Casterbridge* Hardy noted "the walk of the skilled countryman as distinct from the desultory shamble of the general labourer" and the "Saturday afternoon [that] slipped on thus desultorily."

4. The French term **idée fixe** means a fixed idea, a monomania, or obsession. It is pronounced ee-day- FEEKS. Ahab's *idée fixe* was Moby Dick. You would enjoy looking up the story of Berlioz, who used this term to describe his obsession with a beautiful woman—translated into a musical theme that pervades his masterpiece, *Symphonie Fantastique*.

5. A **locus classicus** is a literary passage that is a primary classical example of something, a passage that is typically cited as authoritative or illustrative. *The Iliad* is the *locus classicus* of martial heroism. Oedipus's arrogant inability to understand that he himself could be the source of evil in his city is the *locus classicus* for the Greek concept of hubris.

6. The word **syllogism** comes from the Greek *syllogismos*, a reckoning together or summing up. The stems are *syn* (together) and *logos* (word). In formal logic, a syllogism is a logical structure that contains two premises and a logical conclusion drawn from the two premises. First premise: All men are perplexed. Second premise: Socrates is a man. Conclusion: Therefore, Socrates is perplexed. Note that the truth of the conclusion is not assured if the premises are not true, or if the reasoning is not logical. Examples of false syllogisms: All men have hair; Peggy Sue has hair; therefore, Peggy Sue is a man. Or, All planets have moons; pzx is a newly discovered planet; therefore pzx, must have moons.

In each case below, one of the choices was really the word used by the author in the sentence provided. All of the choices can be found in the example words on the first page of this lesson. Your challenge is to decide which word the author used. This is not a test; it is more like a game, because more than one word choice may work perfectly well. See if you can use your sensitivity and intuition to guess correctly which word the author used. You may need a dictionary.

1. **From E.M. Forster's** *A Passage to India*

    The crowds of Hindus began a _____ move back into town.
    a. euphonic
    b. desultory
    c. bowdlerized
    d. reiterated

2. **From Robert Louis Stevenson's** *Treasure Island*

    "Rout the house out!" _____ Pew, striking with his stick upon the road.
    a. bowdlerized
    b. precursor
    c. euphony
    d. reiterated

3. **From Nathaniel Hawthorne's** *The Scarlet Letter*

    [He was] so _____ by worshipping admirers.
    a. apotheosized
    b. reiterated
    c. bowdlerized
    d. schism

4. **From Henry David Thoreau's** *Walden*

    The tortoise and the frog are among the _____ and heralds of this season.
    a. funambulists
    b. schisms
    c. precursors
    d. euphonies

5. **From Jonathan Swift's** *Gulliver's Travels*

    Gulliver spoke of "our wars by sea and by land, of our _____ in religion."
    a. precursors
    b. schisms
    c. cosmologies
    d. *locus classicus*

Though it is good to have a rich vocabulary, it is not good to abuse that vocabulary by writing verbose, sesquipedalian sentences (such as this one). Those who overuse their vocabularies often do so at the expense both of clarity and of others' patience. Translate the following ostentatious, ponderous passage into graceful, direct English.

THE FOURTEENTH CENTURY COSMOLOGIST, a precursor of contemporary astrophysicists, deduced through careful (though specious) syllogisms that the heavenly spheres made a celestial music as they coursed through the translucent vapors of the imponderable cosmos. This Euphony of the Spheres became an *idée fixe* for the poor scientist (whose lectures were notoriously desultory and were filled with obscure metonymy, boring anaphora, and superfluous reiterations).

Insanity in the cosmologist's family had given him an acute saturnine lyssophobia, which proved to be prophetic: reading a bowdlerized old copy of Lucretius's *De rerum natura*, the *locus classicus* for ancient atomic theory, the cosmologist became convinced—in a blinding epiphany—that the schism between the sacrosanct Ptolemaic (geocentric) and the perfidious Copernican (heliocentric) theories was a false dichotomy. In fact, he concluded (mistakenly reifying his metaphors) that both are true: the music of the spheres clearly shows that both orbital systems take place in simultaneous cosmic balance, like a funambulist stepping through the circumambient stars. In a strange apotheosis, the cosmologist came obsequiously to revere Lucretius as an omniscient, divinely inspired prophet who delineated non-anthropocentric ideas to incredulous neophytes.

Unfortunately, pusillanimous and condescending *bon vivants* ridiculed the cosmologist, mocking his sesquipedalian loquacity, his suspirations and lucubrations, and his heterodox ratiocinations. The truth, they vivaciously averred, was a Cacophony of the Spheres: all heavenly bodies make rude and disagreeable sounds as they course through the firmament.

superfluous

Reading Comprehension

1. In Translation 38, the author's attitude is best described as:
   A. tongue in cheek
   B. reverent
   C. sober and factual
   D. inquiring

2. With which statement would the author likely agree:
   A. Deductive, *a priori* reasoning can be treacherous.
   B. Cosmology is filled with nonsense.
   C. The heavenly spheres produce sound as they move in space.
   D. Too much thinking can cause insanity.

Analogies

3. REITERATE : DESULTORY ::
   A. repeat : discursive
   B. restate : desert
   C. review : recapitulation
   D. remind : euphony

4. SYLLOGISM : ANAPHORA ::
   A. art : poetry
   B. reason : mathematics
   C. cosmology : poetry
   D. logic : rhetoric

Antonyms

apotheosis

5. APOTHEOSIS :
   A. objurgation
   B. ostracism
   C. lionization
   D. vilification

6. DESULTORY :
   A. logical
   B. focused
   C. intelligible
   D. sequential

divergence

An **idée fixe** is an obsession, a fixed idea or monomania that dominates a person's mind. Ahab's obsession with the white whale, Moby Dick, is an example. The time traveler in H.G. Wells's *The Time Machine* has an *idée fixe* with his incredible invention, and he eventually vanishes into the future, never to return. Think of other famous examples of *idée fixe*, either historical or fictional. How many can you think of? As a second imaginative stage of this idea, what are some other things people could become obsessed over? Fudgesicles? Parrots? Rocket engines? Geometry? Mystery novels? Mozart? Robert Frost's poetry? Wildflowers? Ferns? Computers? Leatherbound books? Hiking? Painting? Make an imaginative list of things one might have an *idée fixe* over. Think of the possibilities for a short story about a person with an *idée fixe* over something really rare!

ethics

In 1818 the English editor, Thomas Bowdler, published a censored (**bowdlerized**!) edition of Shakespeare, removing passages that he found to be offensive to his view of public decency. Consider the ethical decisions involved in altering an artistic masterpiece for such purposes. Would you ever support altering the language of a great novel? Would you support altering a great painting? A work of sculpture? What are the rights of the artist? What are the rights of society? What are the rights of an individual who is offended by a painting or a passage in a work of literature?

As an interesting case-study in conflicting standards, you might look up the story of artist James McNeill Whistler, who sued John Ruskin for libel after Ruskin wrote that Whistler had flung a pot of paint in the public's face with his painting *Nocturne in Black and Gold: The Falling Rocket*.

aesthetics

Euphony is beautiful sound, such as the wind in the trees, or the bubbling of a brook, or the rising music of Mozart's clarinet concerto. In *Walden*, Henry David Thoreau includes an entire chapter on the sounds he heard near Walden Pond, including train whistles, birds, and wind. Thoreau urged us to stand at the meeting of two eternities, the past and the future, and to improve the nick of time, the present moment. One way to improve upon the nick of time is to listen to the euphony that often surrounds us. What are some examples of euphony in our world—beautiful sounds that we may listen to every day, if we only turn our attention to them?

Neologist's Lexicon

Use the stems in this list to create a new word (neologism). Give the word, the pronunciation, the part of speech, the etymology, and the definition(s). Keep a record of the neologisms you create from list to list. Here are some examples:

cosmophobia (kosmo fobia) n. [cosmo (universe), phobia (fear)]   1. the pathological fear of space travel 2. the fear of escaping the earth's gravitational field

prephoria (pre for' ia) n. [pre (before), phor (carry)] n. 1. the ecstatic certainty that something is about to happen 2. an unexplained foolish confidence in the future

Sesquipedalian Poetry

Use words from List 38 (and previous lists if you like) to write a poem. This time, use visual and typographical devices to add emphasis to the meaning. Lighten up! Be inventive and courageous. Have fun. An example:

LoCUS psychus for the Desultory   Funambulist   , Op. 5, in C major

              mental universe
                    self precursor takes a peek, this self, this idée fixe
planets of my M I N D, mine. My mined
========black h o l e OOOOOOh!!!
Lies! Reeks, Bowdler eyes @$%^&, whys?
          ((((inTERnal))) cosmoSSSSSSSSSSSSSSSSssssssssssss.............._____
waveform apotheosis of desultory EUphony/sound of reason?/syllogism---SCHISM []
              { . . . . nihilism . . . .}
sound of syllogism....oh **lyssoPHOBIA be a foe be an afff be anaphora whoa+++++**
      What sound [euphony?]
            do thoughts reiterate,,,,,,,,,,,,
          as they course through
              the psyche? All A is B **whooosshh**
                C is A **zzzzzzzzzzzzzzzzzzzzzzz**
                    therefore C is A **whwhwhwhwhwhwhwh**

• *pro*	(forward)	prolix	• *ism*	(doctrine)	narcissism
• patr	(father)	patrician	• mis (G)	(bad)	miscreant
• cred	(believe)	miscreant	• *gno*	(know)	physiognomy
• ous	(full of)	sententious	• loco	(place)	in loco parentis
• miss	(send)	manumission	• sta	(**stand**)	apostasy
• *viv*	(life)	on the qui vive	• *phys*	(nature)	physiognomy
• sanct	(holy)	sanction	• terr	(land)	terra firma
• *syn*	(together)	synopsis	• *opia*	(sight)	synopsis
• co	(together)	colloquy	• loqu	(talk)	colloquy
• in	(in)	in loco parentis	• *hedon*	(pleasure)	hedonism
• *apo*	(away)	apostasy	• **liqu**	(flow)	prolix

prolix (tediously wordy) His tiring conversation was both prolix and vacuous.

narcissism (self-infatuation) He had a narcissistic love of his own reflection.

miscreant (evil unbeliever) A gang of assassins and miscreants attacked the caravan.

physiognomy (facial character) To read the physiognomy is no art, thought Duncan.

patrician (aristocratic) The dignitary's patrician aloofness offended some people.

apostasy (desertion of principle) Worse than disloyalty is apostasy.

hedonism (devotion to pleasure) His ascetic discipline degenerated into hedonism.

sententious (full of maxims) The novelist's sententious prose style bored her.

on the qui vive (on the alert) Be on the *qui vive* for a sign of compromise from the enemy.

manumission (release from slavery) The refusal was an act of self-manumission.

• • •

sanction (authorize) We do not sanction the use of our firm's nàme.

terra firma (firm land) It's good to stand on *terra firma* after a rough voyage.

synopsis (summary) She wrote a brief synopsis of the course for the students.

colloquy (conversation) They enjoyed a private colloquy in the corner.

in loco parentis (in place of the parents) Schools often act *in loco parentis*.

As Used by James Fennimore Cooper in *The Last of the Mohicans*

Another long and deliberate pause succeeded these **sententious** questions.

Parts of Speech:	adj.	adj. conj.	adj.	n.	v.	adj.	**adj.**	n.

Parts of Sentence:				subject	AVP			direct object

Phrases: ----no prepositional, appositive, or verbal phrase----

Clauses: ---------------------------------independent clause---------------------------------
one independent clause, a simple declarative sentence

Here Cooper uses the adjective *sententious* to modify the direct object, the plural common noun *questions*.

Pronunciation

prolix	pro LIX	**on the *qui vive***	KEE VEEV
narcissism	NAR sih sizz em	**manumission**	MAN yoo MISH un
miscreant	MISS kree ant	**sanction**	SANK shun
physiognomy	fizz ee O no mee	***terra firma***	TERR ah FIR ma
patrician	pah TRISH an	**synopsis**	sin OP siss
apostasy	ah POSS ta see	**colloquy**	KOLL o kwee
hedonism	HEE don izm	***in loco parentis***	in LO ko pa RENT iss
sententious	sen TEN shuss		

Spanish Cognates

narcissism	narcisismo	**prolix**	prolijo
hedonism	hedonismo	**apostasy**	apostasía
sententious	sentencioso	**patrician**	patricio
colloquy	coloquio	**synopsis**	sinopsis

1. **Terra firma** is fun to use. It is exotic and reminds us of exploration, of setting foot on solid (firma) ground (terra) at last, after a voyage on the high seas. But we can also use **terra firma** in wonderful metaphorical ways, such as comparing the *terra firma* of philosophical realism and scientific method to the flights and perils of philosophical idealism and deductive, *a priori*, reasoning. Be creative in your use of **terra firma**.

2. The adjective **patrician**, historically, referred to the ancient Roman noble class and is the opposite of the adjective **plebeian**, the ancient Roman lower class. Today, we still refer to aristocratic people as **patrician** and to the common people as **plebeian**, but great care should be used with these words, because they possess connotations that are offensive to our democratic values. The word **plebeian** suggests that someone is coarse, vulgar, unrefined, and ignorant. It gives offense and should be avoided when no offense is intended.

3. Narcissus was the beautiful youth in Greek mythology who first fell in love with Echo (read Ovid's *Metamorphoses*—I like the Rolfe Humphries translation—for the wonderful story) and later fell in love with his own beautiful reflection in the water. When he could not find the person he saw in the water, he pined away and metamorphosed into the narcissus flower. **Narcissism** is extreme self-infatuation with one's own appearance or accomplishments.

4. It is interesting to compare **physiognomy** with **countenance** and **visage**. The **visage** is what you look (vid, vis) at: the physical features and form of the face. The **countenance** is the contents of the face, the feelings that are contained or held (tenere) together (con) in the features of the face. In *King Lear*, Kent tells Lear that there is "something in your countenance which I would fain call Master." The **physiognomy** (fizzy O nomy) is knowing (gno, gnom) the nature (phys) of the person by looking at the face. These words have subtle differences and overlapping meanings. At times, all three are used to refer to the expressions and emotions of the face, but we tend to slightly separate the meanings. A person might have a red visage, an angry countenance, and a noble physiognomy.

5. **Hedonism**, which comes from the Greek word for pleasure (hedone), refers to a philosophical ethical doctrine that the chief aim of life is pleasure—that the pursuit of pleasure is what contributes to the greatest happiness of the individual and of society. This idea of pleasure as good is in striking contrast to many other ethical systems that regard pleasure as bad and regard various forms of asceticism or self-mortification as good.

6. A **Classic Word**: The noun **physiognomy** derives from a Greek word for judging a person by the features of his or her face. Vide note 4, above. We find **physiognomy** in the novels of Walter Scott, the Brontës, Hawthorne, Stowe, and Melville. The philosopher-humorist Melville used the word in a way that both was, and was not, a reference to the physical features of the face: "Physiognomically regarded, the Sperm Whale is an anomalous creature. He has no proper nose." Yes, but then again, Melville was an anomalous creature, who had no proper knows, either, and I doubt if his physiognomy would have revealed much besides a marine depth and the intimation of things moving below the surface.

In each case below, one of the choices was really the word used by the author in the sentence provided. All of the choices can be found in the example words on the first page of this lesson. Your challenge is to decide which word the author used. This is not a test; it is more like a game, because more than one word choice may work perfectly well. See if you can use your sensitivity and intuition to guess correctly which word the author used. You may need a dictionary.

1. **From Joseph Heller's** *Catch-22*

   He's the one who tipped me off that our prose was too _____.
   a. narcissistic
   b. prolix
   c. hedonistic
   d. patrician

2. **From George Orwell's** *1984*

   "Thoughtcrime is a dreadful thing, old man," he said _____.
   a. narcissistically
   b. on the *qui vive*
   c. *in loco parentis*
   d. sententiously

3. **From Mark Twain's** *The Prince and the Pauper*

   But let these _____ look well to themselves.
   a. miscreants
   b. hedonists
   c. apostates
   d. narcissists

4. **From John F. Kennedy's** *Profiles in Courage*

   The *Greenfield Gazette* called him an _____.
   a. apostate
   b. patrician
   c. miscreant
   d. synopsis

5. **From Henry James's** *The American*

   [He had] a prominent blue eye, a German _____, and a massive watch-chain.
   a. colloquy
   b. physiognomy
   c. narcissism
   d. prolixity

Though it is good to have a rich vocabulary, it is not good to abuse that vocabulary by writing verbose, sesquipedalian sentences (such as this one). Those who overuse their vocabularies often do so at the expense both of clarity and of others' patience. Translate the following ostentatious, ponderous passage into graceful, direct English.

BACK ON TERRA FIRMA after his officially sanctioned voyage to Io, the narcissistic hedonist gazed with pleasure at the reflection of his patrician physiognomy in the mirror. With a slow suspiration, he remembered the sententious miscreants and apostates whose prolix colloquies had disrupted his speech to the Solar Assembly. His topic, "An Argument for the Manumission of Robots," had not been well received, especially his theory that the state should act *in loco parentis* for all robots during the first year after their construction. His synopsis of the ethical problems of advanced robotics was misunderstood and greeted with an incredulous cacophony, despite his reiterations that the rights of robots should never supersede the legal rights of *Homo sapiens sapiens*.

Even this did not mollify the acerbic and undisciplined autodidacts. It was an obvious *a priori* truth, he felt, that principles of ethics should apply to inanimate beings—there being a clear dichotomy between right and wrong—but the demotic masses demanded *a posteriori* evidence. You had to show them. In this introspective and saturnine mood, he perambulated off, wondering if a Solar Confederacy plagued with nihilists and neophytes could long endure.

incredulous

Reading Comprehension

1. For Translation 39, which of the following does the passage suggest:
   A. In general, hedonists are ethical individuals.
   B. Principles of ethics should apply to inanimate beings.
   C. The hedonist is unwilling to consider that his ideas might be flawed.
   D. Most people don't listen to the ideas of others.

2. Which of the following best describes the passage:
   A. An insecure intellectual unfairly blames others for his own poor work.
   B. A group of Philistines treats a thoughtful and philosophical presenter unfairly.
   C. Individuals fail to give each others' sides fair consideration.
   D. Colonists on Jupiter's moons suffer a breakdown in civilization.

Analogies

3. **NARCISSISM : HEDONISM ::**
   A. pleasure : self-infatuation
   B. happiness : misery
   C. self-admirer : sybarite
   D. narcolepsy : sleep

4. **PROLIX : COLLOQUY ::**
   A. verbose : interlocution
   B. provide : telescope
   C. promote : cosponsor
   D. lecture : acerbic

Antonyms

apostasy

5. **PATRICIAN :**
   A. fatherly
   B. plebeian
   C. pariah
   D. brahmin

6. **APOSTASY :**
   A. treachery
   B. chauvinism
   C. loyalty
   D. compliance

evaluation

Which is a more serious fault in a person's conversation: to be **prolix** or to be **sententious**? Explain the criteria by which you judge this to be a fault.

analysis

Explain why the noun **physiognomy** means what it means, based on its etymology or stem construction. Similarly, explain the meaning of **apostasy** and of **colloquy**. You may use a dictionary for extra information.

analysis

Read *Macbeth*, and notice Duncan's line about the treacherous Thane of Cawdor. Duncan says that there is "no art to find the mind's construction in the face," and says that the Thane of Cawdor was "a gentleman on whom I build an absolute trust." Is Duncan referring to the Thane's **visage**, **countenance**, or **physiognomy**? Do you understand why Duncan's line is ironic?

application

The noun **synopsis** refers to a brief summary, such as a fifty-word summary of the plot of a novel. You will see synopses of novels, of plays, and of college courses (a longer, more detailed description of a college course and its requirements is called a **syllabus**). Obviously, in order to write a synopsis, one must clearly understand and dramatically condense—one must, as Striver notes in Dickens's *A Tale of Two Cities*, "extract the essence." Write a synopsis of fifty words or fewer of a classic novel or play you have read this year.

convergence

If you were to become a regular user of either the word **sententious**, the word **apostasy**, or the word **narcissism**, which word would you choose? Explain why.

imagination

Creative writing is a wonderful way to use imagination—the process of creating images. Use one of the words in List 39 as the basis for a lush descriptive paragraph or short story in which you imagine a scene as vividly as possible. For example: A shipwreck survivor finally reaches **terra firma**, the sandy beach of a desert island. In great detail, describe the survivor's experience at that moment.

Neologist's Lexicon

Use the stems in this list to create a new word (neologism). Give the word, the pronunciation, the part of speech, the etymology, and the definition(s). Here are some examples:

gnostasis (no stay' sis) n. [gno (know), sta (stop), sis (condition)]   1. having one's opinions or ideas fixed and unchangeable 2. the condition of being closed-minded

liquhedonism (lick yu hee' don ism) n. [liqu (flow), hedon (pleasure)] 1. the inordinate love of streams and waterfalls 2. an obsession with flowing water

Sesquipedalian Hemingway Prose (??)

The Twentieth-Century American writer Ernest Hemingway was known for his terse, journalistic style. Hemingway's style was to emphasize nouns and verbs; to write simple, declarative sentences; to develop flow through run-on sentences; to avoid long words; and to describe characters' behavior rather than their thoughts. Read one of Hemingway's Nick Adams stories, and then try to imitate his writing—Example:

Big Two-Handed River

Rick sat in colloquy with himself on the sand of the bank of the river. The big two-handed river. The river was cold and the water of the river slipped down through the *terra firma* of the mountains where the rain fell quickly on the high slopes and the sententious thunder never sounded prolix, not even to Rick. The river ran straight and clear and cold and wet and flowed on both sides of the island covered with saplings and Rick sat on the moist sand of the bank and felt the pure patrician hedonism of the moment and knew instinctively that the sun was striking the top of his head, making a shadow in the water of the river that ran in front of his face and moved quickly down its bank into the valley below.

On the *qui vive*, Rick sensed that the river flowed to the left of the island and flowed to the right of the island, like a water god with two big hands, a god of water with a liquid and rippling physiognomy, a face you could look into and not feel the pain. Rick felt comfortable here. And he did not feel the pain. The sand of the river gave a cool manumission from the narcissism of life down in the town, down in the valley, where the streets ran parallel in the sun and the miscreants' houses stuck up between the streets, covered by roofs, like an apostasy from nature. The god of water did not visit the streets of the town.

Something in Rick began to move, to sanction a change, and Rick reached for his tackle box and took the line and cool metal hook and pushed the bait carefully onto the hook, carefully so that the fish would take it. He could not see the fish, but the fish would be there, in the shadow of the birches on the far bank, and the fish was there now, waiting for him, *in loco parentis*, to teach him things that his parents never taught him. He could not remember his parents, but he could remember the fish, and he played out the line and cast it into the cool water in the shade of the birches on the far bank, and the fish came and took the bait, as Rick knew it would. I am sorry, Fish, Rick said. It is you who must feel the pain so that I do not need to feel it. And the river moved, and continued to move, on the left hand of the island of birches and on the right hand.

• **vale**	(farewell)	valediction		• dict	(say)	valediction
• *proto*	(first)	protagonist		• *agon*	(actor)	protagonist
• mal	(bad)	maladroit		• *ism*	(doctrine)	stoicism
• *sarco*	(flesh)	sarcophagus		• *phag*	(eat)	sarcophagus
• *gno*	(know)	ignominious		• sur	(over)	surrealistic
• *ana*	(up)	analect		• *lect*	(gather)	analect
• ex	(out)	expository, exegesis		• pos	(put)	expository
• magn	(great)	magnum opus		• mort	(death)	moribund
• super	(over)	supercilious		• miss	(send)	emissary

valediction (farewell speech) Read Donne's "Valediction, Forbidding Morning".

protagonist (leading person) Oedipus is the protagonist of Sophocles's tragedy, *Oedipus Rex*.

maladroit (clumsy) His maladroit groping for the handle was humorous to observe.

stoicism (indifference to sensation) His austere stoicism helped him overcome the pain.

sarcophagus (stone coffin) The sarcophagus's cold, sculpted surface was mossy.

ignominious (disgraceful) The convicted traitor faced a future of ignominious oblivion.

surrealistic (unrealistically imaginary) Dali's dreamy, surrealistic art is popular.

analects (selected writings) She loved reading *The Analects* of Confucius.

expository (explanatory) His essay was expository, not creatively descriptive.

exegesis (critical interpretation) Her brilliant exegesis of *The Inferno* impressed us all.

• • •

magnum opus (great work) Dante's *magnum opus*, *The Divine Comedy*, is a classic.

moribund (dying) The moribund economy affected the stock market.

supercilious (scornful) His arrogant, supercilious manner irked us.

diction (word choice) Her scholarly Latin diction was impressive to the students.

emissary (messenger) An emissary sent out from the Queen suddenly arrived.

As Used by Maya Angelou in *I Know Why the Caged Bird Sings*

	I	spoke	in	**supercilious**	accents.
Parts of Speech:	pron.	v.	prep.	**adj.**	n.
Parts of Sentence:	subject	AVP			

Phrases: -----------prepositional phrase----------

Clauses: --------------------------------independent clause-----------------------------------
one independent clause, a simple declarative sentence

Here Angelou uses the adjective *supercilious* to modify the object of the preposition, the plural common noun *accents*. Note that *accents* cannot be a direct object, because it is the object of the preposition; it cannot be both.

Pronunciation

valediction	val eh DICT shun	**expository**	ex POZZ ih tory
protagonist	pro TAG on ist	**exegesis**	ex eh JEE siss
maladroit	MAL ah droit	***magnum opus***	mag num OP us
stoicism	STO ih sizzem	**moribund**	MORE ih bund
sarcophagus	sar KOFF a guss	**supercilious**	super SILL ee us
ignominious	ig no MIN ee us	**diction**	DICT shun
surrealistic	sur re a LISS tik	**emissary**	EM iss ary
analects	AN ah lekts		

Spanish Cognates

stoicism	estoicismo	**ignominious**	ignominioso
moribund	moribundo	**exegesis**	exégesis
emissary	emisario	**protagonist**	protagonista
sarcophagus	sarcófago	**surrealistic**	surrealista

1. A **Micropoem**: The adjective **supercilious** means scornful or haughty and comes from the Latin *super* (over) and *cilium* (eyebrow)—raised eyebrow. In other words, the word describes the scornful facial expression of the contemptuous person! Notice that we see **cilium** in other words, such as the cilia of the cell we study in biology.

2. The noun **stoicism** comes from *ism* (doctrine) plus the Greek *stoa* (porch or colonnade), and refers to the philosophy of Zeno, who taught in the shade of a colonnade in Athens in about 308 B.C. Zeno believed that all things are controlled by immutable natural laws and that the wise person should simply follow virtue and nothing else. This means that the wise person would focus on virtue and be indifferent to all but virtue: indifferent to pleasure, to pain, to passion, to emotion. When we say that someone is stoical, we mean that this person resembles the Greek Stoics in his or her austere indifference to sensation or emotion. If you are interested in reading a marvelous ancient work of stoicism, read *The Meditations* of Roman emperor Marcus Aurelius, who was a student of Epictetus (eh pick teet' us), his slave, whose writings we also still read. By the way, do you remember Zeno's paradox? A paradox is a true contradiction (!), such as Socrates's famous paradox, "I only know that I know nothing." Zeno's paradox is that if you move toward something in steps, going half the distance that remains in each step, you will never get there! If you do, you have cheated by going more than half the distance.

3. We call a stone coffin, especially an elaborate or monumental one, a **sarcophagus**. This noun comes from the Greek word *sarkophagos*—*sarx* (flesh) and *phagein* (to eat)—and refers to the Greek and Roman practice of burying the dead in great limestone coffins because limestone contributed to the rapid breakdown of the body placed in the coffin. The Greeks and the Romans often carved, inscribed, and elaborately ornamented the sarcophagi.

4. A **protagonist** is a first (proto) actor (agon). The **agon** in the word **protagonist** actually traces back to the Greek *agonistes* (actor), but earlier, the **agon** was a contest, which reminds us that the early Greek tragedies were performed as contests, with leading tragedians such as Sophocles, Aeschylus, and Euripides competing against each other for top prize. The protagonist in a drama is often confronted, of course, by an **antagonist**. The foe of the brave protagonist, Popeye, is the boorish antagonist, Bluto, whom all admirable people detest.

5. You would not expect **stoic** to be a good **Classic Word**, since it seems so philosophical and scholarly, even arcane. But **stoic** has been used by Defoe, Scott, Cooper, the Brontës, Melville, Hardy, Crane, Wharton, and Wilder. One of the best sentences is from Defoe, who in his 1719 novel, *Robinson Crusoe*, wrote, "It would have made a stoic smile to have seen me and my little family sit down to dinner." Charlotte Brontë wisely noted that "The sternest-seeming stoic is human after all." Stephen Crane described the martial "cheerings, moblike and barbaric, but tuned in strange keys that can arouse the dullard and the stoic." Melville, with characteristic mock-solemnity, reasoned, "This Right Whale I take to have been a Stoic; the Sperm Whale, a Platonian, who might have taken up Spinoza in his latter years." Hardy's Yeobright "was an absolute stoic in the face of mishaps which only affected his social standing."

In each case below, one of the choices was really the word used by the author in the sentence provided. All of the choices can be found in the example words on the first page of this lesson. Your challenge is to decide which word the author used. This is not a test; it is more like a game, because more than one word choice may work perfectly well. See if you can use your sensitivity and intuition to guess correctly which word the author used. You may need a dictionary.

1.   **From Aldous Huxley's** *Brave New World*

He had imagined himself..._____ accepting suffering without a word.
a. maladroitly
b. surrealistically
c. superciliously
d. stoically

2.   **From Charles Dickens's** *Great Expectations*

He there delivered his _____ remarks.
a. valedictory
b. ignominious
c. expository
d. maladroit

3.   **From Rachel Carson's** *Silent Spring*

The few birds seen anywhere were _____; they trembled violently.
a. moribund
b. supercilious
c. stoic
d. surrealistic

4.   **From Jane Austen** *Pride and Prejudice*

Elizabeth still saw _____ in their treatment of every body.
a. surrealism
b. diction
c. stoicism
d. superciliousness

5.   **From Herman Melville's** *Moby Dick*

A German _____ supposes that Jonah must have taken refuge in the floating body of a dead whale.
a. stoic
b. exegetist
c. emissary
d. sarcophagus

Though it is good to have a rich vocabulary, it is not good to abuse that vocabulary by writing verbose, sesquipedalian sentences (such as this one). Those who overuse their vocabularies often do so at the expense both of clarity and of others' patience. Translate the following ostentatious, ponderous passage into graceful, direct English.

AS THE LOQUACIOUS and gregarious audience came to silence, the curtain rose behind the proscenium. Strange lighting effects, translucent panels, and monolithic forms gave the scene a surrealistic and moribund look. A great limestone sarcophagus carved with the face of a lycanthrope and incised with the single word VALEDICTION stood at the right. With a supercilious physiognomy a patrician protagonist, Agonistes, glared down condescendingly at an obsequious and pusillanimous emissary from the Great Mooboo, a high-ranking and lionized official in the hierarchy of the plutocracy.

"Speak, ignominious neophyte," said Agonistes.

"Noble Sir," replied the emissary, "I am instructed to summon you to my Worship's palace and to say that you must answer for your perfidious writings."

"Tell your 'worship,' if that's what he is, you miscreant," said Agonistes with sangfroid, "that my expository exegesis of his sententious analects—that vacuous so-called *magnum opus*, HA!—is none of his concern. Wait until he sees my synopsis of his soporific self-proclaimed classic! That egocentric autodidact! His delineation will soon be the *locus classicus* for *non sequiturs* and false syllogisms! I will not be summoned by you or by him. If he sees no dichotomy between my sedate stoicism and his narcissistic hedonism, then he is nothing more than a maladroit and nihilistic apostate who has abandoned the sacrosanct ideas of our official cosmology."

"How prolix!" whispered the abased emissary, in a *sotto voce* suspiration.

"Is that a soliloquy," retorted Agonistes, "or is it merely your demotic diction that makes you so inaudible? Perambulate back to your worship, and tell him I will not mollify his acerbity."

Reading Comprehension

1. In Translation 40, it can be inferred that:
    A. The Mooboo misjudged how Agonistes would respond to his emissary.
    B. Agonistes is making a terrible mistake in speaking so to the emissary.
    C. Agonistes is playing a clever role to conceal his fear.
    D. The emissary is actually the Mooboo in disguise.

2. The author does all of the following EXCEPT:
    A. describe the appearance of the sarcophagus
    B. reveal the philosophical difference between Agonistes and the Mooboo
    C. explain what is perfidious about Agonistes's writings
    D. show Agonistes's opinion of the Mooboo's writings

Analogies

3. **IGNOMINIOUS : MALADROIT ::**
    A. heinous : inept
    B. ignorant : malcontent
    C. disgraceful : shameful
    D. clumsy : ostracized

4. **SUPERCILIOUS : STOIC ::**
    A. haughty : scornful
    B. indifferent : superior
    C. patronizing : impassive
    D. superior : stolid

Antonyms

supercilious

5. **EXPOSITORY :**
    A. revealing
    B. fantastical
    C. poetic
    D. factual

6. **VALEDICTION :**
    A. salutation
    B. welcome
    C. introduction
    D. explanation

analysis and application

If you read *The Meditations* of Marcus Aurelius, you will find that he expresses his **stoicism** through the repetition and rephrasing of several principal ideas. Read *The Meditations*, and make a list of the three ideas you find most commonly reoccurring. Then consider what you have learned about stoicism, and describe a situation in life when stoicism would be an appropriate or appealing posture.

intuition

In order to develop a vivid sense of what the adjective **surrealistic** means, look at a book of Salvador Dali's paintings, with their melting clocks and anthropomorphic landscapes. Then drift into your own imagination, and write a short story that takes place in a dreamy, surrealistic world of your own invention.

synthesis and emotion

Read John Donne's poem "**Valediction**, Forbidding Morning." What other poems can you think of that have similar themes to this poem? Similar styles? How would you describe the emotional tone of the poem? If you were reading the poem aloud, how would you read it in order to properly convey the emotion of the poem? Do you feel the emotion as you read the poem?

ethics

To be **supercilious** is to be scornful and condescending, looking down one's nose with one eyebrow (cilia) raised (super). Is it unethical to behave in a supercilious manner? Is it merely a matter of style? Can you think of a single instance in which supercilious condescension would be the right and good way to behave?

Neologist's Lexicon

Use the stems in this list to create a new word (neologism). Give the word, the pronunciation, the part of speech, the etymology, and the definition(s). Keep a record of the neologisms you create from list to list. Here are some examples:

superlection (soo pur lek shun) n. [super (over), lect (gather), tion (act)]   1. acquiring possessions until you become unaware of what you possess 2. compulsive, indiscriminate collection of seashells, including every mediocre and pedestrian seashell on the beach.

sarcoposition (sar ko po zish' un) n. [sarco (flesh), pos (put), tion (act)]   1. sitting in the middle of a seat for two, so that no one else will sit down, as on a bus 2. sprawling out with arms and legs in a movie theater seat, so that a stranger will not sit in either seat next to you.

Sesquipedalian Shakespeare

Using words from List 40, write a short satirical exchange that captures some of the flavor of a famous scene from a Shakespearean play. Remember to include some of the wonderful archaic language that we find in the plays. An example:

Romero and Juleen

Romero enters and sees Juleen leaning against the Classic Coke machine. She sees him too, whispers to her friend, laughs, and looks demurely at a music video on the television. Instantly a star-crossed lover, Romero tremulously whispers, "Oh, she doth teach the video to glow!" He walks over to Juleen, reaches out, and touches the tip of his index finger to the tip of her index finger.

Romero: If I profane, with my maladroit hand, this *magnum opus*, my lips, two expository emissaries, ready stand to conduct you to the realm of surrealistic forgiveness.
Juleen: Good Emissary, you do wrong your protagonist's lips too much in this, for a scholarly exegesis is how the truly forgiving kiss.
Romero: But have not supercilious scholars lips?
Juleen: Aye, Emissary, lips that they forsooth must use in valediction.
Romero: Oh, brave stoic, then no move make, while my valediction I take. (kisses her)
Juleen: Until this night, I have not known the true diction of a valediction. If this be farewell, prithee let me read all your final analects! (kisses him)
Romero: And yet my mind misgives some moribund end, yet hanging in the ignominious stars, to my despised life, and methinks I do presage the vile chill of a cold sarcophagus. (They kiss again.)

finis

Because English and Spanish are made from
many of the same ancient word fragments,
the two languages are strikingly alike,
especially in their advanced words.
In fact, studying Spanish is one of the
best ways to strengthen your English vocabulary.
This also means that studying Latin stems
will help you learn Spanish as well as English.

xenophobia

anthropomorphic

xenophobia

specious

expedite

mellifluous

malediction

hagiography

• *eu*	(good)	euthanasia		• *thanatos*	(death)	euthanasia
• mir	(wonder)	mirabile dictu		• in	(not)	ineffable
• *hagio*	(saint)	hagiography		• *graph*	(write)	hagiography
• patr	(father)	patronize		• *auto*	(self)	autochthonous
• **mel**	(honey)	mellifluous		• flu	(flow)	mellifluous
• inter	(between)	inter alia		• dict	(say)	mirabile dictu
• ped	(foot)	expedite		• spec	(look)	specious
• bell	(war)	bellicose		• *anthropo*	(man)	anthropomorphic
• mal	(bad)	malediction		• *morph*	(shape)	anthropomorphic
• *xeno*	(stranger)	xenophobia		• *phobia*	(fear)	xenophobia

euthanasia (mercy killing) She was opposed to euthanasia on moral grounds.

ineffable (inexpressible) His overwhelming love for her was ineffable.

expedite (hasten) Please expedite this matter, as time is short.

expatiate (to elaborate) He loved expatiating on his deeds of valor.

hagiography (saint's biography) This biography is too flattering; it is a hagiography.

mirabile dictu (wonderful to say) He was, *mirabile dictu*, still alive after the fall.

mellifluous (honeyed) Read the poet's mellifluous language.

patronize (condescend to) He resented their patrician, patronizing attitude.

autochthonous (native) Alexander honored the country's autochthonous inhabitants.

inter alia (among other things) On the raft there were, *inter alia*, seven ducks.

• • •

bellicose (warlike) The bellicose barbarian tribes in Gaul feuded constantly.

anthropomorphic (man-shaped) The Greek gods were anthropomorphic.

malediction (a curse) We heard the convict's muttered malediction.

xenophobia (fear of foreigners) The xenophobic public hated the immigrant.

specious (false) The specious argument looked to be true, but it was not.

As Used by Bram Stoker in *Dracula*

	He	smiled	with	an	**ineffably**	benign	superiority.
Parts of Speech:	pron.	v.	prep.	adj.	**adv.**	adj.	n.

Parts of Sentence: subject   AVP

Phrases: --------------------prepositional phrase--------------------

Clauses: --------------------------------independent clause----------------------------------
one independent clause, a simple declarative sentence

Here Stoker uses the adverb *ineffably* to modify an adjective, *benign,* that in turn modifies the object of the preposition, the singular common noun *superiority*.

Pronunciation

euthanasia	YOO than AZH ia	autochthonous	aw TOCK thon us
ineffable	in EFF uh bul	*inter alia*	inter AY lee ah
expedite	EX peh dite	bellicose	BELL ih kose
expatiate	ex PAY shee ate	anthropomorphic	AN thro po MOR fik
hagiography	hey jee OG raff ee	malediction	MAL uh dict shun
mirabile dictu	mir AH bee lay DICT oo	xenophobia	ZEE no FO bee ah
mellifluous	meh LIFF loo us	specious	SPEE shus
patronize	PAT ron ize		

Spanish Cognates

euthanasia	eutanasia	bellicose	belicoso
malediction	maldición	mellifluous	melifluo
xenophobia	xenofobia	specious	especioso
autochthonous	autóctono	hagiography	hagiografía
expedite	expedito	ineffable	inefable

1. A **Micropoem**: The adjective **autochthonous** is from the Greek and means of the land (chthon) itself (auto). We have an image of original peoples rising naturally from the earth, like grasses or trees. One of the reasons that Alexander the Great of Macedon was so successful in his conquests was that he made a point of honoring the autochthonous inhabitants wherever he went. In fact, after defeating Darius, the Persian emperor, Alexander discovered that he had captured Darius's family: his mother, wife, and daughter. Alexander honored and respected them, even calling Darius's mother, Sisygambis, by the title Mother. (Later, when Alexander died, she turned to the wall, refused to eat, and died in four days.) Alexander would pay homage to local gods and religious shrines, and he even adopted styles of Persian dress, to his own army's mortification. In one case, Alexander even appointed a Persian general he had just defeated as the ruler of a captured city. This trust and respect earned Alexander the devotion of many peoples.

2. The noun **hagiography** can refer to the actual biography of a saint, but you are more likely to see it used metaphorically, as to describe a biography that is so respectful that it has lost all of its objectivity. There are a number of such reverent biographies on our library bookshelves, often written by those who wish to promote their political philosophies by making heroes out of their favorite governmental leaders. This raises the interesting possibility of the autohagiography (a neologism), the self-adulating autobiography of an egotist or narcissist!

3. The adjective **specious** is interesting to analyze. It refers to reasoning that is false, but by looking at the stems, we better understand the exact nature of specious reasoning. Specious reasoning is full of (ous) looks (spec). An obviously stupid or repulsive argument is not specious; a specious argument is appealing and cogent; it a false argument that looks good.

4. **Classic Words**: **patronize** and **expatiate** are two words that get plenty of use in the classics. *Peter Pan's* Wendy sometimes speaks just a little patronisingly (yes, the word is sometimes spelled with an *s*). Henry Fleming, in *The Red Badge of Courage*, adopts an air of patronizing good humor. Melville's Pequod sometimes sails near the snug patronizing lee of churches. In *Uncle Tom's Cabin*, Marks patronizes a joke by a quiet introductory sniggle. Harriet Beecher Stowe liked **patronize** and used it often—but then, her vocabulary was so brilliantly colossal that she used many words often.

Expatiate seems to be an improbable verb for frequent use, and yet it is often used in the classics. We find it in Kenneth Grahame's *The Wind in the Willows*, in Thomas Hardy's *The Return of the Native*, in Herman Melville's *Moby Dick*, in Harriet Beecher Stowe's *Uncle Tom's Cabin*, and in Nathaniel Hawthorne's *The Scarlet Letter*. In his whale of a book, Melville was certainly to prove the truth of his own words: "From his mighty bulk the whale affords a most congenial theme whereon to enlarge, amplify, and generally expatiate." In fact, Melville even used **expatiate** to describe the whale's behavior! Melville hoped that the whale would "outlast all hunting, since he has a pasture to expatiate in, which is precisely twice as large as all Asia, both Americas, Europe and Africa, New Holland . . . ." Exactly what a whale would do while expatiating is one of the imponderable mysteries.

In each case below, one of the choices was really the word used by the author in the sentence provided. All of the choices can be found in the example words on the first page of this lesson. Your challenge is to decide which word the author used. This is not a test; it is more like a game, because more than one word choice may work perfectly well. See if you can use your sensitivity and intuition to guess correctly which word the author used. You may need a dictionary.

1.   **From F. Scott Fitzgerald's** *The Great Gatsby*

    A universe of _____ gaudiness spun itself out in his brain.
    a. bellicose
    b. ineffable
    c. xenophobic
    d. specious

2.   **From E.M. Forster's** *A Passage to India*

    He did not _____ on his wrongs now, being happy.
    a. expatiate
    b. patronize
    c. expedite
    d. euthanize

3.   **From Toni Morrison's** *Song of Solomon*

    Out of the toothless mouth came the strong _____ voice of a twenty-year-old girl.
    a. ineffable
    b. anthropomorphic
    c. autochthonous
    d. mellifluent

4.   **From Charles Dickens's** *Great Expectations*

    London gentlemen cannot be expected to _____ local work.
    a. expatiate
    b. patronize
    c. expedite
    d. euthanize

5.   **From Emily Brontë's** *Wuthering Heights*

    Mr. Heathcliff...rose and _____ made the tea himself.
    a. ineffably
    b. mellifluously
    c. expeditiously
    d. speciously

It is good to have a rich, expansive vocabulary, but it is not good to abuse that vocabulary by writing or speaking abstruse, verbose, sesquipedalian sentences. To overuse your vocabulary is to do so at the expense of clarity. Translate the following ostentatious, ponderous passage into graceful, direct English. Do not use slang, but do use words that seem familiar and comfortable.

FOR YEARS, the explorer had searched in the jungle for signs of its autochthonous inhabitants, a bellicose, xenophobic tribe known for their deceptively mellifluous war chant, a euphony that could sometimes be heard over the top of the steamy rain forest canopy. Specious rumors, vacuous guides, and patronizing government officials, *inter alia*, had delayed and frustrated the explorer, who tried to be stoical. No one had been willing to expedite the search, though everyone wanted to expatiate on what he or she would advise. But now, *mirabile dictu*, there appeared to be a change in luck.

A clue, an *obiter dictum* in a molding Spanish hagiography discovered in the Museo Antropologico had led the explorer to this remote valley. In the damp dawn, the fortissimo cacophony of the night creatures had abated into a sotto voce suggestion of circumambient life moving on all sides. Parting a tangle of heliotropic vines, the explorer gazed into the inanimate physiognomy of a monolithic, anthropomorphic, stone god, whose unmoving eyes communicated an ineffable malediction to all strangers. "Go beyond this point into my sacrosanct forest," the omniscient figure seemed to say, "and your death will be no euthanasia. Contravene this interdiction at your peril."

Beside the monolith, a gray sarcophagus protruded through the interstices of the jungle foliage. On its surface, an ancient bas-relief delineated a lost anthropocentric cosmology.

This surrealistic thanatopsis was too much even for our protagonist, the intrepid explorer. "Consider me," she thought in silent soliloquy, "an emissary from the outer world, and accept my benediction." Having obsequiously mollified the anger of the jungle god, she turned back with sangfroid and a valedictory suspiration of relief, and perambulated down the tortuous jungle path for home.

Reading Comprehension

1. For Translation 41, which of the following best expresses the main idea:
    A. An explorer retreats from the jungle in cowardice.
    B. An explorer respects tribal wishes and departs.
    C. An explorer lacks the will and strength of character to continue.
    D. An explorer misunderstands the elements of the problem.

2. The author's attitude is best described as:
    A. objective and journalistic
    B. satirical
    C. pedantic
    D. awed

Analogies

3. **INEFFABLE : MALEDICTION ::**
    A. speech : silence
    B. nothing : bad
    C. good : bad
    D. praise : curse

4. **EXPATIATE : EXPEDITE ::**
    A. expand : express
    B. hurry : elaborate
    C. elaborate : express
    D. elaborate : facilitate

Antonyms

hagiography

5. **HAGIOGRAPHY :**
    A. biography
    B. autobiography
    C. monograph
    D. hatchet job

6. **PATRONIZE :**
    A. condescend
    B. stoop
    C. venerate
    D. admire

intuition and imagination

You find yourself on a distant planet, with intelligent lifeforms very different from terrestrial ones. One of the alien species has a highly developed religion, with idols of its strange gods scattered across the undulating terrain. The gods are not **anthropomorphic**. You have never seen anything like them. Describe the way they look.

ethics

The expressed values of the United States are tolerant and inviting, as the inspiring words of the Statue of Liberty convey. "Give me your tired, your poor, your huddled masses, yearning to breathe free. I lift my lamp beside the golden door." This maternal, caring statue has been a tearful and joyful sight for millions of immigrants as they sailed into New York harbor. We see ourselves as the melting pot of many peoples, united in the liberty of a great democracy, pursuing happiness. And certainly, no nation in world history has done more to make freedom and equality real. And yet, there is sometimes a paradoxical **xenophobia** in America, too. Our most cherished civil rights have not come easily, or without price. Tolerance has had to struggle with intolerance. Do you think that there is a difference between America's official ideals and its social values, or not? What are the ethical precepts of our democracy, as expressed in our greatest national documents? Which of these do you regard as most important?

A separate ethical question. The possibility of **euthanasia** is being debated more and more, especially since medical science is able to keep people alive longer and longer, but under conditions that many people are unwilling to accept. What do you think the precise ethical issue is in the question of euthanasia? Do you feel that it would be immoral under all cases, or not? Explain what criteria you think should be used to decide the issue.

analysis

What is the difference between **patronizing**, **condescending**, and being **supercilious**? Clearly, these are near synonyms, but by carefully reflecting on the stems in the words, you can detect subtle differences in tone and meaning. Discuss these differences.

synthesis

Can you think of five different things that are **ineffable**? What are they? What makes them ineffable? Can you think of five different common ideas that are specious?

application

Since none of the words on List 41 are rare, think about what type of document would actually be likely to use each word. For example, you might see **euthanasia** in a discussion of ethics in a philosophical journal. You might see **autochthonous** in an article in *Foreign Affairs*. You might see **inter alia** in a legal brief. Try to give at least two possible documents for each word.

Neologist's Lexicon

Use the stems in this list to create a new word (neologism). Give the word, the pronunciation, the part of speech, the etymology, and the definition(s). Keep a record of the neologisms you create from list to list. Here are some examples:

melography (mel ah' gra fee) n. [mel (honey), graph (write)] 1. handwriting characterized by rounded forms, elaborate curlicues, and circles in place of dots and periods 2. melograph: a short message filled with extremely sentimental clichés

euphobia (yoo fo' bia) n. [eu (good), phobia (fear)] 1. pathological dependence on the high levels of emotion associated with tragedy and misfortune, resulting in a fear of good news 2. fear that good opportunities will require change

Sesquipedalian Creative Writing

Using words from List 41, write a poem, short story, short play, or other invention of your own choice. You might try something crazy, like sesquipedalian instructions for peeling a tangerine, or sesquipedalian instructions from an airline flight attendant. You could write a sesquipedalian standup comedy routine. As usual, have fun finding amusing ways to use the words you are learning.

Pseudosesquipedaliodrama, OR, the Neologist's Theater

Phase One: Working in groups of two, share and compare the neologisms you have created in these eleven lessons for the Neologist's Lexicon, and then write a joint creative play using the words the two of you have invented! Keep your play short; feel free to be silly or absurd, and turn it in to your teacher with a glossary of the key words and their definitions. (Of course, if you and your teacher want it this way, you could do this as a solo assignment, but it is fun and valuable to work in cooperation with other thinkers, especially on creative projects.)

Phase Two (If you enjoyed Phase One): Depending on the size of the class, divide the class into two to four larger groups, compare the plays that the groups of two wrote in Phase One, pick the favorite play of the group, and prepare a performance of the play, after elaborating or refining as much as you like. Perform the plays for the class, after first explaining the neologisms that the audience needs to understand in order to appreciate the play.

Phase Three: If you enjoyed the first two phases, you could work as a single large group to write and perform a single play, combining neologisms from everyone in the class and involving everyone in a part. This would require great cooperation, patience, creative thinking, and a real understanding of the Greek and Latin stems present in the words.

Before you go on to List 42, think carefully about word creation. Notice how logical and creative it can be. Notice the insight and humor that can be contained within a word. Notice how difficult it can sometimes be to get a word right, so that the stems really support the meaning you intend. Notice what an important part this is of the intellectual richness of language.

• par	(equal)	nonpareil		• mal	(bad)	malefic
• non	(not)	nonpareil		• equi	(equal)	equilibrist
• bas	(low)	bas-relief		• super	(over)	superannuated
• *psych*	(soul)	metempsychosis		• post	(after)	postprandial
• *gen*	(origin)	biogenesis		• *meta*	(change)	metempsychosis
• fic	(make)	malefic		• punct	(point)	punctilio
• ann	(year)	superannuated		• tract	(pull)	intractable
• greg	(group)	egregious		• ex	(out)	egregious
• ab	(away)	abjure		• jur	(swear)	abjure
• *bio*	(life)	biogenesis		• *algia*	(pain)	analgesic
• dis	(away)	discursive		• curs	(run)	discursive
• *an-*	(without)	analgesic		• in	(not)	intractable
• tig	(touching)	contiguous				

nonpareil (something unequaled) A unique achievement is a nonpareil.

malefic (causing harm) Notice Iago's malefic influence on Roderigo in Shakespeare's *Othello*.

contiguous (touching) We especially need to make good treaties with contiguous nations.

metempsychosis (transmigration of souls) Some believe in metempsychosis or reincarnation.

biogenesis (theory of life from life) Pasteur proved that the theory of biogenesis was true.

bas-relief (low-relief sculpture) The face was cut in bas-relief from a marble slab.

postprandial (after dinner) The contented guests enjoyed a postprandial stroll.

equilibrist (tightrope walker) The equilibrist did his daring highwire act between the buildings.

punctilio (point of conduct) Her high-society world was a treacherous thicket of punctilios.

superannuated (obsolete) We saw his rusted, superannuated farm implements at the auction.

• • •

intractable (stubborn) You can't pull that bigot away from his intractable opinions.

egregious (blatant) The egregious act of vandalism shocked the large crowd.

abjure (renounce) It is painful to abjure one's former beliefs.

analgesic (painkiller) He took an extra-strength analgesic for the pain.

discursive (rambling) The illogical, discursive speech was difficult to follow.

As Used by William Shakespeare in *Macbeth*

	If	thou	didst	it,	thou	art	the	**nonpareil.**
Parts of Speech:	conj.	pron.	v.	pron.	pron.	v.	adj.	**n.**
Parts of Sentence:		subject	AVP	direct object	subject	LVP		subject complement

Phrases: -----no prepositional, appositive, or verbal phrase------

Clauses: ---------dependent clause-------- -----------independent clause------------
a D,I complex declarative sentence

Here Shakespeare uses the noun *nonpareil* as the subject complement, joined by a linking verb to the subject. This complex sentence shows the difference between a direct object with an action verb and a subject complement with a linking verb.

Pronunciation

nonpareil	non par ELL	**punctilio**	punk TIL ee oh
malefic	mal EFF ik	**superannuated**	super ANN yoo ated
contiguous	kon TIG yoo us	**intractable**	in TRAK tah bel
metempsychosis	met em sy KO sis	**egregious**	ee GREE juss
biogenesis	bio JEN e sis	**abjure**	ab JOOR
bas-relief	BAH re LEEF	**analgesic**	an al JEE zik
postprandial	post PRAN dee al	**discursive**	diss KUR siv
equilibrist	ee KWIL ih brist		

Spanish Cognates

contiguous	contiguo	**punctilio**	puntillo
abjured	abjurado	**contiguous**	contiguo
intractable	intratable	**analgesic**	analgésico
equilibrist	equilibrista	**metempsychosis**	metempsicosis
bas-relief	bajorrelieve		

1. A. **Micropoem**: **Intractable** is a wonderfully expressive adjective. It is not made of *intra* (within); it is made of *in* (not) and *tract* (pull). It suggests a mule-like stubbornness so firm that even pulling is of no avail. To be intractable is to be resistant to persuasion, logic, coercion, or compromise. Prejudice and bigotry are two of the most obvious intractable human phenomena, since they are so resistant to change. Adherence to political dogma is another often intractable behavior. The word **incorrigible** can also refer to a kind of stubbornness, but it really refers to misbehavior that can not be corrected or improved. If you are incorrigible, we find it impossible to teach you better. Another word that refers to stubbornness is **refractory**. A refractory person breaks (fract) the rules and breaks them again (re), regardless of supervision. The stems in the words provide the best guide to the fine connotations that distinguish these words from each other. All three refer to someone who is stubborn, but the intractable person is not pullable, the incorrigible person is not correctable, and the refractory person breaks the rules again.

2. The history of the science of biology provides the most interesting ground for understanding the noun **biogenesis**. It was long thought that many species came into being through **spontaneous generation**, the idea that life-forms could be spontaneously created from inanimate substances. Some scientists thought, for example, that maggots were spontaneously generated by the chemical processes of decay in dead animals. Others believed that life could only be created (genesis) from similar life (bio) in a process called **biogenesis**. The argument raged back and forth between thinkers such as Redi and Spallanzani, and was finally quieted by an ingenious experiment devised by Louis Pasteur, who proved to everyone's satisfaction that life would not generate, even in rich culture, unless other life could get to it first. Of course, this argument is only a partial consideration, since it still ignores the question of the generation of the first life on earth, which could not have come through biogenesis, unless we are all the descendants of extraterrestrials! If the first life on earth arose through chemical combinations in a primal sea bombarded by ultraviolet light and lightning, then that would be a real case of spontaneous generation.

3. **Bas-relief** is different from other sculpture because it creates an illusion of depth without being really carved in depth. This technique was used widely by the ancient Greeks and Romans to illustrate the stories of gods and goddesses and to depict the battles and heroes of the Roman empire. Bas-reliefs were carved into the friezes of the temples. These works of art, such as the Elgin marbles that are now in the British Museum, are among the most prized in the world.

4. A **Classic Word**: To observe punctilios is to be punctilious. Military order is punctilious: Kipling's Kim's regiment is "always punctilious in matters of millinery." Discipline on the high seas is similarly rigorous: on Melville's Pequod, "the punctilious externals, at least, of the quarter-deck are seldom materially relaxed." Social etiquette is filled with punctilios; in *Uncle Tom's Cabin*, characters linger, "with needless punctiliousness, around the arrangements of the table." In the classics we find "an inflexible, driving, punctilious business man" (Stowe), a very stately punctilious gentleman (Melville), and a character possessed of an unfortunate quality that "was continually breaking through his punctilious manner in the shape of restlessness" (Fitzgerald).

In each case below, one of the choices was really the word used by the author in the sentence provided. All of the choices can be found in the example words on the first page of this lesson. Your challenge is to decide which word the author used. This is not a test; it is more like a game, because more than one word choice may work perfectly well. See if you can use your sensitivity and intuition to guess correctly which word the author used. You may need a dictionary.

1. **From Henry James's** *The American*

    His _____ demitasse cost him a penny extra.
    a. contiguous
    b. superannuated
    c. analgesic
    d. postprandial

2. **From Robert Penn Warren's** *All the King's Men*

    The figure of an angel, with wings and flowing drapery, had been executed in _____.
    a. biogenesis
    b. metempsychosis
    c. bas-relief
    d. punctilio

3. **From Thomas Hardy's** *Jude the Obscure*

    They begin with the _____, and gradually comprehend the universal.
    a. contiguous
    b. discursive
    c. malefic
    d. egregious

4. **From Jack London's** *White Fang*

    He observed the law more _____.
    a. discursively
    b. punctiliously
    c. intractably
    d. contiguously

5. **From Charles Dickens's** *David Copperfield*

    There was a black barge, or some other kind of _____ boat, not far off.
    a. contiguous
    b. postprandial
    c. superannuated
    d. egregious

It is good to have a rich, expansive vocabulary, but it is not good to abuse that vocabulary by writing or speaking abstruse, verbose, sesquipedalian sentences. To overuse your vocabulary is to do so at the expense of clarity. Translate the following ostentatious, ponderous passage into graceful, direct English. Do not use slang, but do use words that seem familiar and comfortable.

EIGHTY STORIES above the cacophonous *terra firma* of the xenophobic city, the intractable equilibrist, without valediction, stepped out for a feat of postprandial funambulism on the wire that stretched between the buildings. He gazed at the unsightly chips in the bas-relief frieze of the opposite monolithic tower, a superannuated skyscraper of stone and translucent plastic; some malefic miscreant had fired egregiously at the building with a hand weapon, damaging the sculpture, but the sacrosanct punctilios of the city's patronizing and supercilious elite had prevented more than a token punishment of the egocentric youth.

The equilibrist, in a stoical but discursive soliloquy, had abjured analgesics, and now his head began to pulse *fortissimo* with the magnitude of the challenge that had become his *idée fixe*, a nonpareil: to cross the wire to the farthest building. It would be his *magnum opus*. He would be lionized as the metempsychosis of Houdini. Hagiographies would be written in his honor, for this distance was no interstice, and the buildings were by no means contiguous. In supercilious sangfroid, he stood over the man-made abyss.

Far below, the mellifluous, *sotto voce* hum of the traffic—exiting the city in confluent streams of red tail lights—signaled that the city had not yet settled into sedate night. Far above, the omniscient physiognomy of the constellations twinkled its imponderable benediction on the equilibrist as he stepped, with the incredulous joy of a neophyte, forward on the wire.

omniscient

Reading Comprehension

1. It can be inferred from Translation 42 that:
   A. The equilibrist feels superior to others.
   B. The equilibrist wishes to gain the adulation of others.
   C. The equilibrist is indifferent to the opinions of others.
   D. The equilibrist is a convivial person who feels an *esprit de corps* with others.

2. Translation 42 could be best described as:
   A. the interior monologue of a hero
   B. an eccentric person on the edge of despair
   C. the exciting adventure of a professional risk taker
   D. a study in what some will do for acceptance and approval

Analogies

3. **DISCURSIVE : EGREGIOUS ::**
   A. wander : nomad
   B. irresponsible : delinquent
   C. unfocussed : outrageous
   D. gregarious : cursive

4. **EGREGIOUS : PUNCTILIO ::**
   A. barbarian : regulation
   B. prompt : punctual
   C. eccentric : conforming
   D. blunt : pointed

discursive

Antonyms

5. **CONTIGUOUS :**
   A. adjacent
   B. disconnected
   C. irrelevant
   D. congruent

6. **SUPERANNUATED :**
   A. infantile
   B. callow
   C. pristine
   D. new

evaluation

The **punctilios** that govern the niceties of our social lives form an interesting system of do's and don'ts. One does, for example, go to the door and knock to pick up one's date; one does not sit in the car and honk the horn! One does say hello and look another in the eye when being introduced; one does not look at the floor and mumble. Punctilios do change from time to time and from society to society; behaviors that are rude in one culture are expected in another. Punctiliar relativity. In class discussion make a list of some common punctilios that the members of the class accept, and then rank them in importance, after selecting at least three criteria of behavior chosen by the group.

analysis

Look up the etymologies of the words **discursive** and **desultory**, and decide what the difference is between the two words. Why would you choose one word over the other? Do the other students in the class agree with your analysis?

Can you explain the difference between **abjure** and **adjure**? How can you remember the difference between these two words?

synthesis

The Romans and Greeks created **bas-relief** sculptures, adorning their public buildings with art that depicted their gods, goddesses, heroes, and victories. If the United States were to employ a sculptor to create a great bas-relief for the National Gallery of Art, depicting national achievements of the past ten years, what events should be carved in the sculpture?

application

A **nonpareil** is a unique, unparalleled achievement. What would be an example of a nonpareil in high school academics?

intuition

An idea for a short story: your character suddenly senses that through an accident of **metempsychosis** he has received the soul of another being, in addition to his own! He now has two personalities in one mind! Elaborate.

Neologist's Lexicon

Use the stems in this list to create a new word (neologism). Give the word, the pronunciation, the part of speech, the etymology, and the definition(s). Keep a record of the neologisms you create from list to list. Here are some examples:

> **annefic** (ah nef' ik) adj. [ann (year), fic (make)] 1. being so outstanding as to make one's year 2. totally, like, you know, wow

> **cursalgic** (kurs al' jik) adj. [curs (run), algia (pain)] 1. so discursive in speech as to cause physical pain in the brains of the listeners, resulting in uncontrollable flight 2. speaking continuously so as to be unaware of one's own symptoms

Sesquipedalian Bulwer-Lytton

Bulwer-Lytton is the British author who is satirized in the Peanuts comic strip when Snoopy begins his latest novel with the formula line, "It was a dark and stormy night. Suddenly a shot rang out. Somebody screamed!" Using words from List 42 and others, write a corny opening paragraph in Bulwer-Lytton style. An example:

A Dark and Malefic Night

It was a dark and malefic night. In the distance, somebody retorted acerbically. The analgesics hadn't worked, and Arnold smeared the palm of his hirsute hand slowly over his low forehead, knocking the steel helmet from his head to the sidewalk, where it clattered cacophonously into the contiguous gutter. Egregiously, a shot broke the sedate tranquility of the intangible evening, and the neon lights seemed to punctuate the sound, glowing on the bas-relief of the cloud bottoms, which hovered low and lurid over the building tops. A discursive monologist wandered obsequiously out of an alley, declaiming to no one, twenty yards ahead of Arnold. Abjuring confrontation, Arnold turned away with an epigram: "Leave the intractable to themselves," he muttered, "but I'll be back." But even as he walked away, he knew—whether through metempsychosis, epiphany, or introspection he couldn't tell—that something was wrong. Dead wrong. He was soon to learn that he was right. Dead right.

• re	(again)	remonstrate	• sub	(under)	sublime
• sol	(alone)	solipsism	• *ism*	(doctrine)	solipsism
• in	(not)	ineluctable	• ex	(out)	ineluctable
• **luct**	(struggle)	ineluctable	• super	(over)	supererogatory
• rogat	(ask)	supererogatory	• infra	(beneath)	infra dig
• terr	(land)	disinter	• ject	(throw)	disjecta membra
• ob	(against)	obloquy	• loqu	(talk)	obloquy
• pugn	(fight)	pugnacious	• cise	(cut)	incisive
• *dia*	(across)	diatribe	• trib	(pay)	diatribe
• *acro*	(high)	acronym	• *nym*	(name)	acronym

remonstrate (plead in protest) Her earnest, repeated remonstrations were in vain.

solipsism (doctrine: only self exists) His narcissistic solipsism was amusing.

ineluctable (not escapable) You must face the ineluctable consequences.

truculent (fiercely savage) His truculent nationalism was undiplomatic.

supererogatory (beyond what's asked) His supererogatory efforts annoyed us.

infra dig (beneath dignity) It was considered *infra dig* even to ask.

recondite (abstruse) The recondite subject was beyond his intellect.

disinter (unearth) The crew slowly disinterred the buried home.

disjecta membra (scattered fragments) Only the *disjecta membra* of her work remained.

obloquy (verbal abuse) Hester received the obloquy of the community.

•   •   •

abrogate (annul) It is preferable not to abrogate a firm agreement.

acronym (initials-name) NATO, RADAR, and SCUBA are acronyms.

pugnacious (combative) The pugnacious youth always started fights.

incisive (sharp) Her incisive questions cut to the heart of the issue.

diatribe (abusive speech) The senator's public diatribe reflected his rage.

As Used by F. Scott Fitzgerald in *The Great Gatsby*

	The	policeman	looked	over	with	**truculent**	eyes.
Parts of Speech:	adj.	n.	v.	adv.	prep.	**adj.**	n.
Parts of Sentence:		subject	AVP				

Phrases: -----prepositional phrase------

Clauses: ----------------------------------independent clause----------------------------------
one independent clause, a simple declarative sentence

Here Fitzgerald uses the adjective *truculent* to modify a noun, *eyes*, that is the object of a preposition. The prepositional phrase modifies the verb.

Pronunciation

remonstrate	re MON strate	*disjecta membra*	dis JEK ta MEM brah
solipsism	SOLL ip sizm	**obloquy**	OB lo kwee
ineluctable	in ee LUCK ta bel	**abrogate**	AB row gate
truculent	TRUCK yoo lent	**acronym**	ACK row nim
supererogatory	super eh ROGG atory	**pugnacious**	pug NAY shus
infra dig	IN fra DIG	**incisive**	in SIE sive
recondite	RECK un dite	**distribe**	DIE ah tribe
disinter	dis in TUR		

Spanish Cognates

truculent	truculento	**recondite**	recóndito
pugnacious	pugnaz	**acronym**	acrónimo
diatribe	diatriba	**abrogated**	abrogado
solipsism	solipsismo	**incisive**	incisivo
disinterment	desenterramiento		

1. I admit it: **disjecta membra** is an erudite term that you will rarely see, but it's still fun to look at a word such as this sometimes. And it is good to begin to have a sense of what these very scholarly terms are like. You might see this term if you are studying, say, a classical poet, such as Sappho, whose work only exists in scattered fragments, leaving us wishing that we still possessed her other poems that we know existed, but that have been lost.

2. It will be easy to remember what the noun **obloquy** means because the word is such a literal construction of its pieces. If you are receiving the obloquy of the community, people are talking (loqu) against (ob) you. You are the object of unfavorable discussion—most unpleasant.

3. A **Micropoem**: Imagine absolute and final solitude. Well, **solipsism** is the doctrine (ism) that you're alone (sol). It's the philosophical idea that only the self exists (only I exist and everyone else is merely a figment of my imagination). It seems to be a ridiculous idea—until you try to disprove it. And then you begin to see the value of the idea. Attempting to disprove solipsism is a fascinating intellectual experience because in doing so, you realize the difficulty of thinking deeply. If you cannot prove that solipsism is false, do you really know that it is false? And if you cannot prove something so seemingly obvious, how can you hope to prove or know other things that are apparently far more difficult and complex?

    After thinking about **solipsism**, you become more careful with the word **obvious**. Bertrand Russell and Alfred North Whitehead labored for years on *Principia Mathematica,* in which they attempted to prove that the foundation of mathematics and arithmetic was sound. This task proved to be so difficult that Russell later said it had permanently reduced his intelligence; he claimed never to be as sharp again, which brings up the well-known fact that most mathematicians make their major contributions to mathematics while they are young.

    And another thing. The old stereotype that boys need to study more mathematics than girls do is superannuated—obsolete. In the challenging economy of the future, mathematics will be more important than ever, and there is no reason why bright boys and girls should not equally study and profit from as much advanced mathematics as they can possibly learn. Hundreds of exciting futures will be closed to the ill-advised student who takes the low and short road in mathematics. Bright girls are hereby urged to ignore limiting stereotypes and pursue academics.

4. **Truculent** refers to behavior that is more than hostile or violent. It describes behavior that is disturbingly brutal, fiercely savage, such as the attacks that Mr. Hyde makes on a little girl and an old man in Robert Louis Stevenson's *Dr. Jekyll and Mr. Hyde.*

5. A **Classic Word**: To **remonstrate** is to try emphatically or over and again (re) to show (monstrare) someone something, as someone who is pleading in protest does. Since **remonstrate** is a word that possesses energy and human emotion, we would expect it to be a common word in the classics, and it is; Barrie, London, Conrad, Wells, Crane, Dickens, Melville, Stowe, Hawthorne, the Brontës, and Scott all used it. In *Jane Eyre*, Miss Temple seemed to remonstrate, while Jane eschewed upbraiding and curtailed remonstrance. In *Ivanhoe*, the Saxon remonstrated strongly with his friend upon the injudicious choice he had made of his party.

In each case below, one of the choices was really the word used by the author in the sentence provided. All of the choices can be found in the example words on the first page of this lesson. Your challenge is to decide which word the author used. This is not a test; it is more like a game, because more than one word choice may work perfectly well. See if you can use your sensitivity and intuition to guess correctly which word the author used. You may need a dictionary.

1. **From James Joyce's** *Portrait of the Artist as a Young Man*

   He drove his soul daily through an increasing circle of works of _____.
   a. truculence
   b. solipsism
   c. supererogation
   d. *disjecta membra*

2. **From Upton Sinclair's** *The Jungle*

   I am not to be silenced by poverty and sickness, not by hatred and _____.
   a. obloquy
   b. pugnacity
   c. truculence
   d. diatribe

3. **From George Orwell's** *1984*

   The word you are trying to think of is _____.
   a. solipsism
   b. diatribe
   c. ineluctable
   d. remonstrate

4. **From Alan Paton's** *Cry, the Beloved Country*

   The pain was deep, deep and _____.
   a. recondite
   b. ineluctable
   c. incisive
   d. truculent

5. **From James M. Barrie's** *Peter Pan*

   "Wendy," _____ Michael, "I'm too big for a cradle."
   a. abrogated
   b. disinterred
   c. remonstrated
   d. truculent

Though it is a good thing to have a rich vocabulary, it is not a good thing to abuse that vocabulary by writing verbose, abstruse, sesquipedalian sentences. Those who overuse their vocabularies often do so at the expense of clarity. Translate the following showy, ponderous passage into graceful, direct English. Do not use slang, but do use words that seem familiar and comfortable.

AS THE RUSTY, MONOLITHIC ROCKET settled into the dusty *terra firma* of the moribund planet, the crew could see archaeological excavations scattered over the tortuous landscape, disinterring the ruins of the autochthonous truculent civilization that had once developed there. Incisive scientists had come to the ineluctable conclusion that the pugnacious and malefic society had finally become too bellicose for its own survival; had abrogated all of its treaties; had contravened galactic interdictions; had received the remonstrations, objurgations, obloquies, diatribes, and finally the maledictions of all neighboring planets, and had fallen into the ignominious and solitary decadence that it condignly deserved. The collapse was so complete that it had become *infra dig* to mention it in polite society.

A recent discovery, however, cast a new light on things. The *disjecta membra* of an ancient hagiography were slowly being pieced together by archaeologists and poets working together. Recondite, sesquipedalian, and sententious, the *magnum opus* appeared to offer *a posteriori* evidence (in mellifluous assonance) of metempsychosis on the warrior planet, and could become the omnibus *locus classicus* for the new science of psychocosmology, the study of the universe as a solipsistic manifestation of the omniscient mind of the Divine Emissary, which is what the planets in this wing of the spiral galaxy (known as Messier Object M33 or by the acronym ELVIS, for Extragallactic Lifeform VIral Situ) called their anthropomorphic deity.

Descending the gangplank into the mauve, circumambient, translucent atmosphere, the crew felt the nonplussed xenophobia of the neophyte. Fair enough, they were beginners, after all, and they were uncertain what supererogatory efforts would be expected of them, but nothing, they knew, could ever make them abjure their duties to the planetary confederacy.

Reading Comprehension

1. Which of the following best expresses the main idea of Translation 43?
   A. Political violence is most destructive to the society that employs it.
   B. Loyalty to one's superiors is the only thing that matters.
   C. Science is the most powerful weapon in the search for truth.
   D. An ethical life can only be circumvented at great cost.

2. With which statement would the author likely agree?
   A. If you are going to use military force, use enough or don't use it.
   B. Do not use military force to assert your goals over other societies.
   C. Military force is necessary in political affairs because the end justifies the means.
   D. Military force should be strictly confined to defensive purposes.

Analogies

3. TRUCULENT : PUGNACIOUS ::
   A. 8 : 5
   B. wolf : rabbit
   C. murderer : pugilist
   D. cannibal : anthropophagite

4. RECONDITE : INCISIVE ::
   A. obscure : keen
   B. erudite : perspicuous
   C. reclaim : include
   D. smart : astute

incisive

Antonyms

5. REMONSTRATE :
   A. expostulate
   B. acclaim
   C. ignore
   D. stolid

6. INELUCTABLE :
   A. rife
   B. omnipresent
   C. rare
   D. capture

synthesis

Can you use the adjectives **pugnacious** and **incisive** to describe the same thing? Think of a way to use them both in a sentence to modify the same noun. What things can you think of that are both **truculent** and **ineluctable**? Can you think of a behavior that is both **infra dig** and **supererogatory**?

How many words from List 43 can you apply to Shakespearean characters or plays? Hamlet's mind, for example, is **incisive**. Could any of these words describe characters or events in *Julius Caesar*, *A Midsummer Night's Dream*, *Romeo and Juliet*, or *King Lear*?

imagination and intuition

As the desert sun rises over the Nile, you gaze at the pits where the crew members are **disinterring** one thing after another. Describe some of the wonderful artifacts that are being unearthed.

emotion, imagination, and intuition

Imagine, as vividly as you can, that you are desperately **remonstrating** with someone, but the person is **intractable**. Write a short story that gives elaborate detail about this scene.

divergence

How many **acronyms**, such as NATO, SCUBA, and RADAR, can you think of? Make a long list of acronyms, and then invent some! Try to invent an acronym that is funny or witty, such as STICK: Strict Teachers of Incorrigible Children in Kindergarten.

emotion

What if you suddenly realized, with complete certainty, that **solipsism** was true, and that you actually were the only living thing, and that everything else, living and inanimate, was only your imagination! How would you feel?

pugnacious

Neologist's Lexicon

Use the stems in this list to create a new word (neologism). Give the word, the pronunciation, the part of speech, the etymology, and the definition(s). Keep a record of the neologisms you create from list to list. Here are some examples:

terraluction (terr' a luck shun) n. [terr (land), luct (struggle) tion (act)] 1. the struggle to live off of the land 2. farming, especially operating a family farm under economic conditions that are unfavorable to profitability

loqucism (low' kyew sism) n. [loqu (talk), cism (cut) 1. a form of obloquy in which the victim is cut to shreds by what is said 2. the art of offensive criticism

Sesquipedalian Fiction

Using at least one word from this week's list in every sentence, write a short play, scene, or story. You may also use words from previous lists if you like. Feel free to be imaginative, silly, or absurd. Do not let your critical or judgmental faculties interfere with your creative ideas.

Sesquipedalian Poetry

Using at least one word from this week's list in every (or almost every) line, write a short poem. You may use regular meter, or end rhyme, or other poetic devices, or not! You can even experiment with creative punctuation!

me disjecta membra

scattered fragments of memory
disjecta membra
mind present, mind lost, mind losing, ineluctable fragments . . .
da doo ron ron ron da doo ron ron
disinterred recollections reinterred
autoincisive self-awareness.
it has become/infra dig to/become meself
becoming/infra dig
in a solipsism of gentle truculence¿

• *logy*	(science)	epistemology		• *apo*	(away)	apocryphal
• *anti*	(against)	antinomy		• **mis**	(hatred)	misogynist
• trans	(across)	transom		• *morph*	(shape)	morphology
• fid	(faith)	diffident		• tempor	(time)	temporize
• ize	(make)	temporize		• string	(bind)	stringent
• *gyn*	(woman)	misogynist		• cogn	(know)	cognizant
• somn	(sleep)	somnambulist		• ambul	(walk)	somnambulist
• **epist**	(knowledge)	epistemology		• *crypt*	(hidden)	apocryphal
• *nomy*	(law)	antinomy		• **tauto**	(same)	tautology

tautology (needless repetition) The phrase *required essentials* is a tautology.

antinomy (contradicting reasonable principles) Plato's antinomies are perplexing.

eschatology (theology of last things) Immortality is a question of eschatology.

opprobrium (disgrace) The traitor lived in a state of public opprobrium.

apocryphal (not authentic) The recently discovered writings proved apocryphal.

transom (window or door crossbar) He hung, apelike, from the door's transom.

commiserate (sympathize) She commiserated with him in his distress.

epistemology (study of knowledge) Ex: Descartes asked, " How do you *know* you exist?"

misogynist (hater of women) We deplored the misogynist's intransigence.

morphology (study of form) The biologist studied the morphology of eyes.

• • •

diffident (shy) His diffident glance gave her confidence.

cognizant (aware) It is important to be cognizant of the rules.

stringent (binding) Stringent regulations are very restrictive.

temporize (delay) Please begin without temporizing.

somnambulist (sleepwalker) The critic discussed Lady Macbeth's somnambulism.

As Used by Pearl S. Buck in *The Good Earth*

	Wang Lung	stood	**diffidently**	on	the	edge	of	the	circle.
Parts of Speech:	n.	v.	**adv.**	prep.	adj.	n.	prep.	adj.	n.
Parts of Sentence:	subject	AVP							
Phrases:				---prep. phrase---			---prep. phrase---		
Clauses:	-----------------------------------independent clause---------------------------------								
	one independent clause, a simple declarative sentence								

Here Buck uses the adverb *diffidently* to modify the verb. The verb is also modified by a prepositional phrase, *on the edge,* and the object of the preposition *edge* is modified by a second prepositional phrase.

Pronunciation

tautology	taw TAW lo jee		**misogynist**	miss AH jin ist
antinomy	an TIN o mee		**morphology**	more FAH lo jee
eschatology	ess ka TAW lo jee		**diffident**	DIF fi dent
opprobrium	oh PRO bree um		**cognizant**	COG nih zant
apocryphal	a PAH krih fal		**stringent**	STRIN jent
transom	TRAN sum		**temporize**	TEM por ize
commiserate	ko MIZZ er rate		**somnambulist**	som NAM byoo list
epistemology	ee pis tem AW lo jee			

Spanish Cognates

opprobrium	oprobio		**apocryphal**	apócrifo
misogynist	misógino		**tautology**	tautología
somnambulist	somnámbulo		**antinomy**	antinomia
commiseration	conmiseración		**eschatology**	escatología
morphology	morfología			

1. In his dialogue *The Parmenides*, Plato employed **antinomies** to use reason itself to question the validity of reason! Plato constructed two separate logical arguments that began with the same premise, and then, reasoning without error, reasoned to two contradicting conclusions! This is the sort of powerful intellectual pyrotechnics that students of philosophy are accustomed to expect from Plato, and it helps to demonstrate to the neophyte what the excitement about Plato is all about. Incidentally, *The Parmenides* is a terribly difficult dialogue; if you doubt it, try to read ten pages with comprehension. (As a friend of my childhood used to say, I double-dog dare ya.) A student who wants an introduction to Plato would do better to begin with *The Apology*, which is not really an apology, but Socrates's defense before the Athenians; he had been accused of corrupting the youth and of believing in false gods. In this dialogue, Socrates explains what his philosophical life has been about. He clarifies the meaning of his famous paradox: I only know that I know nothing. The jury found him guilty anyway, and he chose to drink poisonous hemlock rather than be exiled, since he knew that exile was an evil, but not that death was an evil!

2. **Epistemology** is the philosophical study (logy) of how we know anything that we know (epist). (An epistemologist would ask me how I know that.) One of the most interesting examples in the history of epistemology comes from Descartes (de KART), who determined that he would methodically doubt everything he could doubt until he finally found a solid and undoubtable truth. Then, beginning with this self-evident *a priori* truth, he would begin reasoning upward, building a large edifice of truths based on the bedrock he found at the beginning. The result of his effort is a well-known statement: *cogito ergo sum*—I think, therefore I am. Descartes decided that it was impossible to doubt that he was doubting, and that this proved that he existed. If this seemed too easy to be true, it was. Descartes has been accused of circular reasoning—also known as **begging the question**—because he assumed his conclusion (I, myself) in his premise (I think). If you are trying to prove the existence of yourself, you cannot begin with "I think!"

    The real value of Descartes's work was that he demonstrated how fiendishly difficult it can be to prove anything whatsoever, and this helps everyone who is attempting to think clearly to be far more rigorous and consistent.

    In most words, the stem *epist* means letter, as in epistle or epistolary. In **epistemology** the stem comes from the Greek *episteme*, knowledge, rather than *epistole*, letter.

3. If you would like to learn about an interesting case of alleged **misogyny**, study the paintings and the life of Pablo Picasso. Many of Picasso's cubist paintings depict women in terribly unflattering, animal-like, ugly, and even horrifying ways. Picasso, despite his artistic genius, has been condemned for his treatment of women that he knew, and for the way that he painted them. A very unsympathetic biography, *Picasso: Creator and Destroyer* by Arianna Stassinopoulos Huffington, explores these issues in detail. This would make a worthy subject for a student research paper. The Huffington book, by the way, contains fascinating stories. When Paris was liberated from the Nazis, Picasso, who had spent the war in Paris, was visited by Hemingway. Picasso was not at home, but the concierge asked Hemingway if he, like everyone else, had brought Picasso a gift. Hemingway darted back to his car and returned with a box of *hand grenades*, inscribed, "To Picasso, from Hemingway"!

In each case below, one of the choices was really the word used by the author in the sentence provided. All of the choices can be found in the example words on the first page of this lesson. Your challenge is to decide which word the author used. This is not a test; it is more like a game, because more than one word choice may work perfectly well. See if you can use your sensitivity and intuition to guess correctly which word the author used. You may need a dictionary.

1.   **From Stephen Crane's** *The Red Badge of Courage*

       They expressed _____ for that part of the army that had been left on the river bank.
       a. misogyny
       b. commiseration
       c. stringence
       d. diffidence

2.   **From Charlotte Brontë's** *Jane Eyre*

       I was loaded with general _____.
       a. opprobrium
       b. epistemology
       c. morphology
       d. eschatology

3.   **From Jane Austen's** *Emma*

       [Emma observed] the feebleness and _____ of the narrative.
       a. tautology
       b. misogyny
       c. diffidence
       d. antinomy

4.   **From Elizabeth George Speare's** *The Witch of Blackbird Pond*

       The letters [were] painted jauntily on the _____.
       a. epistemology
       b. morphology
       c. somnambulist
       d. transom

5.   **From Robert Louis Stevenson's** *Dr. Jekyll and Mr. Hyde*

       The whole business looked _____.
       a. stringent
       b. apocryphal
       c. diffident
       d. cognizant

Though it is good to have a rich vocabulary, it is not good to abuse that vocabulary by writing verbose, sesquipedalian sentences (such as this one). Those who overuse their vocabularies often do so at the expense both of clarity and of others' patience. Translate the following ostentatious, ponderous passage into graceful, direct English.

PAYNE SCHMERZ, who fell into obloquy and opprobrium after being branded a malefic misogynist that perambulated the streets at night, was actually a diffident and philosophical somnambulist, dreamily incognizant of violating stringent social codes. In one (apocryphal) story, he was said to have bumped his head on a low transom, and to have wandered off in audible self-commiseration.

Actually, Payne's nocturnal sesquipedalian ratiocinations went something like this: "Shall I devote myself to morphology, epistemology, or eschatology? My lucubrations must be confined to one of the three; I can temporize, or stall, or delay no longer, to put it tautologically. If I study morphology, shall I specialize in exobiotic, anthropomorphic life forms? If I study epistemology, shall I reason through *a posteriori* induction or through *a priori* deduction, bewaring of antinomies? And how will I know if I know that I know? If I study eschatology, when will I know the merit of my conclusions? Too late. And how can I circumvent the tortuous perils of solipsism? I feel like a philosophical Phaeton trying to drive a too-powerful sun chariot through the dangers of the mind's sky."

This prolix and recondite self-colloquy continued unabated, and Payne wandered on down the street, his physiognomy tranquil in sleep.

obloquy

Reading Comprehension

1. For Translation 44, which of the following does the passage suggest:
   - A. Payne is an innocent and naive dreamer.
   - B. Payne is an overconfident, self-important egotist.
   - C. Payne is an unstable person with psychological problems.
   - D. Payne is a misogynist who is a danger to society.

2. Which of the following best describes the passage:
   - A. the interior monologue of a misunderstood sleepwalker
   - B. a description of an eccentric person's public reputation
   - C. the deplorable ideas of a miscreant
   - D. the nonsensical dream of a sleepwalker

Analogies

3. **DIFFIDENT : CONFIDENT ::**
   - A. cognizance : awareness
   - B. temporize : hesitate
   - C. empty : full
   - D. stringency : license

4. **SOMNAMBULIST : EQUILIBRIST ::**
   - A. string : sedative
   - B. somniloquy : equivocate
   - C. sleep : walk
   - D. dream : balance

Antonyms

cacophonous

5. **OPPROBRIUM :**
   - A. lionize
   - B. apotheosis
   - C. bowdlerize
   - D. nepotism

6. **MISOGYNIST :**
   - A. philanthropist
   - B. philanderer
   - C. anthropologist
   - D. feminist

evaluation

Which would be a more valuable **epistemological** accomplishment: proving that we know a physical object is before us, or proving that another person's emotions are what they seem? Why? Do you think either phenomenon could actually be known for sure? Why or why not?

synthesis

Use eight or more of the words from List 44 to write a creative paragraph or short story. You may also include words from previous lists if you wish. You may use a dictionary to help with usage and parts of speech questions. Feel free to be humorous or fantastic in what you write.

analysis

Look up the words **eschatology**, **epistemology**, and **apocryphal** in a good college dictionary, and explain why these words mean what they mean, based on their etymologies. Analyze the construction of the words.

What is the etymology of the word **commiserate**? How is this word different from the word **sympathize**? Use the stems/etymologies to distinguish fine shades of meaning between the two words.

application

Think, in elaborate detail, about the act of **commiserating** with someone who needs you to sympathize. How does commiseration work? How does it ease the pain of someone who is suffering? Think of at least five hypothetical situations in which it would be important for you to "be there" to commiserate with someone.

convergence

Consider the two words **diffident** and **stringent**. Pick one of these two words to add to the vocabulary you actually use frequently. Why did you pick that word?

imagination and intuition

In Shakespeare's terrifying *Macbeth*, Lady Macbeth utters her famous **somnambulism** soliloquy as the audience watches transfixed. Guilt and horror have driven her to reveal herself in her restless sleep. Imagine that you are writing a play in which a character divulges personal secrets in somnambulistic soliloquy. Describe the scene and the character's actions, explain what the character reveals about himself or herself, and explain how the character's psychological state motivates this event.

Neologist's Lexicon

Use the stems in this list to create a new word (neologism). Give the word, the pronunciation, the part of speech, the etymology, and the definition(s). Keep a record of the neologisms you create from list to list. Here are some examples:

cryptomorphic (krip to mor' fic) adj. [crypto (hidden), morph (shape)] 1. demonstrably real but invisible, such as gravitation or commiseration 2. of undetectable form or structure, as an incondite short story

antifidous (an tif' fid us) adj. [anti (against), fid (faith), ous (full of)] 1. pathologically professing to believe the opposite of whatever one hears 2. spontaneous, disingenuous skepticism

Sesquipedalian Poetry Practice

Using words from List 44 and previous lists, write a poem in which each word is connected to a previous word by either a vowel sound or a consonant sound. If the repeated sound is an entire syllable, such as **plow** and **vow**, then we call that **rhyme**. If the sound is only for a single vowel sound, such as in the words **smite** and **file**, then we call that **assonance**. If the sound is simply a repeated consonant, located anywhere in the word, such as the repeated *b* sound in **baboon** and **lob** and **abashed**, then we call that **consonance**. If the sound is repeated at the beginnings of the words, such as in the words **morphology**, **manumission**, **miscreant**, and **misogynist**, then we call that **alliteration**. Another sound trick that is fun to use is a reversed sound, such as **fine** and **knife**. Use rhyme, assonance, consonance, reversal, and alliteration to write a poem (sort of) that strings each word to the next through sound connections. In this experimental sound poem, do not worry about meaning; just think about sound. Sometimes, if you do that, surprising meanings emerge anyway!

city synopsis

curs circumvent murk.
stringent negative diffidence.
perfidious patrician trap.
manumission mossy somnambulist.
hedonist funambulist newts is news.
apotheosis parthenogenesis finish us.
squeeze *sui generis locus classicus* glassy bus.
assiduous suit tortuous trotting joggers.
vacuous Saskatoon assonance brass.
ablution sir circumlocution.
do the locomotion soliloquy.
unilateral splatter, all nonplussed compulsive.
apocryphal postlude . . .

• *ine*	(nature of)	aquiline	• *mal*	(bad)	malfeasance
• **fac**	(to do)	malfeasance	• monger	(seller)	costermonger
• *gyn*	(woman)	gynecocracy	• *cracy*	(government)	gynecocracy
• *ous*	(full of)	tenebrous	• ego	(I)	superego
• punct	(point)	pungent	• *mega*	(large)	megalomania
• *syn*	(together)	syndrome	• *drome*	(run)	syndrome
• *narco*	(sleep)	narcolepsy	• *eu*	(good)	euphemism
• *mono*	(one)	monograph	• *lepsy*	(attack)	narcolepsy
• son	(sound)	dissonant	• *mania*	(madness)	megalomania

aquiline (eaglelike) The Emperor had a curved, aquiline nose, like an eagle's beak.

malfeasance (public misconduct) The public official was accused of malfeasance.

costermonger (vegetable vendor) London's cockney costermongers sold their fruit.

gynecocracy (government of women) The chauvinist was afraid of gynecocracy.

tenebrous (dark and gloomy) The castle's tenebrous interior frightened Jonathan.

superego (unconscious conscience) Freud thought the id was controlled by the superego.

expostulate (to object earnestly) She ignored his earnest expostulations.

monograph (paper on one subject) The scholar published a monograph on the subject.

lacustrine (of lakes) Yeats longed for the lacustrine environment of Innisfree.

pungent (sharp) The pungent smell of the spice penetrated the room.

• • •

megalomania (delusions of greatness) The megalomaniac had a Napoleon complex.

syndrome (complex of symptoms) Down's syndrome afflicts some children.

euphemism (pleasant name) The term *rest room* is a euphemism.

dissonant (inharmonious) A dissonant clamor arose in the streets below Talleyrand's room.

narcolepsy (attacks of sleep) The sleepy man was a victim of narcolepsy.

As Used by Marjorie Kinnan Rawlings in *The Yearling*

	A	strong	odor	came	to	him,	**pungent**	and	rank.
Parts of Speech:	adj.	adj.	n.	v.	prep.	pron.	**adj.**	conj.	adj.
Parts of Sentence:			subject	AVP					
Phrases:				--prep. phrase--					
Clauses:				independent clause					

-----------------------------------independent clause-----------------------------------
one independent clause, a simple declarative sentence

Here Rawlings uses the adjective *pungent* to modify the noun *odor*, which is also the subject of the sentence.

Pronunciation

aquiline	AH kwil in	**lacustrine**	LACK us trin
malfeasance	mal FEEZ ance	**pungent**	PUNJ ent
costermonger	KOSS ter monger	**megalomania**	mega lo MAY nee ah
gynecocracy	gye ne KOK ra see	**syndrome**	SIN drome
tenebrous	TEN eh bruss	**euphemism**	YOO fem izm
superego	super EE go	**dissonant**	DISS o nant
expostulate	ex POSS tyoo late	**narcolepsy**	NAR ko lepp see
monograph	MON o graff		

Spanish Cognates

tenebrous	tenebroso	**monograph**	monografía
syndrome	síndrome	**euphemism**	eufemismo
narcolepsy	narcolepsia	**dissonant**	disonante
megalomania	megalomanía	**aquiline**	aquilino
lacustrine	lacustre		

1. The adjective **tenebrous** comes from the Latin word *tenebrae,* which meant darkness. In the Roman Catholic Church, Tenebrae is the office of lauds and matins sung during Holy Week to celebrate Christ's Crucifixion. If something is **tenebrific**, then it produces darkness.

2. A **Micropoem**: The noun **superego** is taken from Sigmund Freud's famous trilogy of terms: ego, id, and superego. For Freud, the father of psychoanalysis, these terms represented different aspects of every human personality. The **ego** is the conscious self that is aware of itself and that deliberately governs itself as best it can. The **id** is the collection of subconscious urges and hidden animal drives that secretly motivates many of our intense and compulsive behaviors, including those that are immoral. The **superego** is the subconscious moral self, the unconscious conscience, or higher (super) self (ego) that is opposed to the base, egotistical self-gratification of the id. The conscious ego is forced to mediate between the opposing sides of the unconscious.

3. Aquila, the Eagle, is a northern constellation south of Cygnus, the Swan. A person with an **aquiline** nose has a curved nose, like an eagle's beak. The *ine* suffix also concludes other animal adjectives: ursine, bearlike; canine, doglike; feline, catlike; porcine, piglike.

4. A **Classic Word**: One common synonym for **remonstrate** is **expostulate**. To expostulate with someone is to reason very earnestly but with civility against what that person is doing. If the two words describing objection have a difference in meaning, it lies in tone; **remonstrate** emphasizes the emphatic complaining objection, whereas **expostulate** emphasizes kindly and courteous objection. You expostulate with your respected parents or beloved spouse. Remember that remonstrate literally means *show again*; it emphasizes the objection that won't take no for an answer and keeps arguing. **Expostulate** has been in continual use for centuries and has been used by Defoe, Swift, Scott, Emily Brontë, Hawthorne, Stowe, Melville, Dickens, Hardy, Wells, Conrad, and Fitzgerald. Robinson Crusoe frequently expostulated with his mother and father. Scott's Cedric the Saxon expostulated with his guards. Swift's emperors of Blefuscu frequently expostulated with their ambassadors. We find running murmurs of expostulation (Fitzgerald), an oriental voice in a courtroom expostulating with impassioned volubility (Conrad), the expostulations of two feeble old constables (Hardy), a woman's frantic expostulations at a parting (Wells), expostulations that are mild and rational (Charlotte Brontë), and kind expostulations (Swift). Perhaps the best sentence to illustrate the civil tone of the expostulation, as contrasted with the not necessarily civil tone of the remonstration, is this one from Defoe's *Robinson Crusoe*: "He called me one morning into his chamber . . . and expostulated very warmly with me upon this subject." In this sentence, the word *warmly* seems to have a pleasant double value, carrying both the smiling civility and the heat of the feeling.

5. It is easy to forget the educational power of the Greek and Latin stems. Consider, for example, just a few of the words that contain the stem *syn*: **synaeresis**, **synaesthesia**, **synagogue**, **synaloepha**, **synapse**, **synarthrosis**, **syncarp**, **syncategorematic**, **synchroflash**, **synchromesh**, **synchronic**, **synchroscope**, **synclastic**. To know that *syn/sym* means together is to have a word half-mastered before you ever encounter it.

In each case below, one of the choices was really the word used by the author in the sentence provided. All of the choices can be found in the example words on the first page of this lesson. Your challenge is to decide which word the author used. This is not a test; it is more like a game, because more than one word choice may work perfectly well. See if you can use your sensitivity and intuition to guess correctly which word the author used. You may need a dictionary.

1. **From Virginia Woolf's** *Mrs. Dalloway*

   Those _____ [were] not allowed to stand their barrows in the streets.
   a. megalomaniacs
   b. superegos
   c. narcoleptics
   d. costermongers

2. **From Joseph Conrad's** *Lord Jim*

   Then in the _____ immensity a livid arch appears.
   a. tenebrous
   b. lacustrine
   c. pungent
   d. dissonant

3. **From Mark Twain's** *The Prince and the Pauper*

   This, in the eye of the law, is..._____ in office.
   a. euphemism
   b. megalomania
   c. expostulation
   d. malfeasance

4. **From John Knowles's** *A Separate Peace*

   No locker room could have more _____ air than Devon's.
   a. aquiline
   b. dissonant
   c. pungent
   d. lacustrine

5. **From Bram Stoker's** *Dracula*

   His face was strong—a very strong—_____, with high bridge of the thin nose and peculiarly arched nostrils.
   a. syndrome
   b. pungence
   c. aquiline
   d. narcolepsy

Though it is a good thing to have a rich vocabulary, it is not a good thing to abuse that vocabulary by writing verbose, abstruse, sesquipedalian sentences. Those who overuse their vocabularies often do so at the expense of clarity. Translate the following showy, ponderous passage into graceful, direct English. Do not use slang, but do use words that seem familiar and comfortable.

AMID THE DISSONANT CACOPHONY of the gregarious water birds, the old captain, B.W. Staey, walked out of the tenebrous northern conifer forest onto the lacustrine shore. His aquiline nose still sensed the pungent tang of the green pine boughs, but the fresh lake wind smelled sweet and cold as it blew in *sotto voce* assonance down from the still snowy peaks. A xenophobic tern flew near his head, expostulating with him like a prolix costermonger about getting too near her nest, and in accordance with the subtle gynecocracy of nature, his mollifying superego subconsciously steered him in kindness away from the nest and back toward the lake waters lapping euphonically with mellifluous sounds by the shore.

"If I only knew what is wrong with me," he soliloquized with stoic but nonplussed physiognomy, "then I should have some peace here." Ever since he had assiduously written the euphemism-ridden monograph accusing the megalomaniac Lord Mayor of malfeasance, he had been plagued with a syndrome of saturnine narcolepsy, somnambulism, and even occasional lyssophobia, although he now felt the intangible soporific effect of the lacustrine environment. With desultory perambulation, he continued introspectively down the shore, toward his small cabin of clay and wattles, and his nine heliotropic bean rows, and his hive for the vivacious honey bee.

Reading Comprehension

1. In Translation 45, the author does all of the following EXCEPT:
    A. Imply that females of all species govern nature.
    B. Suggest that the captain's rambling has no real purpose.
    C. Indicate that the captain does not know the cause of his problem.
    D. Imply that the captain has impugned the integrity of an innocent person.

2. It can be inferred from the passage that:
    A. the author feels sympathy for the spirit of the tern
    B. the author feels antipathy for the rough wilderness that needs to be tamed
    C. the author has difficulty sleeping
    D. the author regards excessive introspection as unhealthy

Analogies

3. **AQUILINE : LACUSTRINE ::**
    A. eagle : fish
    B. ursine : alpine
    C. porcine : pig
    D. bovine : lake

4. **PUNGENT : DISSONANT ::**
    A. sharp : knife
    B. pointed : blunt
    C. stab : symphony
    D. aroma : clamor

aquiline

Antonyms

5. **TENEBROUS :**
    A. refulgent
    B. glimmering
    C. translucent
    D. perspicuous

6. **EXPOSTULATE :**
    A. remonstrate
    B. *ex post facto*
    C. congratulate
    D. eulogize

synthesis

Pungent is an important word to know, since many educated people do use it in conversation. In literature **pungent** has been used to describe smells such as the smell of alcohol, but it has also been used to describe the sharp edge of pungent suffering. In *A Separate Peace*, John Knowles used **pungent** to describe the smell of stale sweat that permeated the locker room at Devon School. Think of various smells that are pungent, and then think of experiences other than smells that could be described as pungent.

aesthetics

In William Butler Yeats's poem "The Lake Isle of Innisfree," there are famous lines describing the **lacustrine** environment at Innisfree, a beautiful lake in Ireland. In one line, Yeats describes the "evening full of the linnet's wings," and in another, he hears "lake water lapping with low sounds by the shore." Carefully consider these lines, and explain how the consonants Yeats used support the meaning he intended.

imagination, elaboration, and intuition

Imagine a scene in which the cockney **costermongers** are beginning to hawk their vegetables on an East End London street in the *fin de siècle*. It is early morning, the sun is just coming up, and the great city is just coming to life. Using your most vivid imagination and intuition, write a description, or even a short story, in which you make this scene seem elaborately real.

emotion

Consider the egotistic sociopath, the person who has plenty of (to use Freud's terms) **id** (urges and drives), but not enough **superego** to make him feel sympathy with or pain for others; he feels no guilt or remorse when he causes others to suffer, and so he is too comfortably egocentric. Lacking a conscience, he manipulates other people to get everything he wants, regardless of the effect this has on their lives. Think carefully about the ways in which you really do care about other significant people in your life, and how their happiness makes you happy too, or how their unhappiness makes you unhappy too. Write a short description of one example of this sym-path-y you have felt.

Notice that this superego void is one of the characteristic qualities of monsters in film and literature: monsters tend to be creatures who have human physical characteristics, but who lack human emotional sympathy for others. The stereotypical cavernous, hollow-sounding monster voice is one indication of the hollow heart and soul of the idful monster.

divergence and convergence

The noun **dissonance** refers to sounds (son) that are away (dis) from each other, which are not symphonic or euphonic, which do not harmonize. First, think divergently to imagine a long list of dissonant sounds, such as the squeak of a blackboard (argh), the grinding of a disposal (ugh), the clang of an alarm (ick), and so forth. Then, think convergently to choose the single worst sound of all, the one sound you would least like to have to listen to for the rest of your life.

Neologist's Lexicon

Use the stems in this list to create a new word (neologism). Give the word, the pronunciation, the part of speech, the etymology, and the definition(s). Keep a record of the neologisms you create from list to list. Here are some examples:

egomonger (ee' go mon gur) n. [ego (I), monger (seller)] 1. a vulgar commercialist who plays on individuals' diffidence with television commercials asking them if they would rather be different, implying that being themselves is not satisfactory 2. a person whose *idée fixe* is to advance himself, and who responds to every declarative sentence with a retort beginning, "Well, in my case . . ."

malodrome (mahl' oh drome) n. [mal (bad), drome (run)] 1. one who always answers the sanguine question, "How's it going" with the saturnine answer "Not too good" 2. one who spends every day tired because he jogs at 5 a.m. every morning

Sesquipedalian Mother Goose

Use the words from various vocabulary lists in this book to write a Mother Goose rhyme. Begin with an actual line from one of the famous Mother Goose poems. For example:

Little Miss Muffet

Little Miss Muffet, sat on her tuffet
Feeling acerbity.
Circumambulated a spider,
Sedately beside her,
And gave Miss Muffet an epiphany.

circum**ambulate**

128

• *para*	(beside)	paragon		• *anti*	(against)	antipathy
• *path*	(feeling)	feeling		• *a-*	(without)	abyss
• **simul**	(feign)	dissemble		• sed	(sit)	insidious
• in	(not)	impecunious		• *kin*	(motion)	kinesiology
• fy	(make)	beatify		• ex	(out)	execrate
• sacro	(holy)	execrate		• **plus**	(more)	ne plus ultra
• ultra	(beyond)	ne plus ultra		• voc	(voice)	vociferous
• fer	(carry)	vociferous		• corp	(body)	corpulent
• *peri*	(near)	perihelion		• *helio*	(sun)	perihelion
• *crypt*	(hidden)	cryptic		• sanct	(holy)	sanctimonious

paragon (excellent model) Her computer graphic design was a paragon of geometric form.

antipathy (strong dislike) His fierce antipathy for his rival continued unabated.

abyss (bottomless fissure) The wild mountain gorge seemed an abyss without bottom.

dissemble (conceal through pretense) Do not be fooled by his lying and dissembling.

insidious (sly) The agent entrapped him with her patient, insidious plot.

impecunious (poor) The impecunious spendthrift could no longer afford fudgesicles.

kinesiology (science of motion) The Olympic coach studied kinesiology assiduously.

beatify (make blissfully happy) She spoke his name, beatifying him for ten minutes.

execrate (denounce or curse) He vilified and execrated his arch enemy, Minnie Mouse.

ne plus ultra (peak of perfection) The Mona Lisa is the *ne plus ultra* of portraits.

• • •

vociferous (loud) His vociferous expostulations disrupted her tranquility.

corpulent (full-bodied) The corpulent gourmet continued to indulge in his own creations.

perihelion (orbital point nearest sun) The comet was brightest at perihelion.

cryptic (having hidden meaning) The Celtic runes contained cryptic messages from the Druids.

sanctimonious (affectedly holy) His sanctimonious attitude was offensive to the group.

As Used by George Owell in *1984*

	To dissemble	your	feelings	was	an	instinctive	reaction.
Parts of Speech:	n.	pron.	n.	v.	adj.	adj.	n.

Parts of Sentence:	-------------- subject-------------- predicate	subject complement

Phrases:	----------infinitive phrase---------

Clauses:	----------------------------------independent clause--------------------------------
	one independent clause, a simple declarative sentence

Here Orwell uses *dissemble* in its infinitive form; in this structure it is a noun. The noun *feelings* is the object of the infinitive in the infinitive phrase, which is the subject of the verb. Notice the linking verb *was* and the subject complement *reaction*. An infinitive such as *to dissemble* is regarded as one word.

Pronunciation

paragon	PAIR ah gon		**execrate**	EX e crate
antipathy	an TIP a thee		***ne plus ultra***	nay plus UL tra
abyss	ah BISS		**vociferous**	vo SIFF er us
dissemble	diss EM bel		**corpulent**	CORP yuh lent
insidious	in SID ee us		**perihelion**	pair ih HEE lee un
impecunious	im peh KYOON ee us		**cryptic**	KRIP tik
kinesiology	ki NEE zee OLL o jee		**sanctimonious**	sank tih MOAN ee us
beatify	bee AT ih fie			

Spanish Cognates

antipathy	antipatía		**abyss**	abismo
insidious	insidioso		**beatified**	beato
execration	execración		**vociferous**	vociferante
corpulent	corpulento		**perihelion**	perihelio

1. The family of *helio* words is fun to note. **Perihelion** is the point at which a planet, comet, or asteroid is nearest (peri) to the sun (helio). Comets reach their brightest phase as they approach the sun. **Aphelion** is the point at which planets, comets, and asteroids are farthest from the sun. The solar system, filled with objects moving through their perihelions and aphelions as they circle in their revolutions around the sun, is **heliocentric**, rather than **geocentric**. And sun-loving tourists, who risk their future healths for the benefit of a tan, are **heliophiles**.

2. The noun **paragon** means a model of excellence to be used for purposes of comparison. The paragon is the ideal pattern to which we aspire. This idea is easier to understand when we realize that paragon comes from the Greek *paragein*: to put side by side. Hamlet tells his friends that Man is the paragon of animals.

4. A **Classic Word**: The noun **abyss** comes from the Greek *abyssos*, meaning bottomless. It is made of *byssos* (bottom of the sea) and *a-* as a short form of *an-* (without or not). **Abyss** is used not only to refer to the great depths of the sea, but also to anything that is profound, without bottom, or without end, such as time, hell, or the vast space of the universe. In ancient cosmogony the abyss was the primal chaos that existed before Creation. In classic literature **abyss** has had a distinguished history. It has been used by Fitzgerald, Wells, Hawthorne, Conrad, Hardy (to describe the vast heath), Kipling, Scott, Dickens, Stowe, and Emily Brontë. In Dickens's *A Tale of Two Cities*, Sidney Carton sees a beautiful city and a brilliant people rising from this abyss (revolutionary Paris). Harriet Beecher Stowe describes slavery's abyss of injustice and cruelty. Heathcliff's poignant cry to the dying Catherine in *Wuthering Heights* is, "do not leave me in this abyss, where I cannot find you." In Conrad's *Lord Jim*, sea and sky are compounded into one abyss of obscurity. In *The Time Machine*, the Morlocks' eyes are abnormally large and sensitive, like the pupils of the abysmal fishes.

5. The **ne plus ultra** is the peak of perfection, the highest point, the zenith, the acme. You can go no (ne) more (plus) beyond (ultra) the *ne plus ultra*. This term places even more emphasis on absolute perfection than the word **paragon**. The *Mona Lisa* is the *ne plus ultra* of portraits because Leonardo's lightning-fast eyes allowed him to capture the most subtle and evanescent of glances, the most impossibly slight changes of countenance that occur at the magic moment of attraction between two people. Many artists can capture the primary emotions of anger, joy, or deep reflection, but few artists have had the acute perception to see the delicate phenomena that the subtlest, in-between emotions bring to the face. But then, you would expect such powers of observation from a painter who could draw the swirling currents of a stream.

6. A **Micropoem**: The adjective **insidious** contains a delightful hidden image. Made of *in* (in) and *sed* (sit), it refers to the trap in which the deceitful person sits in ambush, waiting for his or her victim! To be insidious is to deliberately deceive in order to entrap, to **sit in** wait for your intended prey. This word is an outstanding example of the beautiful micropoems that words so often contain and that are unavailable to those who only consider the definitions and not the etymologies.

In each case below, one of the choices was really the word used by the author in the sentence provided. All of the choices can be found in the example words on the first page of this lesson. Your challenge is to decide which word the author used. This is not a test; it is more like a game, because more than one word choice may work perfectly well. See if you can use your sensitivity and intuition to guess correctly which word the author used. You may need a dictionary.

1.   **From E.L. Doctorow's** *Ragtime*

I look about me and smell the sweat of rage, the _____ rebellion of wild unthinking youth.
a. corpulent
b. impecunious
c. sanctimonious
d. vociferous

2.   **From Edith Wharton's** *Ethan Frome*

It was the sense of helplessness that sharpened his _____.
a. abyss
b. kinesiology
c. sanctimoniousness
d. antipathy

3.   **From Thornton Wilder's** *The Bridge of San Luis Rey*

She leaned forward, her face streaming with happy tears, and made the _____ gesture.
a. beatific
b. impecunious
c. dissembling
d. sanctimonious

4.   **From George Orwell's** *1984*

It's _____. It can get hold of you without your even knowing it.
a. cryptic
b. vociferous
c. insidious
d. sanctimonious

5.   **From T.S. Eliot's** *Murder in the Cathedral*

Men will not hate you enough to defame you or to _____ you.
a. beatify
b. execrate
c. dissemble
d. *ne plus ultra*

Though it is good to have a rich vocabulary, it is not good to abuse that vocabulary by writing verbose, abstruse, sesquipedalian sentences (such as this one). Those who overuse their vocabularies often do so at the expense of clarity. Translate the following showy, ponderous passage into graceful, direct English. Do not use slang, but do use words that seem familiar and comfortable.

THIS GLOWING DIAPHANOUS VISION, thought the astrophysicist, was no mere paragon of poetry in motion, no mere metaphor for the theoretical abyss of kinesiology; this was the *ne plus ultra* of all motion. This was perfection itself. She gazed again through the optical eyepiece of BOOGIE (the in-house humorous acronym for Big Old Optical Gathering Instrument of Entropy) the huge telescope at the summit of Mt. Wollstonecraft, at the streaming translucent filaments of the comet's tail, stretching from the comet's perihelion near the sun to far beyond the orbit of Venus, and she felt a beatific peace. Once again, her equations had proved exact, and the beautiful comet had appeared exactly where she had predicted. For her, mathematics *was* nature, and her equations were paintings with which she described the cosmos. This, she thought, was truth; though the cosmos could be cryptic, it could not dissemble (like some of her insidious colleagues who envied her brilliance and accomplishments, and who lost no opportunity to advise her sanctimoniously about how to improve her work).

With a neophyte's joy, she loved studying the glittering cosmos, with its silently vociferous stars; its corpulent, ringed planets; its ineluctable gravitation; its prolix spectra; its gregarious galaxies; its disinterested physics that knew no antipathy or execration. She loved the euphony of the night wind in the observatory dome; it always seemed to her to be the *sotto voce* harmony of the heavenly spheres. Einstein had seen the physiognomy of the Omniscient Spirit in this black abyss of space; The Old One, he had called it. Well, she understood that, too. She had made a career of this research, this lucubration, this astrophysics, but even after a lifetime of work she had to admit that she was impecunious in knowledge. Like Socrates, she had learned that she knew (really) nothing.

And yet, the happiness she felt in this tenuous knowledge was truly beatific. A life of scientific integrity had given her a self-acceptance that amounted almost to a kind of cosmological narcissism, since through her nonplussed mind, the universe was, as *alter ego*, looking at, and in love with, itself.

Reading Comprehension

1. In Translation 46 it can be inferred that:
    A. The astrophysicist's colleagues concur with her conclusions.
    B. The astrophysicist's colleagues collaborate closely at the observatory.
    C. The astrophysicist's mediocre colleagues are envious of her talent.
    D. The astrophysicist uses unsound scientific practices.

2. The author does all of the following EXCEPT:
    A. imply that profound knowledge is difficult to attain
    B. imply that science is of no value
    C. imply that scientists are fallible human beings
    D. imply that scientists can believe in God

Analogies

3. **CRYPTIC : SANCTIMONIOUS ::**
    A. dungeon : church
    B. concealed : pretentious
    C. code : prayer
    D. suggestion : sanctuary

4. **DISSEMBLE : EXECRATE ::**
    A. denounce : pretend
    B. assemble : berate
    C. intransitive : transitive
    D. feign : deprecate

Antonyms

5. **ANTIPATHY :**
    A. eulogy
    B. lionizing
    C. amour
    D. apotheosis

antipathy

6. **IMPECUNIOUS :**
    A. opulent
    B. squalid
    C. aristocratic
    D. affluent

synthesis

An **abyss** is a deep or bottomless space, such as a precipitous mountain gorge or a trench in the ocean. Think of as many abysses as you can, first in the physical world, and then in the emotional or abstract world, as metaphors; i.e., the abyss of his loneliness. The further out and wilder your comparisons are without being meaningless, the more powerful the synthesis. (Thinking of wild comparisons is good, because you are noticing what seemingly different things have in common. This is an important thinking ability in many fields, such as physics.)

analysis

By breaking the words into their component stems, explain the difference between **paragon**, **nonpareil**, and **ne plus ultra**, or between **antipathy**, **objurgation**, and **execrate**. You may use a dictionary to look up the etymologies, if you would like more information than the stems we have studied provide.

intuition for imagination

Imagine that you have been on a quest. You are young, but brave and determined. You follow a misty path to a high mountain ridge, where you suddenly come upon huge stone monoliths, covered with moss, sticking out of the low vegetation. A small, wizened, grizzled man steps out from behind one of the monoliths, offering to help you, but you can tell that he is **dissembling**. Why is he **dissembling**? What is he concealing? Continue the story . . .

ethics

What figure in American political history do you regard as a **paragon** of ethical political behavior? In other words, who do you regard as a highly ethical politician—someone, such as a president, senator, or governor who helped to govern the United States in a moral and principled way? Explain who you choose and why.

divergence and imagination

Divergence is thinking up options or alternatives. One aspect of divergence is to think of lots of alternatives, and another is to think of very creative, original, or unexpected alternatives. Whereas synthesis is thinking of how different things are connected or similar, divergence is thinking of lots of different ways or kinds of things. Synthesis is noticing similarities; divergence is creating choices. Imagine that you are temporarily **impecunious** and that you are going to solve this problem by selling T-shirts with **sesquipedalian** messages on them, such as "I HATE ANTIPATHY." Working in groups, make a list of witty sesquipedalian T-shirt slogans. Use words from any list up to List 46.

convergence

If you woke up in a strange alternative world, where the law required you to use one of the words from List 46 every day, which word would you choose? Why? Imagine how difficult it would be if you had to use one of these words in every single sentence!

Neologist's Lexicon

Use the stems in this list to create a new word (neologism). Give the word, the pronunciation, the part of speech, the etymology, and the definition(s). Keep a record of the neologisms you create from list to list. Here are some examples:

antikinetic (an ti kin et' ik) adj. [anti (against), kin (motion)] 1. having a tendency to immediately propose the opposite of whatever you hear proposed; always reflexively moving the contrary 2. severely and profoundly intractable, such that you never even consider the possibility of changing your mind on any issue whatsoever

sacropathy (sak roh' path ee) n. [sacro (holy), path (feeling) 1. attaching far more importance to everything one does or encounters than is healthy or rational 2. being so emotionally involved with important matters that you lose the ability to think clearly about them.

Sesquipedalian Recipe

Use the words from List 46 and previous lists to write a sesquipedalian recipe for the preparation of any food you like. If you are not a cook, you can write directions for making a peanut butter sandwich or for preparing a bowl of cereal. The point is to have fun using the words. An example:

The Sesquipedalian Gastronome's Famous Chili
by an Autodidact

To prepare the *sui generis* paragon of all chilis, causing your dissembling friends to sink into an abyss of lionizing envy, obsequiously observe the following prolix and omnibus injunctions, contravening none:

1. In a large pot, empty four 28 oz. cans of corpulent whole tomatoes and four drained 16 oz cans of light red kidney beans. To this pungent mixture, add the heterodox ingredients: a sprinkling of oregano, and a half dozen bay leaves, some salt, and some black pepper. Bring to a truculent boil and then simmer beatifically.

2. In a cast iron frying pan, lightly sauté one diced onion in olive oil, and pour the mollified onion into the large pot. Be on the *qui vive*, lest the onion begin to brown.

3. In the same frying pan, assiduously brown a pound or two of ground beef, adding one or two packages of commercial chili seasoning, depending on how hot you like your chili. Use legerdemain to pour out the grease, and add the browned, seasoned beef to the large pot. Stir to expedite the confluence of flavors. Abjure acerbity.

4. Continue to simmer, stirring intractably, for two hours. *In medias res*, relish the circumambient aromas and perform loquacious soliloquies. Temporize.

5. With equanimity and sangfroid, add three tablespoons of honey just before serving. Stir well. This secret ingredient will create the *ne plus ultra* of chilis. Impugn the specious objections of persons who doubt the wisdom of adding honey. They will soon be transmogrified into mellifluous admirers.

6. Serve with supererogatory sourdough biscuits and honey.

7. Stoically accept the benedictions of the incredulous *bon vivants*.

8. Enjoy postprandial perambulation.

9. Be gregarious.

10. Avoid megalomania.

• *ism*	(doctrine)	pharisaism	• *neuro*	(nerve)	neurasthenia
• *a-*	(without)	neurasthenia	• *sthen*	(strength)	neurasthenia
• re	(again)	remunerate	• *pro*	(forward)	proscenium
• *epist*	(knowledge)	epistle	• chron	(time)	anachronistic
• lent	(full of)	feculent	• less (OE)	(without)	feckless
• contra	(against)	contretemps	• tempor	(time)	contretemps
• *hyper*	(over)	hyperbole	• *para*	(beside)	paradigm
• germ	(related)	germane	• fil	(thread)	filigree
• **gran**	(grain)	filigree	• *scen*	(stage)	proscenium

pharisaism (hypocrisy) His pharisaism of aloof pretense but loose behavior sickened us.

neurasthenia (nervous exhaustion) He mocked the bad poet's neurasthenic affectations.

remunerate (repay) Talented people should be well remunerated for their labors.

proscenium (stage forward of curtain) She took a final bow from the proscenium.

epistle (long instructive letter) Read her tiring epistle on the proper way to vacation.

anachronistic (misplaced in time) Notice the anachronistic 20th century details in the novel.

feculent (foul) We drove sorrowfully past the feculent and filthy yards of the shanties.

feckless (without effect) We saw Hector's feckless efforts to overcome fear of Achilles.

anapest (three-syllable foot, stress on third) Ex.: ampu**tee**, insin**cere**, on the **beach**.

contretemps (embarrassing mishap) The chance meeting was a ludicrous contretemps.

• • •

hyperbole (overstatement) His colorful hyperbole amused us.

paradigm (model) Show us an instructive paradigm or example.

germane (related) Her germane comments were vitally relevant to the debate.

filigree (lacy design) It was difficult to clean the gold filigree around the jewel.

chronic (lasting) The chronic illness plagued her for years.

As Used by Jack London in *White Fang*

	Such	things	were	**remuneration**	in	full.
Parts of Speech:	adj.	n.	v.	**n.**	prep.	n.
Parts of Sentence:		subject	LVP	subject complement		
Phrases:					---prep. phrase---	
Clauses:	-----------------------------------independent clause---------------------------------					
	one independent clause, a simple declarative sentence					

Here London uses the noun *remuneration* as the subject complement.

Pronunciation

pharisaism	fair ih SAY izm	**anapest**	ANN ah pest
neurasthenia	noor as THEN ee ah	**contretemps**	KOHN tra TOH
remunerate	re MYOO ner ate	**hyperbole**	hie PURR bo lee
proscenium	pro SEEN ee um	**paradigm**	PAIR ah dime
epistle	ee PIST el	**germane**	jer MAIN
anachronistic	an ack kron ISS tik	**filigree**	FILL ih gree
feculent	FECK yoo lent	**chronic**	KRON ik
feckless	FECK less		

Spanish Cognates

pharisaic	farisaico	**neurasthenic**	neurasténico
remuneration	remuneración	**proscenium**	proscenio
epistle	epístola	**anachronistic**	anacrónico
feculent	feculento	**hyperbole**	hipérbole
paradigm	paradigma	**filigree**	filigrana
chronic	crónico		

1. A **Micropoem**: The noun **anapest** refers to a poetic foot that contains three syllables, with the stress on the third syllable: --'. It comes from the Greek word for strike (pest) back (ana), dadaWHAM. Examples would be *ampuTEE*, *insinCERE*, or *on the BEACH*. Notice that the foot does not have to be a single word. It can be one, two, or three words. It can be made of pieces of words:

    > At the **break** of the **day** when ba**lloons**
    > Rose in **sil**ent as**cent** over**head**,

    The primary forms of poetic foot are the **iamb**, two syllables with the stress on the second: -', the **trochee**, two syllables with the stress on the first: '-, the **dactyl**, three syllables with the stress on the first: '--, and the anapest. Most traditional English verse, such as Shakespeare's sonnets, is in iambic pentameter (-' / -' / -' / -' / -'). Remember Romeo's first iambic pentameter words to Juliet: "If **I** pro**fane** with **my** un**wor**thiest **hand** . . . ." The word **anapest** comes from the Greek *anápaistos*, meaning struck back or reversed (from a dactyl). One of life's loveliest experiences is to gradually learn an ear for the sound of language, for the music of human speech.

2. The noun **paradigm** comes from the Greek *para* (beside) and *deiknynai* (show); the idea is that one shows two things side by side, the one forming a model for the other. Today, we use the word **paradigm** to refer to an intellectual model. Thoreau's reflections on nature in *Walden* form a paradigm for future nature writers and natural philosophers. We do not usually use the word in a physical sense, as to describe a ship model or plane model.

3. A **Classic Word**: The adjective **chronic** is based on the Greek stem *chron*, meaning time. We find this stem in **chronological**, **anachronistic**, **chronometer**, **chronology**, **chronoscope**, **synchronize**, and **chronicle**, to name only a few words. Harriet Beecher Stowe used **chronic** frequently in *Uncle Tom's Cabin*; she described a kind of chronic plague, a sort of chronic remorse, and a chronic feud between Sam and Aunt Chloe that had existed from ancient times. Melville mentions a chronically broken back in *Moby Dick*. And Dickens, in *A Tale of Two Cities*, finds that Sidney Carton is chronically drunk. In *Tom Sawyer* Mark Twain says that the dreadful secret of the murder was a chronic misery, whereas in *The Call of the Wild*, Jack London pities the "outside dogs, whose digestions had not been trained by **chronic** famine to make the most of little." In John Knowles's *A Separate Peace* we find an attitude of floating, chronic disapproval. The most descriptive use, however, of chronic must be attributed to Harper Lee; in *To Kill a Mockingbird* we learn that "the younger children had perpetual colds and suffered from chronic ground-itch." Chronic ground-itch?? Give me chronic famine any day. Of course, it would be nice to be a chronic consumer of apple pie or cheeseburgers. And anyone who has read far enough to discover this sentence is probably a chronic bibliophile. Join the club. I'll see you at the book store.

    By the way, I know that the term *Uncle Tom* has acquired negative connotations in recent decades, and I understand why, but *Uncle Tom's Cabin* is a brilliant book by a brilliant woman; it was written to condemn the horror and hideous immorality of slavery and racial bigotry, and it does that in a profoundly moving way that few other books can equal.

In each case below, one of the choices was really the word used by the author in the sentence provided. All of the choices can be found in the example words on the first page of this lesson. Your challenge is to decide which word the author used. This is not a test; it is more like a game, because more than one word choice may work perfectly well. See if you can use your sensitivity and intuition to guess correctly which word the author used. You may need a dictionary.

1. **From Mary Wollstonecraft's** *Vindication of the Rights of Woman*

    A _____ stream of wealth...has muddied the pure rills of natural affection.
    a. feckless
    b. feculent
    c. germane
    d. chronic

2. **From Jack London's** *White Fang*

    Such things were _____ in full for his ardors and toils.
    a. epistles
    b. pharisaisms
    c. remunerations
    d. contretemps

3. **From Robert Louis Stevenson's** *Kidnapped*

    Ye must be as _____ at the sailoring as I have found ye at the fighting.
    a. feckless
    b. chronic
    c. feculent
    d. hyperbolic

4. **From John Knowles's** *A Separate Peace*

    Yes, huh, yes there was a small, a little _____ at the tree.
    a. filigree
    b. paradigm
    c. contretemps
    d. proscenium

5. **From Frederick Douglass's** *Narrative*

    They attended with _____ strictness to the outward forms of religion.
    a. feckless
    b. chronic
    c. germane
    d. pharisaical

Though is is a good thing to have a rich vocabulary, it is not good to abuse that vocabulary by writing verbose, abstruse, sesquipedalian sentences (such as this one). Those who overuse their vocabularies often do so at the expense both of clarity and of others' patience.

Translate the following ostentatious, ponderous passage into graceful, direct English. Do not use slang, but do use words that seem familiar and comfortable. Notice that much of the passage is actually in anapestic meter, which might be impossible to imitate in your translation. This will give you some insight into the problems that professional translators have when they try to capture the beautifully poetic work of the great novelists, such as Flaubert, who wrote *Madame Bovary* in such euphonic language that he actually shouted each passage aloud to see if it sounded right. Yes, the neighbors thought he was crazy. Flaubert's literary perfectionism was so intense that he has been often satirized: in Albert Camus's *The Plague*, one character is a novelist who throughout the entire story is still writing and rewriting the very first sentence of a novel, never being satisfied enough with it to go on to the next sentence!

THE NONPLUSSED WINNER of the unremunerative annual Magnum Opus Hyperbole Competition was the neophyte author of a semi-poetic epistle, from which the following tortuous sentence, a prolix paradigm of anapestic meter, is taken: "The most TOTally VACuous COMment and UNgermane PERfidy UTtered in ABsolute FECKlessness WAS the comPLETEly anTIi-neurasTHENically BAD phariSAism CALLing the FECulent FILigree OVer the ROTting proSCENium MONey well SPENT when in FACT it was ONly a BAD contreTEMPS, so aDIEU." This odd exaggeration was freely translated as, "Restoring the old stage was a ridiculous waste of bucks, see ya."

When superciliously asked why he had composed the victorious anapests, the discursive, saturnine winner spoke diffidently and with an obsequious voice into the microphone: "Au conTRAIRE, but the REAson I WROTE the imPONderaBLE introSPECTively SPECious anAPHora-FILLED valeDICTion exPATiatING inter ALia OVer inEFfable RECondite MATters is CRYPTic to ME."

At the epiphany of this bizarre postlude, the incredulous audience burst into condescending, loquacious cacophony.

Reading Comprehension

1. For Translation 47, which of the following does the passage suggest:
    A. The winner of the competition cheated.
    B. The winner of the competition was unaware of his own natural talent.
    C. The winner of the competition worked hard and won fairly.
    D. The winner of the competition spoke in clever self-imitation.

2. The passage could be best described as:
    A. an example of irony
    B. an example of paradox
    C. an example of juxtaposition
    D. an example of parody

Analogies

3. ANAPEST : DACTYLIC ::
    A. insincere : hopelessly
    B. trochee : iamb
    C. poem : epistle
    D. germane : anachronistic

4. CHRONIC : EPHEMERAL ::
    A. clock : femur
    B. prolonged : enduring
    C. protracted : transient
    D. remunerate : indemnify

Antonyms

chronic

5. GERMANE
    A. relevant
    B. felicitous
    C. French
    D. malapropos

6. FECKLESS
    A. salutary
    B. useless
    C. defect
    D. perfect

ethics

In the field of ethics . . . [I love the metaphor of the *field*; imagine how it would change our image if someone said, "On the mountain slope of ethics," or "In the blue abyss of ethics," or "On the frosty tundra of ethics," or "On the beach of ethics." We have fields of grass, fields of grain, fields of thought, fields of magnetism, and fields of gravity. We have playing fields, force fields, and ice fields. I keep wondering what, exactly, is meant by a *field* when we apply the word to gravity or magnetism, since these "fields" are so geometrically different from a field of, say, daisies. One of the most resonant areas (meadows?) of language is the vast number of metaphors that we have used for so long that we have forgotten that we are being metaphorical. And of course, we are forced into constant metaphor because the world is so perplexing that we often do not know any *direct* way to describe the phenomenon we have encountered! Now, where was I?] In the field of ethics, the lives, teachings, and parables of the great philosophers, heroes, and religious leaders serve as **paradigms** (pronounce: pair' uh dimes) for our own ethical behavior. We remember, for example, the irascible voice of John the Baptist, shouting in the desert, and his commitment serves as a paradigm of ethical purity against which we inevitably, and perhaps uncomfortably, compare the level of our own commitment. We remember Martin Luther's intractable, indomitable will: "Here I stand, I can do no other." We remember Socrates choosing hemlock over exile. We remember Sidney Carton taking Charles Darnay's place at the guillotine: "Tis a far, far better thing I do than I have ever done." We remember Alexander treating his enemy Xerxes's mother with dignity and respect, as he would wish his own mother to be treated by a conquering enemy. We remember Martin Luther King Jr.'s dream from the mountaintop, and his vision of the promised land of ethical democracy. We remember Patrick Henry only regretting that he had but one life to give for his country. We remember being asked to consider, before doing unto others, what we would choose to have done to ourselves. Each of these stories is a **paradigm**.

One of my favorite ethical ideas is the *categorical imperative* of the philosopher Immanuel Kant (German, 1724-1804), who defined an action as ethical if we can will maxim of the action to be universalized. In other words, if you want to know if an action is moral, see if you can wish that the general principle of what you intend would be adopted by everyone. In other words, see if you can wish that everyone in every similar situation would do what you want to do. For example: Imagine that you think you have very logical and humane reasons for breaking a law because you feel that the law is wrong or discriminatory. Can you really will that all individuals who feel that a law is wrong would ignore the law? Probably not, as galling as that might be. If everyone who sincerely disagreed with a law felt comfortably free to break it, our society would degenerate into chaos. On the other hand, you probably can will that everyone who felt opposed to a law would work with great legal energy to change it. And so the effect of using Kant's categorical imperative is to lift you out of the emotional details of the particular situation and to make you conscious of the universal principle of your action as a general category of action. Kant's categorical imperative, like Jesus's golden rule, requires you to reflect beyond your single self as a unique case and to consider your action as only one example of an entire category of action; if you would not want the category to happen to the world, then you should not do even one example of it. You must follow the imperative (command) of the category.

Neologist's Lexicon

Use the stems in this list to create a new word (neologism). Give the word, the pronunciation, the part of speech, the etymology, and the definition(s). Keep a record of the neologisms you create from list to list. Here are some examples:

prochronolent (pro kron' o lent) adj. [pro (forward), chron (time), lent (full of)] 1. being continually conscious of what one is going to do next or soon 2. the obsessive awareness of time and instruments that measure time, as one who is continually looking at his watch

scenism (seen' ism) n. [scen (stage), ism (doctrine) 1. the idea that all the world is a stage, and all the people in it merely players (vide Shakespeare!) 2. the unwillingness to live anywhere that is not scenically beautiful

Sesquipedalian Homer

Have you read *The Iliad*, Homer's passionate *magnum opus* of epic poetry about the Trojan war, in which Achilles, Agamemnon, Menelaus, and the Achaians attacked Troy because Paris took the beautiful Helen, wife of Menelaus? Troy's great warrior is Hector, a brave soldier but a bully and a braggart, and he is finally killed by the awesome Achilles, who has been sulking off the battlefield in anger against Agamemnon and who only enters the fray to avenge the death of Patroclos, his great friend.

Homer's writing style is unforgettably vivid. He describes in horrific detail the deaths of the soldiers in the Trojan war, but the graphic description of the violence is not for the sake of sensationalism; it is really to honor the individuality of each man who dies. There are no meaningless, impersonal, statistical deaths in *The Iliad*. Instead, each solder who dies is described in mini-biographical detail; he has a name, a family, he is from a specific town, he owes someone money, he will never return to someone who loves him. Each death matters, and lessens the world. And this is not a Hollywood war; the pain and cruelty of death is not minimized or sensationalized; the terrible work of each blade stroke is described—the wound, the entry point, the bones broken, the agony, the internal organs, the fall, the crash of the armor, the dark night closing over the eyes. After reading Homer's story, we understand why even his greatest heroes, Hector and Achilles, are afraid, and they admit it.

The other element that is fascinating is Homer's **epic simile**: his technique of comparing a human event to an elaborately drawn simile. A warrior will whirl and fight *like a lion on a barren mountain, chased by hounds and surrounded as the hunters run up, drawing their bows; the lion knows that his end is near, he struggles desperately to claw the closest dog and to roar loud enough to frighten the others away, but it is no use, and he whirls faster and faster as the dogs gather around him while the hunters draw closer*. See? That's what a Homeric simile or epic simile is like. It's a very detailed simile. (Homer's simile's are better than my imitation; read *The Iliad*. Really.)

Now, pick something from your own life, silly or humorous if you like, and write a Homeric simile for it using words from List 47 and previous lists (Homer, of course used plain language). For example, you might describe, in sesquipedalian heroic terms, a simile for the act of grabbing your toothbrush first thing in the morning, or the way you stagger up after the alarm rings. Pick something interesting or humorous, and then go far afield for an interesting and creative simile. Have fun using the words from the lists.

• in	(in)	inamorata		• **amor**	(love)	inamorata
• inter	(between)	interpolate		• sub	(under)	subjugate
• ex	(out)	*ef*fulgence		• **fulg**	(shine or flash)	effulgence
• sub	(under)	subjacent		• *sym*	(together)	symposium
• pot	(drink)	sym*po*sium		• *nomy*	(law)	nomothetic
• fus	(pour)	effusion		• dign	(worthy)	condign
• vect	(carry)	invective		• fract	(break)	refractory
• *acro*	(high)	acrophobia		• *phobia*	(fear)	acrophobia

inamorata (mistress) She knew the loneliness of the inamorata.

interpolate (insert) It is wrong to corrupt a book by interpolating new passages.

subjugate (bring under the yoke) The tribes were subjugated by the Roman armies.

effulgence (shining out) We saw the reassuring effulgence of the morning sun.

replete (filled) The record was replete with examples of his benevolence.

querulous (full of complaint) His irritating querulous tendencies became chronic.

subjacent (underlying) The edifice rested solidly on its subjacent rock strata.

symposium (conference) The symposium on international amity was in Brussels.

immolate (sacrifice) Her brave speech was an act of political self-immolation.

nomothetic (lawgiving) Read the nomothetic passages of the *Old Testament*.

• • •

effusion (outpouring) His effusion of joyful greetings made us wince.

condign (worthy) The criminal met his condign end—a prison sentence.

invective (bitter denunciation) She stoically endured her opponent's invective.

refractory (stubborn) The refractory child repeatedly broke the rules.

acrophobia (fear of heights) She felt acrophobia on high bridges.

As Used by Jane Austen in *Pride and Prejudice*

	Mrs. Bennett	was	restored	to	her	usual	**querulous**	serenity.

Parts of Speech:	n.	--------v.--------	prep.	pron.	adj.	**adj.**	n.

Parts of Sentence:	subject	------AVP------

Phrases:	------------prepositional phrase------------

Clauses: ----------------------------------independent clause----------------------------------

one independent clause, a simple declarative sentence

Here Austen uses the adjective *querulous* to modify the noun *serenity*, which is the object of the preposition *to*. The action verb *was restored* is in passive voice.

Pronunciation

inamorata	in ah more AH tah	**immolate**	IM o late
interpolate	in TUR po late	**nomothetic**	no mo THEH tik
subjugate	SUB ju gate	**effusion**	e FYOO zhun
effulgence	eh FULL jence	**condign**	kon DINE
replete	re PLEET	**invective**	in VECK tiv
querulous	KWER u luss	**refractory**	re FRAK tory
subjacent	sub JAY sent	**acrophobia**	ack ro FO bee ah
symposium	sim PO zee um		

Spanish Cognates

interpolation	interpolación	**subjugation**	subyugación
replete	repleto	**querulous**	querelloso
subjacent	subyacente	**symposium**	simposio
immolation	inmolación	**effusion**	efusión
invective	invectiva	**refractory**	refractario
acrophobia	acrofobia		

1. A **Micropoem**: The noun **symposium** has an unexpected derivation. A symposium is simply a conference or a meeting, held for the purpose of discussion of some topic of mutual interest. And so we expect **symposium** to have an etymology similar to the word **conference**: bring together. Something mundane. And yet, **symposium** contains more flavor than we anticipate, because it is derived from the Greek *sympósion*, meaning drinking together! In ancient Greece, a symposium was a **postprandial** drinking party.

2. A **Classic Word**: The adjective **querulous** means peevish or full of complaint, and it comes from the Latin *quer* (complaint) and *ous* (full of). You would expect a word with such a meaning to find rich use in the classics to describe all of literature's querulous characters, and you do. **Querulous** was used by John Knowles, Pearl Buck, Edith Wharton, Kenneth Grahame, Joseph Conrad, Stephen Crane, and Emily Brontë, to name a few authors. In Buck's *The Good Earth*, the old man's cough rises querulously out of the dusky dawn. In *A Separate Peace*, a voice falls to a querulous whisper. In *The Wind in the Willows* (what a wonderfully poetic title; hear the assonance and the alliteration?) we learn that when one gets unsettled and depressed, one is inclined to be querulous. A soldier in Crane's *The Red Badge of Courage* breaks out in a querulous way like a man who has mislaid his hat. Emily Brontë, typically, created an unforgettable and charming use of **querulous** in *Wuthering Heights*: "Nothing was stirring except a brindled, grey cat, which crept from the ashes and saluted me with a querulous mew." And Edith Wharton used **querulous** over and over again in *Ethan Frome*; she describes querulous lines from the thin nose to the corners of the mouth, the querulous drone of the voice, and finally asks if Ethan must "wear out all his years at the side of a bitter querulous woman?"

3. The verb **subjugate** is vividly descriptive. It comes from the Latin *sub* (under) and *jugum* (yoke) and implies yoked enslavement, subservience, complete submission. In *The Time Machine*, H.G. Wells describes how things will move faster and faster toward the subjugation of nature. We find the same concept—the subjugation of nature—in Nathaniel Hawthorne's *The Scarlet Letter*, except that the outcome is the reverse; Hawthorne describes "that wild, heathen Nature of the forest, never subjugated by human law." Modern knowledge and concern over the fate of the planet's environment have given new meaning to the idea of the subjugation of nature; what seemed an exciting challenge in the days of going west to the frontier now seems like the reckless destruction of precious species and the common global environment of atmosphere and hydrosphere that all species must share.

4. In Harper Lee's *To Kill a Mockingbird*, we read, to our delight, "Her use of bathroom invective leaves nothing to the imagination." Bathroom invective? The innocent naughtiness of this sentence is a wonderful example of the alert spirit that so often characterizes the mind of the creative writer. The noun **invective** means vehement or bitter denunciation, vituperation, censure, terrific abuse. It comes from the Latin *invectus*, meaning driven (vect) into (in), in the sense of being attacked. Invective is driving criticism into someone, hard.

In each case below, one of the choices was really the word used by the author in the sentence provided. All of the choices can be found in the example words on the first page of this lesson. Your challenge is to decide which word the author used. This is not a test; it is more like a game, because more than one word choice may work perfectly well. See if you can use your sensitivity and intuition to guess correctly which word the author used. You may need a dictionary.

1. **From Pearl S. Buck's** *The Good Earth*

   The old man's cough rose _____ out of the dusky dawn.
   a. effusively
   b. effulgently
   c. condignly
   d. querulously

2. **From Charles Dickens's** *David Copperfield*

   I would hear of no such _____ on the altar of friendship.
   a. interpolation
   b. subjugation
   c. immolation
   d. symposium

3. **From Kate Chopin's** *The Awakening*

   There was a soft _____ in the east.
   a. effulgence
   b. invective
   c. acrophobia
   d. effusion

4. **From Martin Luther King Jr.'s** *Why We Can't Wait*

   American history is _____ with compromise.
   a. interpolated
   b. refractory
   c. replete
   d. immolated

5. **From John Hersey's** *Hiroshima*

   His growing helplessness kept her in _____; she tenderly nursed him.
   a. effusion
   b. subjugation
   c. interpolation
   d. invective

Though it is good to have a rich vocabulary, it is not good to abuse that vocabulary by writing verbose, sesquipedalian sentences (such as this one). Those who overuse their vocabularies often do so at the expense both of clarity and of others' patience. Translate the following ostentatious, ponderous passage into graceful, direct English.

ON THE STEEP ROCK OF THE ALPINE SLOPE, interpolated amidst the effusion of grasses and windtorn shrubbery, an autochthonous heliotropic flower, replete with white petals and yellow center, grew assiduously, like the vivacious inamorata of light from the effulgent sun. The querulous wind, icy and sharp, tore with tautological vociferations and truculent invective at the intractable flower, trying to disinter it from its tenuous, acrophobic grip on the soil and the interstices of the subjacent sedimentary rock that had pushed up for millions of years from the tenebrous geologic abyss of some proterozoic lacustrine scene. But other ancient and imponderable planetary principles, the abstruse and silent graybeards, the insidious and omniscient calculus of the cosmos, the primal nomothetic laws of nature and physics, preserved the flower, subjugated the ineluctable antipathies of season, and gave condign harmony to the system, to the symposium of light, wind, and rain—displaying the cryptic ratiocinations of nature. In this omnibus confluence of circumambient benedictions, even the circumlocution of the cacophonous wind could not bowdlerize the narcissistic flower from the stoic physiognomy of the slope.

Reading Comprehension

1. In Translation 48, the author's attitude is best described as:
   A. bemused
   B. charmed
   C. ironic
   D. aloof

2. With which statement would the author likely agree:
   A. The forces of nature are ultimately destructive.
   B. The forces of nature are blind and indifferent.
   C. The forces of nature are benevolent and involved.
   D. The forces of nature form a systematic ecological balance.

Analogies

3. **SUBJUGATE : ENTHRALL ::**
   A. immolate : vanquish
   B. invective : contumely
   C. acrophobia : height
   D. effulgence : luminous

4. **REFRACTORY : INTRACTABLE ::**
   A. querulous : tractable
   B. inamorata : mistress
   C. interpolate : withdraw
   D. acrophobia : agoraphobia

Antonyms

5. **REPLETE :**
   A. teeming
   B. scarce
   C. repeat
   D. complete

refractory

6. **CONDIGN :**
   A. appropriate
   B. merited
   C. unjust
   D. dignified

divergence

For either the noun **effulgence**, which is the bright shining of an object such as the sun, or for the adjective **condign**, which means worthy, fitting, or appropriate according to accepted standards, such as the fate of Edmund in *King Lear* (Edmund was slain by Edgar, the brother he betrayed), think of as many interesting examples as you can. Remember that when you are thinking divergently, more is better. For any creative situation in which you are trying to come up with a new idea, the more ideas you have to choose from, the more likely you are to find a great idea, a new idea, a creative idea. When you are trying to think of a lot of ideas, you will often find that you can quickly list several; these are the most obvious and generally known ones, and you find them in your memory banks. These are the ideas that everyone recognizes from ordinary experience and commercial culture. But then, the supply of ready-made or easy-to-think of ideas runs out, and a brief period of difficulty ensues—DON'T GIVE UP—on the other side of the desert are the more interesting ideas, the more unusual ones, the more creative ones, and the ones that are more personally and individually you.

emotion

One of the great stories of all time is the story written by Julius Caesar himself in his *Commentaries on the Gallic War*. Caesar describes his campaigns and decisions during the Gallic Wars from 58 to 51 B.C. Caesar's strategies for **subjugating** the Gauls, including the brilliant Arvernian leader Vercingetorix, make fascinating reading. It is worth a moment to consider the experience of subjugation, of forced total subordination to a conquering enemy, and to reflect on what the normal emotional responses of a subjugated person would be. Imagine being subjugated, being under the yoke, being forced to obey the orders of an enemy you hated. Think of the humiliation, the anger, the resentment, the revenge you would plot, the burning intensity of your feelings. To do this will give you more insight into many of the events you learn about from history, such as the slave revolt that Spartacus led against the Romans, or the unimaginable courage of Harriet Tubman, who risked her life repeatedly by sneaking back into the South to help slaves escape to the North. Can you even imagine that a people could be subjugated and not feel these bitter emotions? Consider several different historical examples of subjugation, and imagine how you would really feel if you were in the place of the subjugated people. -Who are some famous historical figures who revolted against subjugation?

reason

Let's write a **syllogism** using a word from List 48. Remember that a syllogism is a logically correct assertion that has the form: All A is C; B is A; therefore, B is C. For example, we might say,

All **effulgence** is bright; radiance is a form of effulgence; therefore, all radiance is bright.

or:

Every **symposium** is a conference; the Cognitute is a symposium; therefore, the Cognitute is a conference.

Neologist's Lexicon

    Use the stems in this list to create a new word (neologism). Give the word, the pronunciation, the part of speech, the etymology, and the definition(s). Keep a record of the neologisms you create from list to list. Here are some examples:

symfulgent (sim full' jent) adj. [sym (together), fulg (shine)]   1. shining more brightly together than individually, as two persons who bring out the best in each other's personality 2. serving as reciprocal catalysts, as two chemicals that each set the other on fire

nomophobia (no mo fo' bee uh) n. [nomy (law), phobia (fear)] n.   1. fear of the law or of officers of the law   2. anxious obsession with the lyrics of the song, "I Fought the Law and the Law Won"

Sesquipedalian Dr. Seuss

    Use words from List 48 and previous lists to imitate your favorite Dr. Seuss story.

The Querulous Cat

The moon didn't shine out
Effulgently bright
So we lay in our beds,
Subjugated all night.
When in jumped the Cat
The refractory Cat,
The querulous
Fearless, intractable Cat.
"Where's your Mother,"
He asked,
As he jumped through the door
And he waltzed with effusion
'Cross the subjacent floor.
To our nonplussed, incredulous
Neophyte minds
That omniscient Cat
Uttered omnibus kinds
Of retorts and strange malapropisms
You see, which we
Couldn't repeat, even in soliloquy.
Then he gathered up all
Of the objects with which
Our house was replete
And he thought he would snitch.
And he made such a face
That we found it condign
When *in medias res*
Mom came in from behind.

• dis	(away)	discern		• mis (G)	(bad)	misnomer
• **nom**	(name)	misnomer		• pugn	(fight)	inexpugnable
• **Sino**	(China)	Sinology		• *entomo*	(insect)	entomology
• per	(through)	perspicacity		• spec	(look)	perspicacity
• *pro*	(before)	prognosis		• *gno*	(know)	prognosis

discern (to mentally separate, identify) We failed to discern the real reasons.

misnomer (wrong name) To call whales *fishes* is a misnomer, according to Melville.

chauvinism (fanatical devotion) Nicolas Chauvin was chauvinistic about France.

inexpugnable (unconquerable) The enemy held an inexpugnable position.

etiology (cause or science of causes) Study the etiology of a social problem.

hebetude (state of dullness) He gaped in lethargic, open-mouthed hebetude.

axiology (study of value) Axiology is the study of axioms of ethics and aesthetics.

congeries (heap) His collection was a disorganized congeries of dusty artifacts.

Sinology (study of China) She longed to study Sinology and diplomacy.

nonentity (a nobody) He was a jabbering nonentity, a superfluous, prolix nobody.

• • •

prognosis (medical forecast) The doctor presented a prognosis of the disease.

entomology (insect zoology) The oft-bitten entomologist lost his collection.

perspicacity (insight) We admired the perspicacity of Susie's scientific mind.

synthesis (combination) The best solution was a synthesis of many ideas.

mobocracy (mob rule) The great revolution degenerated into cruel mobocracy.

As Used by Arthur Conan Doyle in *The Hound of the Baskervilles*

	I	seemed	to discern	some	signs	of	emotion.
Parts of Speech:	pron.	v.	n	adj.	n.	prep.	n.
Parts of Sentence:	subject	LVP	-------subject complement------				
Phrases:			----------infinitive phrase--------			--prep. phrase--	
Clauses:	------------------------------------independent clause--------------------------------						
	one independent clause, a simple declarative sentence						

Here Arthur Conan Doyle uses the infinitive form *to discern* as a noun; the infinitive phrase *to discern some signs* is the subject complement, and in that phrase *signs* is the object of the infinitive. The linking verb *seemed* creates an equation.

Pronunciation

discern	dis SERN	**Sinology**	si NAH lo jee
misnomer	miss NO mer	**nonentity**	non EN tih tee
chauvinism	SHOW vin izm	**prognosis**	prog NO siss
inexpugnable	in ex PUG na bel	**entomology**	en to MAH lo jee
etiology	ee tee AH lo jee	**perspicacity**	per spih KASS ih tee
hebetude	HEE beh tood	**synthesis**	SIN theh siss
axiology	ax ee AH lo jee	**mobocracy**	mob OCK ra see
congeries	KON jer eez		

Spanish Cognates

discernment	discernimiento	**chauvinism**	chauvinismo
inexpugnable	inexpugnable	**etiology**	etiología
axiom	axioma	**congeries**	congerie
sinology	sinología	**prognosis**	prognosis
entomology	entomología	**perspicacity**	perspicacia
synthesis	síntesis		

1. A **Micropoem**: We admire the keen, insightful mind of a scientist like Rosalind Franklin, the brilliant physicist whose precise work was instrumental in helping Crick and Watson solve the structure of the DNA molecule (she died before she could receive a Nobel Prize, which is not awarded posthumously). This power of penetrating insight is beautifully captured by the word **perspicacity**, which is the ability to see (spec) right through (per) something. To the perspicacious person, things that are opaque, tenebrous, or obscure to the rest of us are translucent and intellectually visible. The noun **perspicacity** and its adjective **perspicacious** are to be distinguished from the noun **perspicuity** and its adjective **perspicuous**. Both refer to lucidity and keenness of insight, but the former refers to minds, and the latter refers to products. A perspicacious person would write a perspicuous paper.

2. A **congeries** is a heap, pile, or aggregation. The noun comes from the Latin *congerere*, to collect, which is composed of *con* (together), and *gerere* (to bear or carry). Imagine an archaeology lab that is a congeries of dusty artifacts from many cultures: masks, tools, stone implements, tablets, pottery, figures, scrolls, spears, amphorae, everything heaped in corners and piled on shelves, light pouring in through a big window, with the snow-covered leafless branches of deciduous tress outlined against a bright blue sky beyond.

3. The noun **Chauvinism** is named for Nicolas Chauvin, a blustering fanatical patriot in Napoleon's army. The word implies zealous, belligerent, and even prejudiced adherence to any cause. One of the most typical modern uses is to describe the intractable male-centeredness of the *male chauvinist*, the person who is bigoted against women.

4. The noun **etiology** can either refer to the cause of disease, as in the etiology of tuberculosis, or it can refer more abstractly to the study of causality itself. This word traces back through the Latin to the Greek, in which *aitiologia* meant determining the cause of anything. The genetic etiology of many hereditary diseases is presently unknown, but as scientists proceed with the mapping of human DNA, more and more of these causes will be identified, and then we will have to deal with the questions arising from our ability to alter genetic codes.

5. A **Classic Word**: The verb **discern** comes from the Latin *dis* (away) and *cernere* (to separate), and it describes our ability to make intelligent distinctions, to separate things from other things to which they are connected. Sometimes **discern** implies something physical, such as Defoe's use in 1719 in *Robinson Crusoe*: "and I could easily discern their postures and gestures by my glasses." Usually, **discern** refers to something more subtle. Jane Eyre was able to discern in the course of the morning that Thornfield Hall was a changed place. Melville described an old Manxman who had preternatural powers of discernment. Hardy, Crane, and Wharton used the word as well. The frightened youth Henry Fleming discerned forms begin to swell in masses out of a distant wood. Ethan Frome's eyes, accustomed to obscurity, would discern Mattie as clearly as though she stood in daylight. And Harper Lee described a man who sat on a flagpole for no discernible reason!

In each case below, one of the choices was really the word used by the author in the sentence provided. All of the choices can be found in the example words on the first page of this lesson. Your challenge is to decide which word the author used. This is not a test; it is more like a game, because more than one word choice may work perfectly well. See if you can use your sensitivity and intuition to guess correctly which word the author used. You may need a dictionary.

1. **From Elizabeth George Speare's** *The Witch of Blackbird Pond*

    What William thought, it was impossible to _____.
    a. interpolate
    b. subjugate
    c. discern
    d. misnomer

2. **From John Knowles's** *A Separate Peace*

    I had applied for such a _____ of a job.
    a. nonentity
    b. misnomer
    c. prognosis
    d. synthesis

3. **From Joseph Conrad's** *Lord Jim*

    There was a "shelter of _____ peace."
    a. perspicacious
    b. chauvinistic
    c. discernible
    d. inexpugnable

4. **From Frederick Douglass's** *Narrative*

    I looked at it as the climax of all _____, the boldest of all frauds.
    a. congeries
    b. hebetudes
    c. misnomers
    d. etiologies

5. **From Thomas Hardy's** *The Mayor of Casterbridge*

    The upper part of Durnover was...composed of a curious _____ of barns and farmsteads.
    a. nonentities
    b. synthesis
    c. mobocracy
    d. congeries

Though it is good to have a rich vocabulary, it is not good to abuse that vocabulary by writing verbose, sesquipedalian sentences (such as this one). Those who overuse their vocabularies often do so at the expense both of clarity and of others' patience. Translate the following ostentatious, ponderous passage into graceful, direct English.

WHAT A DILEMMA. The nonplussed freshman stared at the catalog that delineated the course offerings, wondering what to take. The congeries of courses seemed endless. Axiology 101, Entomology, Kinesiology, Cosmology, Sinology, Chauvinism and Prejudice, there seemed to be no end to the possibilities. She tried to concentrate, humorously remembering the prolix, vacuous nonentity who reduced her to hebetude at the freshman party last night; well, party was really a misnomer, she discerned; it was more like inexpugnable boredom!

This looked like an interesting course: Introduction to Etiology. Her perspicacious mind immediately grasped the idea: CAUSES. Disease. Prognosis. Diagnosis. Syndromes. A synthesis of major theories. Causes of diseases. Pathology.

Let's see, she thought, how about Axiology 101. Values, ethics, aesthetics, religion. Imponderable mysteries. Eschatology. Hedonism. Stoicism. Pharisaism. Nepotism. Ethical paradigms. It sounded interesting, and she had never taken a class in philosophy before. What is right, what is beautiful . . . they would probably read Plato's *Dialogues*. Antinomies. Tautologies. Yes, I'll take this course.

Sinology, Sovietology? Hmmm. The other students said that the professor was good. Lots of original sources to read, rather than just textbooks. Lots of discussion and ideas. Plutocracies and mobocracies. Autochthonous populations. Lots of exploration of current events and problems. Questions. And with the world changing, this might be an important subject to know more about.

To know?? Ah, here's Epistemology and the Meditations of Descartes. Another philosophy class. It might be fun: How do you know that this box exists. How do you know the material world is there. Questions like that. *A priori* knowledge, *a posteriori* knowledge. The mind/body dichotomy. Recondite abstractions. *Cogito ergo sum.* A *non sequitur*? She had heard of these ideas, but had not really studied them before. Sounded good.

Advanced Entomology. Bugs. Advanced bugs. Six legs. Joints. Exoskeletons. Compound eyes. Repulsive/attractive. Bug anatomy, bug chemistry, bug analysis. Bug projects . . . catching bugs. Creepy ratiocinations. Gotta take it.

She closed the catalog, introspectively anticipating the lucubrations that awaited her in the semester ahead.

Reading Comprehension

1. For Translation 49, which of the following does the passage suggest:
    - A. The college freshman is bright and intellectually vigorous.
    - B. The college freshman is interested in finding easy classes.
    - C. The college freshman is trying to avoid mathematics and science.
    - D. The college freshman is uncomfortable with abstractions.

2. Which of the following is the best title for the passage:
    - A. An Academic Neophyte Nonplussed by Advanced Academics
    - B. The Intellectual Ratiocinations of an Academic Neophyte
    - C. The Scholastic Soliloquy of a Diffident Intellect
    - D. An Academic Neophyte's Heterodox Interests

Analogies

3. PERSPICACITY : HEBETUDE ::
    - A. dullness : acuteness
    - B. etiology : biogenesis
    - C. brilliance : lassitude
    - D. languor : perspective

4. AXIOLOGY : ENTOMOLOGY ::
    - A. morals : ethics
    - B. scientist : microscope
    - C. axle : biology
    - D. decisions : life forms

Antonyms

5. NONENTITY
    - A. cipher
    - B. nullity
    - C. whippet
    - D. luminary

6. INEXPUGNABLE
    - A. vulnerable
    - B. impregnable
    - C. indomitable
    - D. unvanquishable

entomology

evaluation and aesthetics

Imagine that you are taking an art class, and you are going to do a project in **entomological** art; in other words, you're going to make pretty bugs. They will be sculpture, in a variety of media, designs, styles, and colors. Now, here's the rub: the prize will go to the person who makes the most original insect that is still an insect. This means that every entry must have six legs, three body parts, antennae, compound eyes, and so forth. Of course, even though all insects have some of these basic common elements, they still have vast variation, as the millions of insect species on our planet vividly demonstrate. So there is plenty of room for variation. Your project: First, imagine what your ideas for several very original insects might be. Then, imagine that you are asked to be a judge, and you are instructed to write a list of your criteria for originality. What would be your answers to both of these questions?

synthesis

Since the noun **synthesis** is one of the words in List 49, let's explore this concept in some detail. **Synthesis** is from the Greek *syn* (together) and *tithenai* (to put or place). In synthesis we **put things together**. This putting together can be physical, as in making synthetic materials such as plastics by combining chemicals. But often, the synthesis we describe is in the world of ideas. Einstein used synthesis to combine tensor calculus and modern physics to create the concepts of relativity and space-time. There were already people who knew the calculus, and there were already people who knew the physics, but Einstein noticed the synthetic implications of the one for the other. It is this kind of brilliant noticing—the noticing of unnoticed relevance, the noticing of unnoticed connections, the noticing of unnoticed similarities—which characterizes synthesis at its most brilliant. That is why, to put this advanced idea in ordinary language, we ask students to think of wild, crazy, or silly comparisons. We are trying to stretch the mind into the real thing, into true and original synthesis. Anyone can notice an obvious synthesis, such as that subtraction and taking a bite of chocolate cake are similar, because they both involve the removal of something from a total. But what about less common kinds of synthetic thinking? For example, what are the profound and meaningful things that small children and mature adults have in common? What are the deepest goals and values that men and women have in common? We often think of how children and adults are different, or of how men and women are different, but in what ways, other than some of the most obvious ones, are we the same?

For other examples of brilliant synthesis, consider Homer's epic similes. Or remember Shakespeare's brilliant and terrifying metaphors in *Macbeth*, in which Macbeth compares life to a walking shadow, and to a tale told by an idiot. (Schopenhauer said that the value of metaphors is to explain an unknown relation by a known one. Good, eh?) Without synthesis, would there be poetry or literature? Certainly, there would not be symbolism; it would vanish.

Synthesis is also an important process in other thinking skills; it helps to make them possible. We live in a world of specialization and compartmentalization, and yet we will probably survive and improve our planet better if we can become good at *application* of knowledge and *connection* of various kinds of knowledge, and these things require synthesis. You can't really apply knowledge transfer it from the abstract, chalky classroom to the green and moving world—if you can't notice the connections and similarities between your abstract examples and the particular situations in the real world.

Neologist's Lexicon

Use the stems in this list to create a new word (neologism). Give the word, the pronunciation, the part of speech, the etymology, and the definition(s). Keep a record of the neologisms you create from list to list. Here are some examples:

propugnance (pro pug' nance) n. [pro (before), pugn (fight)] 1. being prematurely combative and belligerent before information verifies the reason for anger 2. the proclivity for hasty and unreasonable combativeness

entomonomy (in toe moe' no me) n. [entomo (insect), nomy (name or law)] 1. the unfortunate habitual reference to one's associates as forms of insects, as gadflies, wasps, social butterflies, busy bees, flies in the ointment, and so forth 2. excessive use of the phrase, "Stop bugging me"

Sesquipedalian Metamorphosis

In Franz Kafka's surrealistic story, *The Metamorphosis*, the main character Gregor Samsa wakes up to find that he has been metamorphosed into a gigantic insect. He is lying on his back with his six legs sticking up in the air, and he finds it difficult to roll off of his exoskeleton onto his feet. As the story evolves, no one seems to care about Gregor, not even his boss, who is only concerned that he be at work on time. Use the words from List 49 and previous lists to describe some similarly strange situation. The situation is up to you. Maybe you wake up as a sock. That's your problem. I'd rather not be a sock. I'd rather wake up as a bowl of cereal and bananas any day. See what you can come up with. Here's an example:

The Metagnosis

One morning, Michael gradually gained consciousness to discover that he had transmogrified overnight into a being of inexpugnable hebetude, a corpulent nonentity, incapable even of the energy and acuteness necessary to be prolix and superfluous. His physiognomy felt flat. The etiology of this alteration was unclear, but he knew intuitively that the prognosis was bad. In the tenebrous corner of his room, he discerned a gregarious mobocracy of entomological life feasting on last night's hedonistic pizza, but his hebetude had transformed the axiological dictum that would have made him care. So different was his personality that he felt unlike his usual perspicacious self and more like a synthesis of the intelligences visible in fish eyes and lizard's postures, but perhaps intelligence is a misnomer in those cases; blank reactions might be more accurate. Even the congeries of clothes beside the bed failed to disturb Michael's normal obsession with neatness and organization.

He lay there for a long time, nonplussed, wondering if it mattered if he lay there for a long time, nonplussed, wondering if.... Through the window, he could hear the loquacious neighbors in their daily gregarious colloquy. "That Michael," said one in a condescending and supercilious lilt, "he certainly has a soporifically sesquipedalian vocabulary." "*Au contraire*," replied the other, "you're just smarting under his assiduous objurgations." On they went, in desultory perambulations and vacuous vociferations. Michael slowly turned to the wall, tracing gingerly through the soliloquy that would lead him out of this malefic mood and back to his typical mellifluous, sanguine disposition.

• re	(again)	refulgent		• fulg	(shine or flash)	refulgent
• mal	(bad)	mal de mer		• mar	(sea)	mal de mer
• *neo*	(new)	neophilia		• *phil*	(love)	neophilia
• culp	(blame)	mea culpa		• *cracy*	(government)	timocracy
• ante	(before)	antediluvian		• fract	(break)	fractious
• surg	(rise)	insurgence		• duct	(lead)	induction
• **luvi**	(wash)	antediluvian		• tion	(act or state)	fulguration
• tude	(state of)	solicitude		• *agora*	(marketplace)	panegyric

refulgent (shining) Achilles strode forth to meet Hector, refulgent in his new armor.

mal de mer (seasickness) She sailed with no fear of the *mal de mer*.

timocracy (government based on honor) It is not a meritocracy but a timocracy.

neophilia (love of the new) Her home was a monument to neophilia—no antiques there.

mea culpa (my fault) Include a *mea culpa* at the beginning of the difficult lecture.

fulguration (flashing) The fulgurations of the lightning storm continued.

repartee (quick, witty reply) We were amused by Austen's quick repartee in *Pride and Prejudice*.

dissident (one who disagrees) The Soviet dissident mentally "sits apart."

subliminal (below consciousness) He has a subliminal fear of darkness.

solicitude (state of concern) We much appreciate your earnest solicitude.

• • •

antediluvian (from before the Flood) He rejected their superannuated, antediluvian attitudes.

panegyric (elaborate eulogy) His speech to the crowd was a panegyric on his friend's merits.

induction (factual reasoning) Science uses a process of induction, and some deduction, too.

fractious (unruly) The fractious mob clamored when Sidney approached the guillotine.

insurgence (uprising) The riotous insurgence was defeated as soon as it began.

As Used by W.H.D. Rouse in his translation of *The Odyssey of Homer*

	You	are	full	of	antediluvian	wisdom.
Parts of Speech:	pron.	v.	adj.	prep	adj.	n.
Parts of Sentence:	subject	predicate	subject complement			

Phrases: ----------prepositional phrase----------

Clauses: -----------------------------------independent clause---------------------------------
one independent clause, a simple declarative sentence

Here Rouse uses the adjective *antediluvian* to modify the singular common noun *wisdom*, which is the object of a preposition.

Pronunciation

refulgent	re FULL jent	**subliminal**	sub LIM in al
mal de mer	MAL deh mair	**solicitude**	so LISS ih tood
timocracy	tim MOCK ra see	**antediluvian**	an tee di LOO vee an
neophilia	nee o FILL ee ah	**panegyric**	pan eh JIR ik
mea culpa	MAY ah KUL pah	**induction**	in DUCK shun
fulguration	FUL gyoor AY shun	**fractious**	FRACK shus
repartee	re par TAY	**insurgence**	in SIR jence
dissident	DISS ih dent		

Spanish Cognates

refulgent	refulgente	**timocracy**	timocracia
fulgurant	fulgurante	**dissident**	disidente
subliminal	subliminal	**solicitude**	solicitud
antediluvian	antediluviano	**panegyric**	panegírico
induction	inducción	**insurgent**	insurgente

1. A **Micropoem**: The adjective **subliminal** is a psychological term that refers to our ability to respond to, be affected by, or enjoy stimuli of which we are not really conscious. How does this meaning emerge from the etymology of the word? Well, it's really interesting. To understand, we must look at the words **sublime** and **sublimate**. The adjective **sublime** means elevated or lofty, exalted, noble, grand, supreme . . . HIGH. Huh? Why would a SUB word mean HIGH? Because **sublime** comes from the Latin *sublimis*, which comes from the stems *sub* (under) and *lim* (lintel). You still don't get it? Well, a lintel is a horizontal architectural feature that spans the two sides of a door or fireplace, supporting the wall up above the door. In other words, you would reach UP to hang something HIGH up under the lintel. Under the lintel is high. Ah. Our ideals of honesty, integrity, and lifelong devotion are sublime human ideas. Now, to **sublimate** is to psychologically redirect some basic form of human of energy, such as sexual energy (remember our discussion of ego, superego, and id?), upward to some higher social or moral goal. We might say, for example, that some creative person's powerful creative urge is actually driven by his sublimated (elevated, see?) sexual energy. To sublimate something is to redirect it higher, up to lintel level. And so **subliminal** refers to this process, that in our sublime endeavors we are sometimes moved by sublimated feelings emerging subliminally from the subconscious mind, which is a lot of meaning to squeeze out of the image of a lintel.

2. A **panegyric** is an elaborate eulogy, an oration or writing that expatiates on the merits or virtues of the subject. The noun traces back to the Greek word *panegyrikos*, solemn assembly, which is made of *pan* (all) and *agyris* (gathering). The image is that all have gathered to praise; in my mind, I see a central fire, the yellow flickering light on the solemn physiognomies, the voice of the panegyricist beginning to ring in stentorian tones. Walter Scott refers to a doleful panegyric, and Swift has Gulliver reply, "you have made a most admirable panegyric upon your country."

3. If you studied Volume *1 of The Word Within the Word*, you will remember what a wonderful micropoem **antediluvian** is; it literally means so antiquated as to date before (ante) Noah's Flood (luvi). Melville used **antediluvian** repeatedly in *Moby Dick*, to describe the antediluvian Hindoo; an old, crutch-like, antediluvian wheezing humorousness; and an archaeological, fossiliferous, and antediluvian point of view. Hardy also used the term in *The Return of the Native*: "The number of their years may have adequately summed up Jared, Mahalaleel, and the rest of the antediluvians, but the age of a modern man is to be measured by the intensity of his history."

4. A **Classic Word**: The noun **solicitude** has a major place in literature. It was used by Scott, Cooper, Charlotte Brontë, Stowe, Melville, Dickens, and Hardy, to name only a few. We see serious solicitude, professions of solicitude, gentle solicitude, looking with solicitude, fargazing solicitude, fatherly solicitude, conscientious solicitude, superfluous solicitude, melancholy solicitude, kind solicitude, and anxious solicitude. Solicitude comes from the Latin *sollicitudo*, uneasiness of mind, which traces back to *sollicitus*, agitated, which traces back to *sollus*, whole, and *ciere*, to arouse. We feel solicitude when we are in the state of (tude) being wholly aroused in concern.

In each case below, one of the choices was really the word used by the author in the sentence provided. All of the choices can be found in the example words on the first page of this lesson. Your challenge is to decide which word the author used. This is not a test; it is more like a game, because more than one word choice may work perfectly well. See if you can use your sensitivity and intuition to guess correctly which word the author used. You may need a dictionary.

1. **From James M. Barrie's** *Peter Pan*

   I, George Darling, did it. _____, _____.
   a. *mal de mer, mal de mer*
   b. antediluvian, antediluvian
   c. *mea culpa, mea culpa*
   d. subliminal, subliminal

2. **From Marjorie Kinnan Rawlings's** *The Yearling*

   But the convalescence, the _____ of his mother and father, was definitely pleasant.
   a. dissidence
   b. solicitude
   c. repartee
   d. refulgence

3. **From Walt Whitman's** *Leaves of Grass*

   I loiter enjoying his _____ and his shuffle and break-down.
   a. repartee
   b. neophilia
   c. insurgence
   d. panegyric

4. **From Charlotte Brontë's** *Jane Eyre*

   Brontë describes the "_____ dawn of the tropics."
   a. subliminal
   b. antediluvian
   c. refulgent
   d. fractious

5. **From Mary Shelley's** *Frankenstein*

   He concluded with a _____ upon modern chemistry.
   a. *mea culpa*
   b. insurgence
   c. fulguration
   d. panegyric

Though it is good to have a rich vocabulary, it is not good to abuse that vocabulary by writing verbose, sesquipedalian sentences (such as this one). Those who overuse their vocabularies often do so at the expense both of clarity and of others' patience. Translate the following ostentatious, ponderous passage into graceful, direct English.

AFTER THE CACOPHONOUS FULGURATIONS of last night's storm, Captain Arson thought, the tranquil effulgence of the tropical dawn was comforting. The sails were filling now, and Arson's *mal de mer* had passed as the foaming Homeric black seas had receded, trailing after the querulous storm as it vanished with *sotto voce* rumbles over the horizon. With the typical meteorological neophilia of the great storm, this storm had left the sky, and even the smell of the air, new and fresh, oxygen-rich, like an atomic ambrosia to be inhaled by the gods of the future.

But this was no time for a panegyric on the inexpugnable powers of nature or for sublime expressions of the subliminal forces within him. This was a time for inductive reasoning, for stoic ratiocination on the blunt facts that would insure survival on the seas. This was a time for— "NeeeCHUH!!," he sneezed—strength of will, for digging deep into his will for the sangfroid he would need to face the assiduous challenges of the wind and waves. But then, willpower was his forte, or his name wasn't Will F.L. Arson.

After their mutinous insurgence, the fractious dissidents had left him alone on the superannuated ship, *The Lyssophobia*. Alone with the rigging, the wooden decks, and the salt spray—alone with his feckless dreams of timocracy . . . how naive those ideals seemed now. Alone at the helm. Alone with his maps. Alone with his hungry dog, Londonjack, who gazed at him with canine solicitude, and who answered his inquiries in mute repartee, lifting one ear and cocking his furry physiognomy. "*Mea culpa*, London," Arson thought, "I got you into this."

Perambulating down the salty deck past the hatchway that opened into the tenebrous hold, he found it difficult to forget the insidious perfidy of his dissemblingly obsequious crew, who had impugned his sincere commiserations and accused him of megalomania. The narcoleptic London, vacuously watching his master withdraw through a haze of hebetude, failed to discern the etiology of the problem.

Reading Comprehension

1. In Translation 50, it can be inferred that:
    A. Arson was not perceived by his crew as he thought he was perceived.
    B. Arson was a cruel taskmaster who deserved the mutiny he got.
    C. The crew took advantage of Arson's kindness to enrich themselves.
    D. Arson, London, and *The Lyssophobia* will soon visit the depths of the abyss.

2. The author does all of the following EXCEPT:
    A. imply that Arson is egocentric
    B. imply that Arson is intelligent
    C. imply that London loves Arson
    D. imply that Arson has no solicitude for London

Analogies

3. **FULGURATION : REFULGENCE ::**
    A. blink : stare
    B. red light : green light
    C. fill : refill
    D. dissident : loyalist

4. **ANTEDILUVIAN : SUBLIMINAL ::**
    A. dissident : insurgence
    B. repartee : *mea culpa*
    C. waves : *mal de mer*
    D. time : awareness

Antonyms

refulgence

5. **DISSIDENT :**
    A. thief
    B. rascal
    C. adherent
    D. toady

6. **PANEGYRIC :**
    A. diatribe
    B. *obiter dictum*
    C. eulogy
    D. soliloquy

analysis and application

Consider what you know about the scientific method. We begin nonplussed by a fact of nature, then we create a hypothesis, then we design an experiment that will test the veracity of the hypothesis, then we collect a congeries of data, then we ratiocinate about the data, then we determine whether the hypothesis is verified or not verified, and then we report the result of the experiment. Now, **induction** is *a posteriori* factual reasoning, leading (duct) objective facts into (in) the mind, where as **deduction** is *a priori* reasoning in which we begin with a truth we cannot impugn and allow our reason to lead (duct) logically down (de) from the truth with which we began. The question to analyze is, is the scientific method purely inductive or purely deductive, or is it a synthesis of induction and deduction? Explain your answer, and specifically identify which stages of the scientific method you regard as inductive or deductive. Breaking things down into pieces this way is analysis.

intuition

Your parachute gently lowers you to the lurid surface of a **refulgent** and **fulgurating** environment. Continue.

synthesis and emotion

Jack London has been called the most widely read American writer in the world. In his classic novels, such as *White Fang*, *The Call of the Wild*, and *The Sea Wolf*, London described a nature without solicitude, red of tooth and claw, struggling under a blank and indifferent freezing cosmos, in which only those possessed of a Nietzschean ferocity of willpower can survive. In London's merciless geographies, the protagonists had better get their fires built, because the cosmos will freeze the good and the bad, the young and the old, the kind and the cruel, alike. This is a world in which "To Build a Fire" can be the difference between survival and annihilation. How does this pessimistic naturalism of London's books make you feel? What other books can you think of that have similar fierce survival conditions, in which the characters can count on nothing but their own intelligence and will to survive a malefic environment?

divergence, evaluation, and convergence

Imagine that you have a severe case of **neophilia** and are obsessed with everything that is most modern, most new, most recently invented. Your house is a congeries of gleaming contemporary objects. First, brainstorm a long and divergent list of the new things that your imaginary house includes. Don't just be fluent (listing lots); also be flexible (listing different kinds of things) and original (listing un-thought-of kinds of things). In this brainstorming stage, be wild and crazy, don't try to judge the ideas, and piggyback on each other's ideas. Then, use congenial discussion to select five good criteria for deciding which new items are worth most—not necessarily in monetary terms, though you may use that criterion if you like. List your criteria in hierarchical order, from most important at the top to least important at the bottom. Then, apply the five criteria you chose to select the single most valuable new item in your imaginary house. If you like this process, you would love studying brainstorming techniques, such as the classical Osborn-Parnes Creative Problem-Solving model or Torrance's Future Problem Solving program. [Do study them. (You'll really like them. (I'm serious. (I am. (Trust me. (OK?)))))]

Neologist's Lexicon

Use the stems in this list to create a new word (neologism). Give the word, the pronunciation, the part of speech, the etymology, and the definition(s). Keep a record of the neologisms you create from list to list. Here are some examples:

luvitude (loo' vee tood) n. [luvi (wash), tude (state of)] 1. the sanguine pride that characterizes one who is squeaky clean 2. the physical condition of one who has spent the day surfing

philocracy (fill ah' krass see) n. [phil (love), cracy (government)] 1. a government or society that elects the candidate who cares most about people 2. a government in which only individuals named Phil are eligible for public office

Sesquipedalian Television

Using the words from List 50 and previous lists, write a spoof of the language of one of the television programs you watch, if you watch any. Do you? Yes, you probably do.

HelioTrek: A Panegyric to Neophilia

SPACE.

The final frontier.

These are the voyages of the starship *Mal de Mer*, in which brave men and women risk their lives to probe the surreal reaches of the fulgurating cosmos, to be emissaries of anthropomorphic peace and anthropocentric values, and to bring the benediction of peace to the internecine conflicts of fractious and dissident autochthonous miscreants on the omnibus *terra incognitas* of the vast abyss.

Dirk.

James D. Dirk.

The perspicacious commander of the starship *Mal de Mer*, who would have perished long ago, with his ecumenical crew in his gleaming high-tech sarcophagus, if he were not omniscient, narcissistic, and more than a match for the callow neophytes who obsequiously and mellifluously adhere to the patronizing *ex cathedra* injunctions emitted from his handsome physiognomy.

Spot.

The alien Spot.

The sedate and supercilious pointy-eared stoic, whose syllogisms, saturnine lucubrations, and sententious ratiocinations provide expository epiphanies to all of the lesser intellects on the *Mal de Mer*. Spot is the favorite candidate for euthanasia, in the mind of the next protagonist

Stones.

Doc Stones, the xenophobic and querulous physician, who loses no opportunity for retorts and emotional diatribes against the enemy he most execrates, alien Spot. The Stones/Spot schism and character dichotomy provides internecine drama for the voyages of the starship *Mal de Mer*.

Foggy.

Engineer Foggy, Expediter, the portly but diminutive engineer whose obsequious fawning on Captain Dirk only irritates the entire crew, especially vivacious First Mate Bee Meeyup.

Space. The final frontier.

These are the voyages of the starship *Mal de Mer*.

These are the vacuous heroes whose apotheosis is the stuff of apocryphal hagiographies.

Much of the ancient world is still standing—
in our landscapes and in our language.

amorphous

neologism

equivocate

superfluous

geosynchronous

toponym

synergy

equinox

• *syn*	(together)	synergy		• *protero*	(early)	hysteron proteron
• *epi*	(on)	epithet		• *nym*	(name)	toponym
• *topo*	(place)	toponym		• *hysteros*	(latter)	hysteron proteron
• *equi*	(equal)	equinox		• **nox**	(night)	equinox
• *geo*	(earth)	geosynchronous		• *chron*	(time)	geosynchronous

synergy (combined force) The synergy of their personalities lifted them both to new abilities.

epithet (disparaging or descriptive name) "I'm Diogenes the Dog," he retorted to Alexander.

toponym (place name) He was a master of toponyms, national capitals especially.

equinox (sun crosses equator) At the equinox, day and night are of equal duration.

ailurophobia (fear of cats) Her ailurophobia caused her great anxiety in the presence of cats.

intestate (with no will) Unfortunately he died intestate, leaving his family penniless.

syntax (grammatical arrangement) The syntax of your sentence is ungrammatical.

hysteron proteron (begging the question) His circular argument is a case of *hysteron proteron.*

geosynchronous (stationary in orbit) The geosynchronous satellite never moved in the sky.

epistolary (made of letters) Bram Stoker's scary *Dracula* is an epistolary novel.

• • •

amorphous (without shape) The ruins formed an amorphous mound of broken rubble.

neologism (new word) He was fond of coining neologisms, such as *televoracity.*

circumspect (cautious) His circumspect reply made us wonder what he was concealing.

equivocate (to hedge) The cautious politician began to equivocate in his answer.

superfluous (unnecessary) The extra information was superfluous.

As Used by James Watson in *The Double Helix*

	Most	of	my	words	to	her	were	**superfluous.**
Parts of Speech:	n.	prep.	pron.	n.	prep	pron.	v.	**adj.**
Parts of Sentence:	subject						LVP	subject complement
Phrases:		----prep. phrase-----		--prep. phrase--				
Clauses:	-----------------------------------independent clause--------------------------------							
	one independent clause, a simple declarative sentence							

Here Watson uses the adjective *superfluous* as a subject complement to modify the noun *most*. The linking verb *were* links *superfluous* to its noun/subject.

Pronunciation

synergy	SIN er jee	**geosynchronous**	gee o SYN kron us
epithet	EP i thet	**epistolary**	ee PIST o lery
toponym	TOP o nim	**amorphous**	ah MOR fuss
equinox	EE kwih nox	**neologism**	nee OH lo jiz em
ailurophobia	ay LOOR o FO be ah	**circumspect**	SIR com spekt
intestate	in TEST ate	**equivocate**	ee KWIV o kate
syntax	SIN tax	**superfluous**	su PURR floo us
hysteron proteron	HISS ter on PRO ter on		

Spanish Cognates

epithet	epíteto	**toponym**	topónimo
equinox	equinoccio	**intestate**	intestado
syntax	sintaxis	**epistolary**	epistolar
amorphous	amorfo	**neologism**	neologismo
circumspect	circunspecto	**equivocation**	equivocación
superfluous	superfluo		

1. An **epithet** is a descriptive name or a disparaging name used invectively, but the stems give us a clearer idea of how the word works. An **epithet** is a name which is put (tithenai) on (epi), especially a name added on to the common name, such as *Peter the Great* or Zeus *Cloudgatherer*. An epithet can also be a simple disparaging adjective. The word **epithet** was used by Kipling, Conrad, Cooper, and Scott. Charlotte Brontë and Emily Brontë used it in their novels. Jane Eyre remarks, "You missed your epithet. I am not a pagan." Scott refers to the epithets holy, noble, and Black Sluggard. A fine use of **epithet** is from Stephen Crane's *Red Badge of Courage*: "This cold officer upon a monument, who dropped epithets unconcernedly down, would be finer as a dead man, he thought."

2. A **Micropoem**: The verb **equivocate** is a vividly descriptive word, depicting the dodging, hedging, deceiver speaking (voc) equally (equi) out of both sides of his mouth. Equivocate is given prominence in Shakespeare's *Macbeth*, in which the porter cries, "Faith, here's an equivocator that could swear in both the scales against either scale."

3. A **Micropoem**: To be **circumspect** is to be cautious, but in this word we see the cautious person looking (spect) cautiously around (circum), on the *qui vive*, the eyes moving from side to side. **Circumspect** has been used in the classics for centuries. It was used in the earliest novels, such as Daniel Defoe's 1719 classic, *Robinson Crusoe* and Jonathan Swift's 1726 satire, *Gulliver's Travels*. Robinson Crusoe finds that he has to be a little more circumspect, whereas Gulliver looks circumspectly and walks with the utmost circumspection to avoid treading on stragglers in Lilliput. The special image of looking around that **circumspect** contains can be easily seen in one of the sentences from Stevenson's great children's classic, *Treasure Island*: "and I walked more circumspectly," says young Jim Hawkins, "keeping an eye on every side."

4. A **Classic Word**: Very few words are more frequently found than **superfluous**, the word that means unnecessary, but that communicates an image of overflow, of excess flowing (flu) over (super) the top. **Superfluous** was used by Shakespeare four centuries ago; the distraught King Lear beseeches his thankless daughters not to give reasons why he does not need the hundred knights he has retained in giving up his kingdom, for, Lear cries, "Our basest beggars/Are in the poorest thing superfluous." Scott referred to superfluous wealth, Emily Brontë to superfluous company, and Charlotte Brontë to superfluous solicitude. Nathaniel Hawthorne's Hester Prynne bestowed all her superfluous means in charity. Melville used **superfluous** over and over in *Moby Dick*; we find superfluous scientific words and physical superfluousness, but no superfluous beard. Thoreau sharpened his wit to a point in *Walden*, noting that "Superfluous wealth can buy superfluities only." Thoreau also described the superfluous energy of the day, a superfluous and evitable wretchedness, and goodness which was not a transitory act but a constant superfluity. He remarked superfluous glow-shoes (?), superfluous property, and another alternative than to obtain the superfluities. In *The Return of the Native*, Hardy notes that someone's presence could be superfluous, and describes a woman's head in a large kerchief, "a protection not superfluous at this hour and place." And in London's *The Call of the Wild*, Hal, Charles, and Mercedes are reduced to "the inexorable elimination of the superfluous" from their sled, which had been weighed down by congeries of ponderous non-necessities.

In each case below, one of the choices was really the word used by the author in the sentence provided. All of the choices can be found in the example words on the first page of this lesson. Your challenge is to decide which word the author used. This is not a test; it is more like a game, because more than one word choice may work perfectly well.

1.   **From Rudyard Kipling's** *Kim*

He called it a Moon of Paradise, a Disturber of Integrity, and a few other fantastic _____ which doubled her up with mirth.
a. epithets
b. toponyms
c. neologisms
d. syntaxes

2.   **From William Makepeace Thackeray's** *Vanity Fair*

I have the honour (_____) to introduce to her ladyship my two friends.
a. superfluously
b. epistolarily
c. amorphously
d. circumspectly

3.   **From Thomas Hardy's** *The Return of the Native*

Wildeve had died _____, and she and the child were his only relatives.
a. circumspectly
b. equivocally
c. superfluously
d. intestate

4.   **From W.E.B. Dubois's** *The Souls of Black Folk*

In failing thus to state plainly and _____ the legitimate demands of their people...
a. circumspectly
b. unequivocally
c. superfluously
d. amorphously

5.   **From F. Scott Fitzgerald's** *The Great Gatsby*

That ashen, fantastic figure glid[ed] toward him through the _____ trees.
a. superfluous
b. amorphous
c. circumspect
d. equivocal

Though it is a good thing to have an expansive vocabulary, it is not a good thing to abuse that vocabulary by writing abstruse, verbose, sesquipedalian sentences. Those who overuse their vocabularies often do so at the expense of clarity.   Translate the following showy, verbose, ponderous passage into graceful, direct English. Do not use slang, but do use words which seem familiar and comfortable.

ON AN AMORPHOUS ASTEROID in geosynchronous orbit around an effulgent but moribund star in the constellation Aquila, Cyrus the Circumspect cautiously approached the impecunious philosopher Erik the Equivocator to see if Erik's epithet was a condign appellation. Eric was known throughout the galaxy for his ironic malapropisms, perspicacious neologisms, superfluous objurgations, circumlocutions, and deliberate *hysteron proteron*. Originally an epistolary novelist, Eric had resorted to hardier philosophy when nonplussed critics had maligned his syntax.

Erik was known for sitting outside the asteroid capital (toponym Stellopolis) on a congeries of superannuated computer chips. "I am a voice," Erik resounded vociferously from his rusty congeries, "declaiming in the abyss! Is there an honest colonist among you? NO!"

Cyrus walked up to Erik and said with cool sangfroid, "I am Cyrus the Circumspect! Answer my questions and do not dissemble, or you will die intestate."

"By the laws of Cosmic Synergy and the omnibus interdictions of our glorious timocracy," replied Erik with acerbity, "I will obey and I will not."

Cyrus endured the repartee with equanimity. "When," asked Cyrus condescendingly, "is the next equinox?"

"Today," replied Erik cryptically, "for each day gives us equal knocks. It is an equalknocksious cosmos, if you ask me."

"Don't try your imponderable neologisms on me," replied Cyrus with antipathy. "I want answers. One more chance. What is the etiology of my ailurophobia?"

"Easy," replied the dissident stoic, "a CATastrophe."

"You lie, nihilist," Cyrus impugned, "but I exculpate you because of your bravery. I admit it: if I were not Cyrus the Circumspect, I would be Erik the Equivocator." And off he perambulated, looking circumspectly to the left and to the right. The saturnine philosopher sat on his chip pile, soliloquizing a diatribe against megalomaniacs.

Reading Comprehension

1. In Translation 51, which of the following best expresses the main idea?
    A. We admire the fortitude of the dissident.
    B. Maladroit neophytes should receive supercilious epigrams.
    C. The social hierarchy must be superseded by a timocracy.
    D. To be wise is to be nonplussed.

2. The author's attitude in Translation 51 is best described as:
    A. regarding this event as a ludicrous contretemps
    B. distant and unsympathetic to either character
    C. presenting this story as a paradigm for tolerance
    D. contemptuous of those who are obsequious

Analogies

3. TOPONYM : NEOLOGISM ::
    A. river : book
    B. pseudonym : *nom de plume*
    C. map : science fiction
    D. syntax : diction

4. SYNERGY : DIFFUSION ::
    A. epithet : encomium
    B. epistolary : romantic
    C. circumspect : mincing
    D. *hysteron proteron* : syllogism

Antonyms

5. AMORPHOUS :
    A. geometric
    B. square
    C. inchoate
    D. rectilinear

amorphous

6. EQUIVOCATE :
    A. impugn
    B. declaim
    C. retort
    D. aver

synthesis

Synergy is combined energy or action, as when two muscles work together or two talents create together. Think about two muscles pulling together to combine their energies, and then think of other situations which are analogous, either physically or metaphorically.

reason

We have previously studied the **syllogism**, which is a paradigm for logical ratiocination. But now we must consider **hysteron proteron**, or begging the question, which is the logical error of assuming as one's premise the very conclusion which is to be proved! An example of *hysteron proteron* would be to argue that we must all be ethical because morals are important. It is not that morals are not important; it's just that the logical properties of this sentence do not prove anything. This sentence only repeats itself in circular reasoning, saying, in essence, *morals are important because morals are important.*

The famous philosophical example of *hysteron proteron*, some would say, was French philosopher/mathematician René Descartes's dictum, "*Cogito ergo sum.*" (I think, therefore I am.) The story is worth reviewing: Descartes (1596-1650) was attempting to found his philosophical system on a bedrock of certainty, and so he decided that he would begin by doubting everything which he could doubt. He began a process of systematic doubting and finally asked whether he knew for certain that he even existed, or whether he could doubt it. His answer was, I am thinking, therefore I exist. Eureka! He thought he had found a certain fact that he could not doubt. And yet, he was guilty of *hysteron proteron*, of begging the question, because whether he existed or not was the question—it was not something he was logically allowed to assume in his premise. If I am uncertain whether I exist, then I do not know if it is I thinking or not. Descartes's assertion actually took the form, I EXIST THEREFORE I EXIST. I therefore I.

Why is **hysteron proteron** called *hysteron proteron*? *Hysteros* means latter, and *protero* means former. Begging the question is putting the latter former; it is including what you should prove later in the beginning of your argument.

Begging the question is not always as easy to detect as you might imagine, because the same idea can be phrased in different ways, and so we can phrase both the premise and the conclusion in different words, cleverly concealing the fact that they are only different words for the same idea. Examples of deceptive *hysteron proteron* would be sentences such as "Education is important because knowledge is valuable," "I am nonplussed because phenomena perplex me," and "Everyone should vote because participating in democracy is important." These statements are actually circular; they are disguised repetitions.

The *hysteron proteron* fallacy has been recognized as a logical error from the beginning of philosophical time. Also known as the fallacy of *circulus in probando*, it was described by Aristotle (384-322 B.C.), pupil of Plato and teacher of Alexander the Great.

Think carefully about *hysteron proteron* (begging the question, putting the latter former, circular reasoning, *circulus in probando*) and then write an example which illustrates the illogical circularity—which shows how the result reached depends on the result being assumed to begin with. Then, think more carefully, and explain what non-circular, effective, and valid reasoning would need to be, and how this is different from *hysteron proteron*. Once this distinction is vividly clear to you, you will begin to notice that the world is replete with *hysteron proteron*!

Neologist's Lexicon

Use the stems in this list to create a new word (neologism). Give the word, the pronunciation, the part of speech, the etymology, and the definition(s). Keep a record of the neologisms you create from list to list. Here are some examples:

hysteronym (hiss' ter oh nim) n. [hysteros (latter), nym (name)]   1. the invective or incisive epithet which you think to apply to your opponent only afterwards, when it is too late to deliver it 2. any epithet preceded by the words, "I should have said . . ."

noxochronic (nox o kron' ik) adj. [nox (night), chron (time)]   1. becoming obsessively nocturnal, as a bibliophile who reads every summer night until dawn   2. being unable to sleep unless the sun is shining through the curtains

Sesquipedalian Epistolary Story

An epistolary novel is one such as Bram Stoker's *Dracula*, which uses the device of the letter to give the novel a documentary feel, as though the story were really true and you were only reading someone's letters about what actually happened. This is one reason why *Dracula* is so shockingly vivid and credible. There is no difficulty in making Coleridge's suspension of disbelief when one is reading *Dracula*; even though the content is incredible, the reader becomes credulous, in part because the epistolary technique enhances the illusion. Write a short epistolary story.

Epithetula, the Demon of Diatribe

Dearest Gullibette,

I have only just arrived at the castle here in Transnomia, and already I miss you terribly. The Professor was not present to meet me at the gate, but I was admitted by an obsequious toady of deplorable syntax, who escorted me to my comfortable room. Oh, Gullibette, if only you could see the undulating hills and forests which circumscribe the picturesque castle! I had been in my room unpacking for only a few minutes when the Professor entered. I didn't even hear him come in, but suddenly there he was behind me, Professor Epithetula. I had expected him to be sedate and dignified, but to my shock, he was condescending and supercilious and greeted me rudely with a hissing, adjective-laden diatribe, calling me Mort the Amorphous, Burt the Superfluous, and Porter the Portly. I explained with equanimity that my name was Jonathan Sangfroid, but he continued to abuse me with his vile invective and vociferously called me a Putative Pudd'nhead, Heterodox Heretic, and a Translucent Transient. When I asked him why he abused me thus, he said he knew me for a knave and a villain and would daub the walls of the castle with me! I begged to be excused from his loquacious objurgations, but I soon felt their soporific effects on me, and I fell into a sound and refreshing sleep.

Later, I awoke to find that three weird sisters had entered the hall outside my door and were whispering new sotto voce vituperations in suspirating voices, calling me a Pusillanimous Pussycat, a Neptune of Nepotism, and a Foolish Funambulist. When I opened the door to drive them away, they suddenly transmogrified into parakeets and flew through my room and out the narrow barred window into the night, chirping new epithets as they flew! What a day I'm having. Write soon, Love, Jonathan.

• intra	(within)	intramural	• **mur**	(wall)	intramural
• *penta*	(five)	pentameter	• *meter*	(measure)	pentameter
• reg	(rule)	regicide	• cide	(kill)	regicide
• corp	(body)	incorporeal	• *mega*	(large)	megalith
• *lith*	(rock)	megalith	• per	(through)	perspicuous
• fort	(strong)	fortepiano	• extra	(beyond)	extramural
• fid	(faith)	perfidious	• trans	(cross)	intransigent
• ego	(I)	egomania	• con	(together)	incondite
• **plan**	(smooth)	fortepiano	• cap	(take)	incipient
• **catena**	(chain)	concatenate	• spec	(look)	perspicuous

intramural (within the walls) Intramural activities are held within the school.

extramural (outside the walls) Extramural sports are between different schools.

pentameter (of five measures) The poem was in iambic pentameter, five iambic feet to a line.

fortepiano (loud then soft) The passage should be played fortepiano.

incipient (just beginning) It was an incipient problem, just beginning to cause difficulties.

concatenate (chain together) The concatenated events formed a chain of causes and effects.

incondite (poorly constructed) The neophyte's novels were incondite and shallow.

regicide (killing of a king) Macbeth's regicide of Duncan haunts his conscience.

incorporeal (not consisting of matter) The spirit's essence was incorporeal, not corporal.

megalith (huge stone) The prehistoric megaliths stood in black outline against the red sky.

• • •

ingenuous (innocent and naive) The ingenuous youth, new to the city, was easily deceived.

perspicuous (brilliantly clear) Your perspicuous mind and perspicacious work are appreciated.

perfidious (treacherous) The perfidious act was roundly condemned by the loyalists.

intransigent (not compromising) The intransigent zealot lost everything through stubbornness.

egomania (self-obsession) His irritating egocentrism developed into unendurable egomania.

As Used by Herman Melville in *Billy Budd*

	Some	sort	of	plot	was	**incipient.**
Parts of Speech:	adj.	n.	prep.	n.	v.	adj.

Parts of Sentence:	subject				LVP	subject complement

Phrases: ----prep. phrase-----

Clauses: -----------------------------------independent clause---------------------------------
one independent clause, a simple declarative sentence

Here Melville uses the adjective *incipient* as a subject complement to modify the noun *sort*. We know *sort* is a noun because it is modified by two adjectives, and because it is the subject of the verb, so it must be either a noun or pronoun.

Pronunciation

intramural	in tra MYOOR al	**incorporeal**	in KOR por EE al
extramural	ex tra MYOOR al	**megalith**	MEG a lith
pentameter	pen TAH meh ter	**ingenuous**	in JEN yoo us
fortepiano	FOR tay pe AH no	**perspicuous**	per SPICK yoo us
incipient	in SIP ee ent	**perfidious**	per FID ee us
concatenate	con CAT en ate	**intransigent**	in TRAN si jent
incondite	in KON dite	**egomania**	ee go MAY nee ah
regicide	REJ ih side		

Spanish Cognates

pentameter	pentámetro	**incipient**	incipiente
concatenation	concatenación	**regicidal**	regicida
incorporeal	incorpóreo	**megalith**	megalito
ingenuous	ingenuo	**perspicuous**	perspicuo
perfidious	pérfido	**intransigent**	intransigente

1. The noun **pentameter**, which we have mentioned in previous discussions, refers to a poetic line which contains five (penta) feet (meter: measure). These five feet might be iambs, trochees, dactyls, or anapests. The classic line of poetry in English is **iambic pentameter**, which is the line to be found in the Shakespearean sonnet: three quatrains and a couplet of iambic pentameter, for a total of fourteen lines and 140 syllables, rhyme scheme *abab cdcd efef gg*. Shakespeare's sonnets are overwhelmingly beautiful and are among the great literary treasures of the English language. So powerful is the sonnet that Shakespeare even concealed a sonnet in the dialogue of Romeo and Juliet's meeting. Look again at the play, and see the beautiful sonnet/dialogue, beginning, "If I profane with my unworthiest hand . . . ."

2. The adjective **ingenuous** refers to one who is innocent, naive, who is unreserved, who does not dissemble. An ingenuous girl is sometimes called an **ingénue**, especially as a character on stage. To be ingenuous is to be unspoiled by the cruel world, unjaded, uncynical. The ingenuous person, male or female, is still in (in) original (gen) condition, sincere and optimistic. In Cooper's *The Last of the Mohicans*, Alice is described as ingenuous: "The ingenuous Alice gazed at his free air and proud carriage" . . . "said the uneasy youth, gazing at the ingenuous countenance of Alice" . . . "He was, however, anticipated by the voice of the ingenuous and youthful Alice." We find **ingenuous** in the novels of Hardy, Harper Lee, and the Brontës. There are ingenuous rustics, ingenuous diversions, ingenuous comments, and ingenuous enthusiasm, but the most striking sentence is one from Hardy's *Return of the Native*: "An ingenuous, transparent life was disclosed; as if the flow of her existence could be seen passing within her." You will detect that it is not necessarily a compliment to be described as ingenuous; it can be a kind of epithet, implying that you aren't very smart or observant, that you are easily duped or led by the nose, that you are wide-eyed and waggy-tailed, willing to believe anything a calculating manipulator would tell you. And on the other hand, there is a certain human beauty in the good will and trust of the ingenuous person. The word has range, and might be used in many different situations. Be careful with it.

3. A **Classic Word**: Here is a great word: **perfidious**. It means treacherous (perfidy is the opposite of fidelity), and as you might imagine upon reflection, it has a rich history in exciting adventure novels, where it aptly describes the villains, cutthroats, and deceivers who violate (per) the faith (fid) of those who trust them. We find **perfidious** in *Peter Pan*, *Lord Jim*, *Moby Dick*, and *Gulliver's Travels*—all novels of the sea. We find **perfidious** in *Ivanhoe*, and in *Jane Eyre*. Peter Pan's gang suddenly sees the perfidious pirates bearing down upon them. In *Lord Jim* the perfidious shaft of an arrow falls harmless. In Melville's *Moby Dick* we find perfidious silences and perfidious allies. The stubborn Jane Eyre remembers the perfidious hints given by Mrs. Reed about her disposition.

4. A puzzle: why does the adjective **incipient** mean just beginning, when it is composed of the stems *in* (in) and *cap* (take)? Take in? It doesn't seem to make sense, until you realize that **incipient** comes from the Latin *incipere*, to take in hand, to begin. The image is of hands grasping, closing, taking up the task in order to begin. Thomas Hardy loved the word **incipient** and used it over and over in his novels.

In each case below, one of the choices was really the word used by the author in the sentence provided. All of the choices can be found in the example words on the first page of this lesson. Your challenge is to decide which word the author used. This is not a test; it is more like a game, because more than one word choice may work perfectly well.

1.   **From Kate Chopin's** *The Awakening*

She recognized anew the symptoms of infatuation which she had felt _____ as a child.
a. fortepiano
b. incorporeally
c. perspicaciously
d. incipiently

2.   **From Mary Wollstonecraft's** *Vindication of the Rights of Woman*

[I] learned to think with the energy necessary to _____ that abstract train of thought which produces principles.
a. incipient
b. concatenate
c. pentameter
d. fortepiano

3.   **From John Milton's** *Paradise Lost*

Thus _____ Spirits to smallest forms reduced their shapes immense.
a. incondite
b. intransigent
c. incorporeal
d. incipient

4.   **From Thomas Hardy's** *Jude the Obscure*

The house [was] little more than an old _____ cottage.
a. incondite
b. intramural
c. concatenated
d. megalith

5.   **From Martin Luther King Jr.'s** *Why We Can't Wait*

They were so _____ that Burke Marshall despaired of a pact.
a. perfidious
b. ingenuous
c. incondite
d. intransigent

Though it is a good thing to have a rich vocabulary, it is not a good thing to abuse that vocabulary by writing verbose, abstruse, sesquipedalian sentences. Those who overuse their vocabularies often do so at the expense of clarity. Translate the following showy, ponderous passage into graceful, direct English. Do not use slang, but do use words which seem familiar and comfortable.

NEVER ONE TO JOIN in gregarious activities, either intramural or extramural, the diffident and ingenuous girl worked intransigently alone on her poetry, her *idée fixe*, far from the perfidious egomaniacs who had dissembled and misled her when she had first reached the university. Her incipient poetic talent had matured through a concatenation of influences, and the amorphous and incondite jingles and cryptic metaphors she wrote as a neophyte now seemed maladroit and embarrassing to her, especially in comparison to the controlled and perspicuous sonnets she was writing now on new themes: incorporeal reality, axiological perplexities, the self-regicide of personal growth—lofty transmogrifications of subliminal energies.

She looked at the sonnet she had almost finished. It was a classic: three quatrains and a couplet of iambic pentameter. It had been difficult to subjugate her ideas to the sonnet's stringent meter and rhyme scheme, and she had almost abjured the sonnet form to make the final couplet anapestic tetrameter, but finally decided to adhere to the traditional paradigm—the three-syllable anapests would be too dissonant with the music of the iambic quatrains. When the *disjecta membra* of her work was unearthed in future millennia, she thought, at least the patronizing exegetes would know she could write a proper sonnet.

Her sedentary lucubrations continued thus, late into the night, her introspective creative synergies forming less a soporific than a stimulant, until at last the effulgent dawn came streaming through the window with the euphony of the loquacious songbirds, and she went beatifically to a condign sleep.

Reading Comprehension

1. In Translation 52, the author does all of the following EXCEPT:
   A. suggest that the poet has problems forming healthy friendships
   B. indicate that the poet's talents are still developing
   C. indicate that her poem strictly followed the traditional sonnet form
   D. reveal the theme of the latest poem

2. The author's attitude is best described as:
   A. bored with the frivolity of poetry
   B. condescending toward this poet's mediocre abilities
   C. appreciative of the artistic decisions of poetry
   D. indifferent toward poets and poetry

Analogies

3. **INTRAMURAL : EXTRAMURAL ::**
   A. saturnine : gregarious
   B. introduction : table of contents
   C. wall : moat
   D. introspective : obsequious

4. **REGICIDE : PERFIDIOUS ::**
   A. neophyte : ingenuous
   B. egomania : perspicuous
   C. pentameter : incondite
   D. king : faith

Antonyms

5. **INCORPOREAL :**
   A. substantial
   B. atomic
   C. vaporous
   D. supernatural

6. **FORTEPIANO :**
   A. cacophony
   B. euphony
   C. crescendo
   D. *sotto voce*

perfidious

divergence

The word **incipient** means just beginning, like the incipient dawn of a new day which stirs the incipient breezes and the incipient euphony of the birds, which bring our slumbering consciousness to incipient alertness. Make a long list of other incipient phenomena.

elaboration, evaluation, and convergence

A **concatenation** is a chain of events. The concatenation might be a natural chain of cause and effect events, such as one of the great cycles of ecology, meteorology, or biology, or it might be a chain of human events, such as the tragic concatenations which bring wars into sanguinary and cacophonous being. Long molecules are said to be *catenated*. The idea of a chain presents us with an interesting opportunity for thinking. First, list several concatenations which exist in nature: water cycles, oxygen cycles, cycles which create soil, and so forth. For each one, **elaborate** somewhat on the links in the chain. For example, the sun heats the seas and lakes, which evaporate, the vapor rises, forms clouds, condenses, forms rain, falls, waters the vegetation, runs off into the streams, flows into the lakes and seas, and the concatenation repeats itself.

Once you have a list of four natural concatenations, then use **evaluation by criteria** to choose which of these cycles is most critical to life on our planet. If you could use a magic spell, one time, to magically protect one of these natural chains, so that no harm would ever come to it, which one would you protect first? In order to evaluate these concatenations, you must first decide upon some *criteria* (the singular is *criterion*) which you can use to compare them. For example, you might decide that the important thing is to make sure the planet has fresh water, or fresh oxygen, or clean air, or sunlight with the ultraviolet rays filtered out, or plankton living in the sea . . . there could be many criteria. Make a list of criteria, then discuss what you have listed, narrow to what you feel are the four most important criteria, and then use the four criteria to select the concatenation in nature that you would spend your one magic spell to protect.

In applying the criteria, you might prefer to list them from most important to least important and assign points to each criterion: 4, 3, 2, 1. The Future Problem Solving program, which was developed by Dr. Paul Torrance, uses this technique. You list your criteria vertically on the left and your concatenations horizontally across the top, and then you rank each of the concatenations, *moving horizontally one criterion at a time*, rather than vertically one choice at time. In other words, if your first criterion is oxygen, then you would move across, giving each chain one to four points according to how much that chain contributed to the planet's oxygen supply. Doing it this way, *one criterion at a time*, forces you to compare the merits of the different choices more objectively. When you have evaluated all four choices by all four criteria and assigned all of the points, then the choice which gained the most points wins! As an example, here is a grid which shows why I choose my cat, Heisenberg, as the best animal. Heisenberg is a clear winner over the next best animal, the turtle.

	DOG	CAT	TURTLE	GRAMPUS
FURRY	3	4	1	1
NO TROUBLE	1	2	3	4
CAN LIVE INSIDE	2	4	3	1
PURRS	1	4	1	1
TOTAL	7	14	8	7

Neologist's Lexicon

Use the stems in this list to create a new word (neologism). Give the word, the pronunciation, the part of speech, the etymology, and the definition(s). Keep a record of the neologisms you create from list to list. Here are some examples:

egomuric (ee go myoor' ik) adj. [ego (I), mur (wall)] 1. putting up behavioral or psychological barriers that prevent people from knowing you 2. responding with subterfuges or circumlocutions to all personal questions

metricide (met' rih side) n. [meter (measure), cide (kill)] 1. the act of killing a person who measures or evaluates one's performance, especially if the assessment is unfavorable 2. the act of killing a sanguine game show host who smiles while pronouncing the word sorry

Sesquipedalian House Pets

Using the words from List 52 and previous lists, write a description of an animal. An example:

The Fly of the House: His Malefic Intentions

Perspicacious, omniscient, he knows the location of every crumb, every hiding place, every intramural skypath in the house. Superciliously recognizing my careful food wrapping for the incondite and tortuous inadequacy that it is, he descends like a cacophonouzzzzz six-footed gastronome, giving me chronic entomological nightmares; he is the compound-eyed HouseKing, and I the obsequious dissembling regicide. I strike with bellicose uproar, creating a concatenation of catastrophes. An egomaniac having no incorporeal interests, his *idée fixe* is food, only food, and he lands on that megalith to flies, the bread loaf. He is intransigent and will not be shooed, but returns after each swat, his fortepiano buzz fading as he lands again, perfidiously, on the sacrosanct bread. With *sotto voce* epithets, I insidiously await his next move, my subliminal angers finding a truculent insurgence as they rise to the surface of my consciousness. I will DESTROY, I promise myself incredulously, this inexpugnable fly, this refractory fly, this feculent, corpulent hedonist, this miscreant, this fly. I objurgate and execrate the fly with new invectives, but all diatribe is feckless. The fly is pugnacious and in defiant retort buzzes acerbically past my ear as he vanishes with postprandial equanimity into the tenebrous corners of the room.

In a nonplussed epiphany I suddenly realize the end of all metempsychosis: it is to be reborn as the king of beasts, the paragon of animals, the nonpareil of animate phenomena, the vivacious *bon vivant*: the fly.

• in	(in)	incuse	• **cud**	(strike)	incuse
• cise	(cut)	incise	• **rhino**	(nose)	rhinoplasty
• *plasto*	(molded)	rhinoplasty	• *necro*	(death)	necromancy
• omni	(all)	exeunt omnes	• quadr	(four)	quadrilateral
• aqua	(water)	aqua vitae	• *iso*	(same)	isocracy
• dict	(say)	ipse dixit	• cant	(sing)	recant
• *a-*	(without)	anomaly	• *homo*	(same)	anomaly
• clude	(close)	preclude	• circum	(around)	circumscribe
• sci	(know)	prescience	• *phan*	(appearance)	phantasmagoria

incuse (hammered in) He hammered the incuse design into the copper plate.

incise (cut in) The design was incised into the mahogany furniture.

rhinoplasty (plastic surgery) The expensive rhinoplasty did not correct his broken nose.

necromancy (sorcery) The Haitian necromancer claimed that the dead told her the future.

exeunt omnes (all leave) The stage directions read, "*Exeunt omnes*," so everyone left.

quadrilateral (four-sided) He worked on a plane figure, a quadrilateral polygon.

ipse dixit (arbitrary statement) It was foolishly *ipse dixit*, an arbitrary assertion without proof.

aqua vitae (alcohol) He detected the pungent aroma of *aqua vitae* through the tavern window.

isocracy (all have equal power) The remote tribe was an isocracy and had no appointed leader.

phantasmagoria (rapidly changing images) He saw a phantasmagoria of faces and objects.

• • •

prescience (foreknowledge) His prescience gave him a warning weeks in advance.

anomaly (abnormality) The weather anomaly—green clouds—had no formal name.

recant (retract) He had to recant his statement to sing a geocentric tune about the solar system.

preclude (foreclose) Don't preclude your options too soon; study advanced math.

circumscribe (limit) The few permissible behaviors are carefully circumscribed.

As Used by Jane Austen in *Emma*

	Happiness	must	preclude	false	indulgence.
Parts of Speech:	n.	v.	**v.**	adj.	n.
Parts of Sentence:	subject	-----------AVP---------			direct object
Phrases:	----no prepositional, appositive, or verbal phrase-----				
Clauses:	---------------------------------independent clause----------------------------------				
	one independent clause, a simple declarative sentence				

Here Austen uses *preclude* as the predicate; notice that it is an action verb and transfers the action to a direct object.

Pronunciation

incuse	in KYOOS	**isocracy**	eye SOCK ra see
incise	in SIZE	**phantasmagoria**	fan TAZ ma GOR ee ah
rhinoplasty	RYE no plas tee	**prescience**	PREH shence
necromancy	NECK ro man see	**anomaly**	a NOM a lee
exeunt omnes	EX ay unt OM nays	**recant**	ree KANT
quadrilateral	KWAD ri LAT er al	**preclude**	pre KLOOD
ipse dixit	IP say DIX it	**circumscribe**	SIR come scribe
aqua vitae	AH kwa VI tee		

Spanish Cognates

necromancy	necromancia	**quadrilateral**	cuadrilatero
phantasmagoria	fantasmagoría	**prescience**	presciencia
anomaly	anomalía	**circumscribed**	circunscrito

1. An **anomaly** is an abnormality, an oddness, an incongruity. At first it seems that the word is made of *a-* (not) and *nom* (name) to describe an unusual situation for which there is no name, but actually this noun comes from the Greek *anomalos*, which means irregular, and which breaks down into *an* (not) and *homo* (same). The anomaly is the odd item in the group; it is the one that is not (an) the same (homo) as the others. **Anomaly** was one of Melville's favorite words. He used it repeatedly in *Moby Dick* to describe oddities, such as the curious anomaly of the most solid masonry joining with oak and hemp in constituting the completed ship. (Masonry on a ship?) The best example from Melville concerned the appearance of the sperm whale: "Physiognomically regarded, the Sperm Whale is an anomalous creature. He has no proper nose." I'd have called that *arhinally*.

2. A **Classic Word**: The noun **necromancy** comes from the Greek *nekromanteía* and refers to sorcery, the black (necro) art. We see this word in Swift's *Gulliver's Travels*, Scott's *Ivanhoe*, Hawthorne's *The Scarlet Letter*, Stowe's *Uncle Tom's Cabin*, and Kipling's *Kim*. Swift's sentence gives a chilling sense of the connotations of **necromancy**: "By his skill in necromancy, he has a power of calling whom he pleases from the dead."

3. **Aqua vitae**, which literally means the *water of life*, is alcohol. Though you will not see this term often in literature, you will see it in Shakespeare, such as this sentence from *Romeo and Juliet*: "Give me some aqua vitae, / These griefs, these woes, these sorrows make me old."

4. A **Micropoem**: To **circumscribe** is to limit, and we see the limitation depicted in the word: a circle (circum) is drawn (scrib) around the perimeter of what is permissible. Robinson Crusoe feels himself circumscribed by the boundless ocean and cut off from mankind, whereas the incorrigible Toad in *The Wind in the Willows* feels that his life has become narrow and circumscribed. We also use **circumscribe** in geometry, when we draw one figure around another, touching as many points as possible. A circle circumscribed around a triangle would touch the triangle in three points.

5. To **preclude** is to close (clude) off a possibility beforehand (pre). Ethan Frome feels a sense of relief so great as to preclude all other feelings.

6. The noun **phantasmagoria** refers to a series of phantasms, illusions, or apparitions. It can also refer to any similar scene made up of many changing elements or shifting images. The word comes from the Greek *phántasm* (image) and *agora* (assembly or marketplace) and conveys the idea of an assembly of images. This word reminds us of the noun **agoraphobia**, fear of open spaces. The Greek *agora*, the market place, was where people assembled. If you were in a dream state, watching hosts of images fly past your eyes, that would be a phantasmagoria. We often see such collections of changing images in movies. Macbeth sees a horrific and nightmarish phantasmagoria, but when visions of sugarplums dance in an excited child's head, that is a more beatific phantasmagoria.

In each case below, one of the choices was really the word used by the author in the sentence provided. All of the choices can be found in the example words on the first page of this lesson. Your challenge is to decide which word the author used. This is not a test; it is more like a game, because more than one word choice may work perfectly well.

1.   **From Harriet Beecher Stowe's** *Uncle Tom's Cabin*

There is a dread, unhallowed _____ of evil, that turns things sweetest and holiest to phantoms of horror and affright.
a. isocracy
b. phantasmagoria
c. necromancy
d. prescience

2.   **From Nathaniel Hawthorne's** *The Scarlet Letter*

It was like nothing so much as the _____ play of the northern lights.
a. incuse
b. phantasmagoric
c. anomalous
d. circumscribed

3.   **From Robert Louis Stevenson's** *Kidnapped*

Open the corner cupboard and bring out a great case bottle of _____.
a. *aqua vitae*
b. *exeunt omnes*
c. *ipse dixit*
d. necromancy

4.   **From Herman Melville's** *Moby Dick*

Physiognomically regarded, the Sperm Whale is an _____ creature. He has no proper nose.
a. prescient
b. anomalous
c. rhinoplastic
d. circumscribed

5.   **From Charlotte Brontë's** *Jane Eyre*

Something of serenity in her air..._____ deviation into the ardent.
a. precluded
b. circumscribed
c. recanted
d. incised

Though it is a good thing to have a rich vocabulary, it is not a good thing to abuse that vocabulary by writing verbose, abstruse, sesquipedalian sentences. Those who overuse their vocabularies often do so at the expense of clarity. Translate the following showy, ponderous passage into graceful, direct English. Do not use slang, but do use words which seem familiar and comfortable.

FAR BELOW THE CACOPHONOUS MONKEYS AND GREGARIOUS PARROTS who looked curiously down from the buoyant leaves atop the towering rain forest canopy, the medicine man, *El Viejo*, stood alone, like solipsism reified, in the middle of the thatched village in the clearing, frightened, trying to wash his nonplussed mind of the phantasmagoria which carried his perspicuous, prescient visions. Drawing a quadrilateral figure in the sand before the fire pit, he summoned the malefic powers of necromancy in a final effort to preclude the fearful tragedy he saw approaching his village through the future, but the strange future images continued streaming through his mind: anomalous coins, not incised but with incuse designs stamped into their metal; bottles of *aqua vitae* with cryptic symbols and hieroglyphics; livid physiognomies altered through lurid cosmetics and rhinoplasty; huge anonymous social systems which would destroy the near perfect isocracy of his sacrosanct forest culture; bellicose rulers recanting and abjuring promises to the autochthonous inhabitants of the jungle; stringent legal systems which would circumscribe life in the cool, green forest and prevent the silent, barefoot hunters from following the invisible paths of the forest beings; *ipse dixit* dogma of xenophobic bureaucrats who would never take the interests of the Indians into account; and beyond all of these images from the future, NOTHING. An approaching void. An abyss. He could see no images of his people beyond the phantasmagoria. It was as though his people had all vanished from the forest in a terrible *EXEUNT OMNES*— as though the forest itself had vanished, but how could that be? Why could he not find the rain forest in these images from the far future?

As *El Viejo* gazed into the phantasmagoria of images which had transmogrified from the reassuring *terra firma* he usually saw into the *terra incognita* of an tenebrous abyss, the plaintive call of the monkeys descended like sorrow through the leafy shadows of the canopy, and the parrots rose from their branches and flew silently into the mist, their reds and blues fading into an ineffable, inexpugnable white.

Reading Comprehension

1. Which of the following best expresses the main idea of Translation 53?
    A. Primitive intellects do not comprehend the benefits of technology.
    B. History is a constant progress from wilderness to civilization.
    C. The profit motive is a universal norm in all cultures.
    D. Industrial forces threaten the earth's cultural and ecological resources.

2. With which statement would the author likely agree?
    A. All species are important.
    B. The rights of some species are more important than the rights of others.
    C. All other species exist simply to benefit humanity.
    D. The future is an unknown.

Analogies

3. **INCUSE : INCISE ::**
    A. accuse : incisive
    B. mitosis : meiosis
    C. objurgate : persuade
    D. bludgeon : lacerate

4. **CIRCUMSCRIBE : QUADRILATERAL ::**
    A. limit : intractable
    B. comprehend : imponderable
    C. persuade : incredulous
    D. bilateral : unilateral

Antonyms

5. **NECROMANCY :**
    A. romance
    B. prescience
    C. devotion
    D. augury

circumscribe

6. **ANOMALY :**
    A. quotidian
    B. empyrean
    C. wont
    D. paragon

synthesis

We know that Galileo Galilei, the Italian astronomer and physicist who was born in 1564 and died in 1642, was forced to **recant**, to sing a geocentric song instead of a heliocentric song, by the church hierarchy, which found his eccentric tune to be dissonant with its dogmatic melodies. What other example of intellectual suppression, in history, science, or literature, can you think of?

An **Obiter Dictum**: Galileo was the first to see the moons of Jupiter, and this discovery gave him insights into the workings of the solar system. Today, we can see the moons of Jupiter with even a modest pair of binoculars. If you have never seen them, take a look. For a more challenging task with binoculars, see if you can find our sister spiral galaxy Andromeda, which is visible in the winter in the northern hemisphere; it's even visible to the naked eye, but it makes a ghostly and inspiring sight in a pair of good binoculars. Andromeda, of course, is far (FARRRRR . . . R) beyond Jupiter. In fact, I believe it is the most distant object visible to the naked eye. Do you remember Andromeda from your reading of mythology? Andromeda was Cassiopeia's daughter who married Perseus, who rescued her from a sea monster.

divergence and convergence

Make a list of **anomalies**, either fictitious or real. One example from literature is the anomalous chemical which transmogrifies the nice Dr. Jekyll into the malefic Mr. Hyde. It is especially odd because Dr. Jekyll only thinks he knows what the active chemical is; actually, it is a substance of which he is unaware and which has gotten into his compound without his knowing—unfortunately for him, since he finds himself unable to procure more of a chemical whose identity he doesn't know.

Another example of an anomaly is the fictitious "Bermuda Triangle," which was invented for a creative writing piece in *Argosy* magazine, but which proved to be so sensational an idea that a number of writers made fortunes by convincing credulous neophytes that this fictional strange anomaly is a thrilling reality. Fiction masquerading as nonfiction. Ho hum. If you get a chance, see the NOVA television program on this subject; it will give you an interesting insight into the integrity of scientific thinking. And the next time you read some wide-eyed article about the forces of nature being reversed, dust off your incredulity.

After you have made your list of anomalies, choose your favorite, and explain what you like about it.

aesthetics, intuition, and imagination

Under an effulgent sky, you stumble through the dusty Mesopotamian ruins until you notice, in the interstice between two boulders, something gleaming. Excitedly breaking away rock and clay, you disinter a wall which has not been seen for four millennia and which is covered with designs, both **incuse** and **incised**. Imagine. Use your intuition (ideas from the blue) to write a short creative description of this discovery. Draw some of the designs which you see on the wall.

Neologist's Lexicon

Use the stems in this list to create a new word (neologism). Give the word, the pronunciation, the part of speech, the etymology, and the definition(s). Keep a record of the neologisms you create from list to list. Here are some examples:

> **rhinocusination** (rye no kyoos in aye' shun) n. [rhino (nose), cud (strike) ation (act)] 1. striking the nose, as of an opponent 2. any process which creates pungent, malodorous vapors

> **aquadiction** (ah' kwah dik shun) n. [aqua (water), dict (say), tion (act)] 1. speaking under water 2. attempting to answer a question while using mouthwash

A Sesquipedalian Choice

1. Sesquipedalian Fiction

Using words from List 53 and previous lists, write a short play, scene, or story. Feel free to be imaginative, silly, or absurd. Do not let your critical or judgmental faculties interfere with your creative ideas.

2. Sesquipedalian Poetry

Using many words from List 53 and other lists, write a poem. You may use regular meter, or end rhyme, or other poetic devices, or not! In the past we have written poems with primary attention being paid to sound, rather than sense. This time, concentrate on sense. If you like, you can juxtapose the sesquipedalian lines with contrasting language of other categories, such as the glossy terminology of advertising hype (the NEW SplenDEX HI-TEKK AquaSPlash!), technical or medical language (we excise the necrotic tissue), nursery rhyme, or the foolish nonsense of rock and roll choruses (doo-wopp, doo-lang-doo-lang).

3. Sesquipedalian Revision

Using sesquipedalian words from the lists in this book and from other sources, such as the dictionary, write a sesquipedalian revision of some familiar story, such as "'Twas the night before Christmas . . . ." This will help you think of other words that are similar to the limited list of words we have studied.

4. Sesquipedalian Invention

For those who would rather write their own question/problem/project than do any of the ones listed above: Using other assignments in this book as a model, invent a sesquipedalian thing to do, and do it. (I'd love to know what you come up with; why don't you send it to me through my publisher?)

• **pro**	(for)	pro rata		• *ideo*	(idea)	ideologue
• gen	(origin)	exogenous		• *exo*	(outer)	exogenous
• *gamy*	(marriage)	exogamy		• *endo*	(within)	endogamy
• **tend**	(stretch)	distend		• *dent*	(tooth)	indenture
• *pleo*	(more)	pleonasm		• nom	(name)	nom de plume
• tract	(pull)	tractable		• sangui	(blood)	sanguinary
• luc	(light)	elucidate		• lat	(side)	collateral

pro rata (proportionate) It was not an equal division, but a *pro rata* division.

ideologue (theorist) An ideologue can be an exponent or an idle theorist.

exhortatory (urging) He made an exhortatory appeal to the crowd. (L. *hortari*: urge)

exogenous (originating externally) Exogenous influences changed the group.

exogamy (marriage out of tribe) Exogamy with neighboring villages was the tribe's custom.

endogamy (marriage within tribe) Endogamy had gradually weakened the tribe.

distend (stretch out) The distended stomach of the starving child was heartbreaking to behold.

indenture (written contract) The indenture's copies were notched alike, proving authenticity.

pleonasm (redundancy) It is a true fact that the term "free gift" is a pleonasm.

nom de plume (pen name) Samuel Clemens's *nom de plume* was *Mark Twain*.

•   •   •

tractable (docile) The tractable young gentleman was liked by all.

anthropoid (humanlike) The anthropoid apes gathered hooting around the juke box.

sanguinary (bloody) Homer's graphic descriptions of sanguinary combat are unforgettable.

collateral (side by side) The collateral problems aggravated each other.

elucidate (explain) Please help us by elucidating this matter

As Used by John Milton in *Paradise Lost*

	And	now	his	heart	**distends**	with	pride.
Parts of Speech:	conj.	adv.	pron.	n.	v.	prep.	n.
Parts of Sentence:				subject	AVP		
Phrases:						---prep. phrase---	
Clauses:	------------------------------------independent clause--------------------------------						
	one independent clause, a simple declarative sentence						

Here Milton uses *distends* as the simple predicate; even though it is an action verb, there is no direct object; *pride* cannot be the direct object because it is the object of preposition.

Pronunciation

pro rata	pro RATE ah	*pleonasm*	PLEE o nazm
ideologue	ID ee o log	*nom de plume*	nome de PLOOM
exhortatory	ex ORT a tory	**tractable**	TRACK tah bel
exogenous	ex OJ en us	**anthropoid**	AN thro poid
exogamy	ex OG a me	**sanguinary**	SANG wi nary
endogamy	en DOG a me	**collateral**	ko LAT er al
distend	diss TEND	**elucidate**	e LOOSE ih date
indenture	in DEN ture		

Spanish Cognates

exhortatory	exhortatorio	**exogenous**	exógeno
exogamy	exogamia	**endogamy**	endogamia
pleonasm	pleonasmo	**tractable**	tratable
anthropoid	antropoide	**sanguinary**	sanginario
collateral	colateral	**elucidation**	elucidación

1. A **Classic Word**: To **elucidate** is to explain, to enlighten, to shed light (luc) on a subject. This verb, from the Latin *elucidare*, has been a popular word in the classics of the last century. It was used by Stowe, Melville, Hardy, Conrad, Kipling, and Harper Lee. Melville's Ishmael provides a sentence that elucidates the use of **elucidate**: "All these particulars are faithfully narrated here, as they will not fail to elucidate several most important, however intricate passages, in scenes hereafter to be painted." Usually, **elucidate** is used transitively (taking a direct object): he elucidated his meaning (Conrad), he elucidated the political situation (Kipling), he elucidated principles of whaling laws (who else?).

2. The adjective **sanguinary** means just what you think: bloody. If you have ever read a serious history of the American Civil War, such as any of the books by Bruce Catton, then you realize that the Civil War was unbelievably sanguinary; to read about it is like reading *The Iliad*, except that you have to keep reminding yourself, incredulously, that you are not reading fiction. We do see this adjective in the classics to describe a sanguinary affair (Barrie), a sanguinary shindy (Conrad), sanguinary games (Hardy), and sanguinary predictions (Stowe). One of the most interesting sentences is from (I know this will shock you) Melville: "Quakers are the most sanguinary of all sailors and whale-hunters."

3. A **Micropoem**: The adjective **tractable** means docile, yielding, easily controlled. But the stems reveal that the word contains a wonderful energy: it means pullable, just as the opposite **intractable** means not pullable. In Orwell's *Animal Farm*, the bulls that had always been tractable suddenly turned savage. Conrad describes a character who was gentlemanly, steady, tractable. Stowe describes a sick person to the full as tractable a patient as a sick bison. Gulliver heartily wishes the Yahoos would be so tractable.

4. The adjective **exhortatory** comes from the Latin *exhortari*, greatly urge. The stems are *ex* (out) and *hort* (urge). To **exhort** is to urge, but it can be urgent advice, urgent caution, or urgent discourse. In H.G. Wells's *The War of the Worlds*, the public was exhorted to avoid and discourage panic. Soldiers in *The Red Badge of Courage* issue exhortations, commands, and imprecations. Hawthorne's Hester Prynne is exhorted to confess the truth.

5. The nouns **endogamy** and **exogamy** are two interesting terms from the field of anthropology, the science (logy) of humanity (anthropo). The first refers to a culture's custom of marrying (gamy) someone within (endo) the tribe, and the second refers to the custom of marrying outside (exo) of the tribe. In order to learn about what it means to be human, anthropologists study cultures of all kinds all over the world and write scientific descriptions, called *ethnographies*, of these other societies. One famous ethnography is Jomo Kenyatta's *Facing Mount Kenya*, which is about Kenya's Kikuyu tribe. Anthropologists such as Jane Goodall sometimes study primates other than human beings, such as the **anthropoid** apes: chimpanzees or gorillas. You would enjoy Jane Goodall's book, *In the Shadow of Man*. Some anthropologists, such as Louis Leakey, do archaeology. Leakey spent his life in East Africa, disinterring the remains of prehistoric hominids in Olduvai Gorge. There are many interesting books about this famous dig, both by Leakey and by his wife, Mary. His son, Richard, continued his work after his death.

In each case below, one of the choices was really the word used by the author in the sentence provided. All of the choices can be found in the example words on the first page of this lesson. Your challenge is to decide which word the author used. This is not a test; it is more like a game, because more than one word choice may work perfectly well.

1. **From Frances Hodgson Burnett's** *The Secret Garden*

   His poppy-colored cheeks were _____ with his first big bite of bread and bacon.
   a. anthropoid
   b. exhortatory
   c. tractable
   d. distended

2. **From Henry David Thoreau's** *Walden*

   As if we grew like _____ plants by addition without.
   a. *pro rata*
   b. exogenous
   c. tractable
   d. collateral

3. **From George Orwell's** *Animal Farm*

   Bulls which had always been _____ suddenly turned savage.
   a. tractable
   b. sanguinary
   c. endogamous
   d. anthropoid

4. **From James Hilton's** *Lost Horizon*

   [He had] the detached fluency of a university professor _____ a problem.
   a. distending
   b. exhorting
   c. *nom de plume*
   d. elucidating

5. **From Mary Shelley's** *Frankenstein*

   Thanks to the..._____ laws of man, I had learned now to work mischief.
   a. sanguinary
   b. collateral
   c. tractable
   d. *pro rata*

Though it is a good thing to have a rich vocabulary, it is not a good thing to abuse that vocabulary by writing verbose, abstruse, sesquipedalian sentences. Those who overuse their vocabularies often do so at the expense of clarity. Translate the following showy, ponderous passage into graceful, direct English. Do not use slang, but do use words that seem familiar and comfortable.

DESPITE THE EXHORTATORY HYPERBOLE of the village ideologues who advised her to be endogamous, the young woman, a talented poet who wrote under the *nom de plume* Thalpaivlys, had chosen her husband in an exogamous marriage, and in doing so had helped to initiate a new era of peace between the adjacent villages. Communication had led to cooperation, pharisaism to integrity, execration to benediction, xenophobia to conviviality, and the anachronistic sanguinary and bellicose past had given way to a beatific gregariousness between the two groups of autochthonous inhabitants. For the first time, those who worked hard received a true *pro rata* share of the remuneration, indentures protected the rights of the less powerful, and the intransigent became tractable. Tribal boundaries and other collateral issues were settled in council through careful elucidation of the facts. The distended bellies of the hungry were no longer seen. Tired old pleonasms such as "hated enemies" and "deadly perils" were no longer heard in every trivial conversation. Instead of chronic hebetude, a refulgent social synergy had emerged from the harmony of the villages.

It was a good time to be alive, the young woman thought. The future held much promise. She was assiduously completing a series of story poems for children about a funny and charming anthropoid ape, Fayray, and her antics in the mountain vegetation. The poems were coming well, using the anaphora that all children love because they can call out the lines aloud, and soon she would be singing these poems to the children around the glowing and mellifluous fire. In her mind, she could already see the children's eyes sparkling eagerly in the firelight—eyes, she reminded herself, of children from *both* villages. In this image, the historic dichotomy between the two peoples was finally mollified in a confluence of two cultures.

Reading Comprehension

1. It cannot be inferred from Translation 54 that:
    A. The incredulous should reconsider putative enemies.
    B. The *sotto voce* tones of colloquy can be better than cacophonous soliloquy.
    C. You must abase yourself obsequiously to those who condescend to you.
    D. A social schism can become a malefic *idée fixe*.

2. The worst title for Translation 54 would be:
    A. The Tragic Postlude of a Moribund Schism
    B. How to Abjure a Superannuated Cultural Dichotomy
    C. From Xenophobic Obloquy to Eulogy
    D. The Imponderable Nature of Superfluous and Supererogatory Truculence

Analogies

3. ENDOGAMY : EXOGAMY ::
    A. room : yard
    B. planet : moon
    C. introspective : gregarious
    D. nationalism : globalism

4. PLEONASM : NOM DE PLUME ::
    A. redundancy : *nom de guerre*
    B. reiteration : pseudonym
    C. tautology : pen name
    D. periphrasis : anonym

Antonyms

5. TRACTABLE
    A. incorrigible
    B. obstreperous
    C. intransigent
    D. refractory

6. PRO RATA
    A. apportioned
    B. incommensurable
    C. commensurate
    D. fractious

endogamy

synthesis

List at least three characters from different works of literature who have in common the fact that they are either **tractable** or **sanguinary**.

application

The adjective **exogenous** refers to things that originate externally. Something exogenous has been transplanted, imported. One opposite of **exogenous** is **indigenous,** which means native or **autochthonous**. A continent might have, for example, indigenous plants and exogenous plants. Think of at least three examples in which you could accurately apply the word **exogenous**.

emotion and imagination

What emotions do you associate with the word **sanguinary**? Often, when we study history, we read as though history were only a series of facts, of names, of dates. We can read about the most tragic events that have ever occurred and be unmoved. Why? Because we are reading with our minds, but not with our hearts, and the intellect alone is shallow. To truly understand the profound depths of what we learn, we must use our whole humanity, and this means, for example, that in reading about a great battle we must not only digest the factual detail, but we must imagine the scenes, the sensory realities, and the emotions that would be part of that experience in real life. Now, back to our question: What emotions do you associate with the word **sanguinary**? In your mind, imagine (make an image) a Civil War battlefield on the early morning after a battle. What are the emotions of the survivors, of the wounded, of the commanding officers, of the families who read about the great battle in the morning paper?

To understand, we must think not merely from the mind alone, nor from the heart alone, but from the heart of the mind. For history, one of the most human of all subjects, this is especially important.

aesthetics

Imagine that you are asked to write and direct a television program about an **anthropoid** alien who lands on our planet and makes friends with us, overcoming initial suspicion and fear, and showing us new and wonderful technologies we can use to make our planet peaceful and healthy. The thing is, the alien is only **anthropoid** in the most general way and in most specifics looks very different indeed from *Homo sapiens*. Considering the requirements of the television program, how would you design the appearance of your anthropoid alien? What colors, skin surface, facial features, and so on would you choose? Describe your alien, and draw it, if you would like to.

anthropoid

Neologist's Lexicon

Use the stems in this list to create a new word (neologism). Give the word, the pronunciation, the part of speech, the etymology, and the definition(s). Here are some examples:

lucotraction (luke' oh trak shun) n. [luc (light), tract (pull), tion (act)] 1. being irresistibly drawn to effulgence, as to lights, fame, or stars 2. the irrational compulsion to be on the beach in the dark, so as to see the sun rise over the sea

endonomy (en don' omy) n. [endo (within), nom (name) 1. the practice of selecting names for children only from among the names already given to other family members, such as uncles, grandmothers, or parents 2. the practice of giving children in sequential generations the identical name, distinguished only by the additions, Jr, II, III, and so on

Sesquipedalian Cartoon

Using words from List 54 and previous lists, write a cartoon scene about your favorite cartoon characters. An example:

Elmo Fudd and Entomo Wabbit

Elmo: Be vewy vewy *sotto voce*. I'm a sanguinawy hunter, hunting the perfidious and wascawy Wabbit.

Wabbit: Ehhhhh, What's da putative problem, Doc?

Elmo: Shhhh . . . be vewy vewy circumspect. I'm hunting Wabbits.

Wabbit: Well Doc, I don't mean to impugn your perspicacious perspicacity — pardon my pleonasm — or nuttin, but do you know a wabbit when you see one? I mean, you ain't VACUOUS, are you? I mean, elucidate dis for me, Doc.

Elmo: *Au contraire*, I certainwy do know wabbits! Why are you being so queruwous?

Wabbit: Well Doc, I don't wanna disturb your hebetude or anyting, but are you SURE you can discern a wabbit when you see one? I mean, da world is replete wit wabbits.

Elmo: YES. A wabbit has two BIG ears . .

Wabbit: Like deese?

Elmo: YES, and a wabbit has a big fuzzy tail . . .

Wabbit: Like dis?

Elmo: YES and . . . OHHHH BLAM!! BLAM!!!

Wabbit: Wait!! Doc!! Be tractable why dontcha?? Can't we discuss deese collateral issues wit equanimity? Tink what yer doin, Doc! Ain't dis a little ipse dixit?

Elmo: I'll *ipse dixit* you, you wascawy wabbit! You perfidious, intwansigent, intwactable . .

Wabbit: Hey DOC! You shouldn't concatenate your invectives like dis, I mean . . .

Elmo: You'll die intestate, you dissident, fwactious . . . MEGAWOMANIAC!

Wabbit: STOP!!!!

Elmo: Oh, I'm sowwy. What is it?

Wabbit: Doc, are you trying to hurt my feelings?

Elmo: I'm so nonpwussed. What an embawassing contwetemps.

(*Exeunt omnes*)

• cad	(fall)	cadenza	• cred	(believe)	credence
• man	(hand)	manifest	• se	(apart)	sequester
• ex	(out)	extirpate	• ad	(to)	apprehension
• pre	(before)	apprehension	• **hend**	(grasp)	apprehension
• pro	(before)	proscribe	• scrib	(write)	proscribe
• sur	(over)	surfeit	• fac	(make)	surfeit
• per	(through)	pellucid	• luc	(light)	pellucid
• bell	(war)	belligerent	• inter	(between)	intervene

cadenza (elaborate solo) Wallace Stevens's poem is entitled "Martial Cadenza."

credence (belief) It is not sagacious to give credence to sensational rumors.

lugubrious (full of mourning) His lugubrious howls over the dropped popsicle amused her.

manifest (evident) His concern for her was manifest in his close attention to what she said.

sagacious (full of wisdom) The sagacious comments helped us increase our tolerance.

sequester (set apart) Auden says each nation is "sequestered in its hate."

extirpate (root out) The government attempted to extirpate the rebels.

expiate (make amends for) He attempted to expiate his sins, but his guilt was inexpugnable.

apprehension (anxious foreboding) With apprehension, he stared at the dust on the horizon.

proscribe (forbid) Personal comment on official decisions was proscribed by law.

•   •   •

credible (believable) He is not a credible candidate, being only a ship's dog.

surfeit (excess) There was a surfeit of food and drink at the ceremony.

pellucid (crystal clear) Light shone through the pellucid spring water onto the golden sand.

belligerent (warring) The belligerent student body insulted the obsequious official.

intervene (come between) It is unwise to intervene in this acrimonious dispute.

As Used by Joseph Conrad in *Heart of Darkness*

	His	sagacious	relative	lifted	his	head.
Parts of Speech:	adj	**adj.**	n.	v.	adj.	n.
Parts of Sentence:			subject	AVP		direct object
Phrases:	---no prepositional, appositive, or verbal phrase---					
Clauses:	------------------------------------independent clause-------------------------------- one independent clause, a simple declarative sentence					

Conrad uses *sagacious* as an adjective to modify the noun *relative*, which is the subject of the sentence. The word *his* is here a possessive adjective.

Pronunciation

cadenza	ka DEN za	**apprehension**	app re HEN shun
credence	KREE dense	**proscribe**	pro SCRIBE
lugubrious	loo GOO bree us	**credible**	KRED ih bel
manifest	MAN ih fest	**surfeit**	SUR fit
sagacious	sa GAY shus	**pellucid**	pel LOOSE id
sequester	se KWES ter	**belligerent**	beh LIH jer ent
extirpate	EX tir pate	**intervene**	in ter VEEN
expiate	EX piate		

Spanish Cognates

cadenza	cadencia	**credence**	credencia
lugubrious	lúgubre	**manifest**	manifiesto
sagacious	sagaz	**sequestration**	secuestro
extirpation	extirpación	**expiation**	expiación
apprehension	aprehensión	**proscribed**	proscripto
credible	creíble	**belligerent**	beligerante

1. The verb **intervene** means literally to come (ven) between (inter). It comes from the Latin *intervenire*, made of *inter* and *venire*, to come. Usually we see this word used to describe physical intervention, but not always. Ethan Frome finds that his pride retorts before his reason has time to intervene. In Wells's *The War of the Worlds*, a drifting bank of black vapor intervenes. Wells also refers to intervening time, and in *The Time Machine*, to the interstices of intervening substances. Tom Sawyer wishes he had had no intervening holiday. In *Moby Dick* three years intervenes between the flinging of two harpoons. Robinson Crusoe sees a strange and unforeseen accident intervene, and a cloud or hazy weather intervene. In Thomas Hardy's *The Return of the Native*, we behold the "well-known form [of the reddleman] in corduroy, lurid from head to foot, the lantern beams falling upon him through an intervening gauze of raindrops."

2. A **Micropoem**: The verb **sequester** contains a small drama. It comes from the Latin word *sequestrare*, meaning to put something apart (se) in the hands of a trustee (quester). We see an object passing into the hands of a trustee to be separated. So to sequestrate is to separate something, to set it apart, or to do this to yourself by withdrawing into solitude. In *Ivanhoe*, there is a distant and sequestered turret. In *The Last of the Mohicans*, the scout and Indians were familiar with the sequestered place where they now were. In *Jane Eyre* characters love their sequestered home, and Jane asks, "What crime was this, that lived incarnate in this sequestered mansion?" Hardy used **sequester** repeatedly; in *The Return of the Native* he wrote, "In returning to labour in this sequestered spot he had anticipated an escape from the chafing of social necessities." My favorite example is from W.H. Auden's poem "In Memory of W.B. Yeats": Auden argues that we must "teach the free man how to praise," though the "living nations wait / Each sequestered in its hate."

3. The verb **proscribe** means forbid, but why? It comes from the Latin *proscribere*, which meant to outlaw something by publishing it in writing. Today, we do not always mean a written or published document, but we do mean that to proscribe is to condemn, to outlaw, to denounce, to prohibit, to forbid. In *A Tale of Two Cities* Charles Darnay finds himself to be one of a race proscribed (the aristocrats in the French Revolution).

4. A **Micropoem**: to **extirpate** is to pluck out (ex) by the roots (stirp), from the Latin *extirpare*, plucked up by the stem. In *Ivanhoe* people are commanded to extirpate magic and heresy. But a really beautiful and unforgettable sentence comes from Charlotte Brontë's character Jane Eyre, who finds it "hard to extirpate from my soul the germs of love."

5. The adjective **lugubrious** comes from from the Latin *lugubris*, mournful. In other words, **lugubrious** means full of (ous) mourning. Often this word modifies the words *howling* or *wailing*. Jack London: "Then he fell, and lay where he fell, howling lugubriously." Harriet Beecher Stowe: "when there was the least wind, most doleful and lugubrious wailing sounds proceeded from it." Mark Twain: "Presently the dog set up a long, lugubrious howl just outside." Mark Twain: "That long, lugubrious howl rose on the night air again!" Owooooohhh.

We have seen many wonderful examples of the way words in our lists are used in the classics, but List 55 contains three words— **apprehend**, **sagacious**, and **manifest**— that are replete in literature. To give you a realistic sense of just how often some of the words we have studied are likely to appear in books you will read, let's look in more detail at these three words.

apprehension

The noun **apprehension**—together with its friends the verb **apprehend**, the adjective **apprehensive**, and the adverb **apprehensively**—has been in steady use for the past three centuries. **Apprehension** is a combination of *ad* (to), *pre* (before), and *hend* (grasp). It comes from the Latin *apprehendere*, to grasp, and so it is both a **Classic Word** and a **Micropoem**, since it is really a metaphor, comparing the feelings of understanding a danger beforehand to the physical act of the hand grasping an object and not letting it fall. Apprehension is both mentally grasping the meaning of something and doing so in advance.

In this idea, *the mind is a hand*.

It can grasp a truth, as a hand can grasp a thing.

That is why we love this word; it's the poetry of it.

The delicacy, the articulated fingers of thought closing on the truth.

In the classics, **apprehension** has been used in 1719 by Defoe, in 1726 by Swift, in 1826 by Cooper, in 1851 by Melville, in 1876 by Twain, in 1881 by Stevenson, in 1886 by Hardy, in 1895 by Crane, in 1898 by Wells, in 1903 by London, in 1911 by Wharton, in 1937 by Steinbeck, in 1959 by Knowles, and in 1960 by Lee. Robinson Crusoe is frightened almost to death with the apprehensions of his sad condition. Gulliver suffers depression of spirits caused by the continual apprehension of death. In *Tom Sawyer*, the slow days drift on, each leaving behind a slightly lightened weight of apprehension. Jim Hawkins in *Treasure Island* finds the worst of his apprehensions realized. The youth in *The Red Badge of Courage*, Henry Fleming, hurries in the vague apprehension that one of the swollen corpses on the battlefield will rise and tell him to begone. Jack London's dog Buck watches the people apprehensively. Ethan Frome has no room in his thoughts for vague apprehensions. Curly's wife in *Of Mice and Men* becomes suddenly apprehensive.

We find characters crouching fearfully in the bushes and listening, distracted by apprehension (*The War of the Worlds*), feeling a certain apprehension lest the good name of another should be sucked down in the eddy of a scandal (*Dr. Jekyll and Mr. Hyde*), apprehending that one is rather addicted to profane song (*The Last of the Mohicans*), and feeling a pinprick of apprehension (*To Kill a Mockingbird*).

Apprehension is both an emotion and a comprehension. It is worry. Anxiety. We feel apprehensive, as the examples from classic books reveal, about death, about being badly treated, about danger, about ghastly possibilities, about mischief, about what might happen.

sagacious

    The adjective **sagacious** comes from the Latin *sagax* (wise) and *ous* (full of): full of wisdom. The noun form is **sagacity**, and we see both of these forms often in good books:

    Defoe describes mighty sagacious, tractable creatures. What might he be describing?

    Swift describes a low intelligence below the sagacity of a common hound; the sagacity and smell of a bird that enable him to discover his quarry at a great distance; and bees and ants having the reputation of more industry, art, and sagacity than many of the larger animals.

    Scott describes sagacity and prudence, a knight who resolves to trust to the sagacity of his horse, and a character who possesses the sagacious knowledge of physiognomy.

    Cooper notes such blind marks as are only known to the sagacity of a native; a sagacity that does not deceive; a singular compound of quick vigilant sagacity and of exquisite simplicity; and a measure dictated by the sagacity of a guide, in order to diminish the marks of a trail.

    Emily Brontë creates a character who "must trust to my own sagacity."

    Hawthorne creates a sagacious, experienced, benevolent old physician; and describes the sombre sagacity of age; but wonders if one possesses native sagacity. (The first description, of course, is of the insidious Roger Chillingworth, and is intensely ironic.)

    Melville's *magnum opus* contains wonderful uses of **sagacious**: "snuffing up the sea air as a sagacious ship's dog will, in drawing nigh to some barbarous isle," "an extremely sensible and sagacious savage [Queequeg, our hero]," "does the ocean furnish any fish that in disposition answers to the sagacious kindness of the dog?" "the result of this lowering was somewhat illustrative of that sagacious saying in the Fishery," "But peradventure, it may be sagaciously urged, how is this?" and "I had not a little relied upon Queequeg's sagacity."

    Dickens's wonderful portly character in *A Tale of Two Cities*, Mr. Lorry, is described as the sagacious Mr. Lorry, who has the sagacity of the man of business and who knows that there are questions which no sagacity could have solved.

    Twain's character is half sorry her sagacity had miscarried.

    Hardy describes the sagacious old heads who knew what was what in Casterbridge.

    Crane's Henry Fleming rationalizes that his actions in running away had actually been sagacious things.

    Conrad's characters have eyes that dart sagacious, inquisitive glances and who possess sheer, instinctive sagacity. Lord Jim feels the deep sense of his sagacity crowning every day of his inner life.

    Don't you think it is interesting that many authors have used **sagacious** to describe animals, rather than *Homo sapiens*? We see sagacious horses, sagacious birds, sagacious ants and bees, and sagacious dogs. There is something about the word **sagacious** that gives it a certain surprise value; we feel no special impact in saying that a dog is *smart*, but to say that a dog is *sagacious*, as Melville does, feels bracingly original and refreshing. But Melville adds, *sagacious kindness* . . . Ah, now that is interesting. The sagacious kindness of the dog.

sagacious

manifest

Another word that I would bet you rarely use, or even hear in conversation, and yet that is enormously frequent in the classics is **manifest**, which can be an adjective or a verb and which has a collection of transmogrifications: **manifestly**, **manifested**, and **manifestation**. **Manifest** is a major **Classic Word**, appearing in almost every book of note, a favorite word not just of a few authors, but of most.

Manifest comes from the Latin *manifestus* and literally means struck with the hand! In other words, to have something made manifest is like being slapped! Something is manifest if it is obvious, completely evident, readily perceived and plain. Since this experience is such a vivid and important one, we see **manifest** in constant use for more than four hundred years; it was used by Shakespeare ("Thy heinous, manifest, and many treasons . . .") in *King Lear*, 1606, and it was used by Arthur Miller in *The Crucible*, 1953: "The witch-hunt was a perverse manifestation of the panic which set in among all classes."

In the classics, we find manifest treasons, manifest tokens of wonder, causes manifestly known to be just, manifest alarm, manifestations of weakness, manifest danger of falling down every precipice, manifest pride, manifest sympathy, manifest constraint, the manifestation of wealth in dress and equipage, tittering which continues and manifestly increases, picturesque manifestations, manifestations of jealousy, manifestations of discontent, and on and on. There are far too many examples of **manifest** to try to list or discuss them all, and so let's just focus on some of the best ones:

Henry David Thoreau, in his 1854 masterwork *Walden*, desires to have "A house whose inside is as open and manifest as a bird's nest." This is not only a beautiful image, it also shows Thoreau's genius for connecting words in unexpected ways. Thoreau noted that "the squirrels manifest no concern whether the woods will bear chestnuts this year or not."

Cooper's Hawkeye, in the 1826 adventure *The Last of the Mohicans*, exhorts his friends to "Manifest no distrust" when confronted by the Indians, "or you may invite the danger you appear to apprehend." Of course, this exhortation not to manifest one's apprehensions is sagacious advice.

Harriet Beecher Stowe's Uncle Tom "in various ways manifested a tenderness of feeling, a commiseration for his fellow-sufferers." Despite the pejorative connotations that the term *Uncle Tom* has acquired in recent decades, to read this book is to understand why Stowe's writing enraged the nation against the truculent evil of slavery.

Jonathan Swift's credulous traveler, Gulliver, sojourns to the land of the feculent and vacuous Yahoos and is mortified to learn, "It was manifest I had neither the strength or agility of a common Yahoo." This, you will realize if you read the disgusting Yahoo chapter in Swift's 1726 satire *Gulliver's Travels*, is a sobering epiphany indeed. Don't call any learned person a Yahoo unless you want to see resentment made manifest.

George Orwell's famous pigs, in his 1945 classic *Animal Farm*, are able to rule the farm, partly because they are sagacious enough to comprehend what the other animals only vaguely apprehend. Orwell describes "the pigs, who were manifestly cleverer than the other animals."

To see a word only in a list, with a single example sentence, is very deceptive. Not all of our words are as common as **apprehension**, **sagacious**, and **manifest**, but you will be surprised, once you know the words, at how often you see them and at how many of them you will see, even the ones that seem excessively erudite.

In each case below, one of the choices was really the word used by the author in the sentence provided. All of the choices can be found in the example words on the first page of this lesson. Your challenge is to decide which word the author used. This is not a test; it is more like a game, because more than one word choice may work perfectly well.

1.   **From Sir Walter Scott's** *Ivanhoe*

They were commanded to _____ magic and heresy.
a. manifest
b. expiate
c. proscribe
d. extirpate

2.   **From Henry David Thoreau's** *Walden*

The Roman made an _____ offering.
a. lugubrious
b. credible
c. sagacious
d. expiatory

3.   **From Mark Twain's** *Tom Sawyer*

Presently the dog set up a long, _____ howl just outside.
a. manifest
b. sagacious
c. lugubrious
d. pellucid

4.   **From Stephen Crane's** *The Red Badge of Courage*

His actions had been _____ things.
a. sequestered
b. manifest
c. belligerent
d. sagacious

5.   **From Martin Luther King Jr.'s** *Why We Can't Wait*

The yearning for freedom eventually _____ itself.
a. intervenes
b. manifests
c. surfeits
d. extirpates

Though it is a good thing to have a rich vocabulary, it is not a good thing to abuse that vocabulary by writing verbose, abstruse, sesquipedalian sentences. Those who overuse their vocabularies often do so at the expense of clarity. Translate the following showy, ponderous passage into graceful, direct English. Do not use slang, but do use words that seem familiar and comfortable.

AFTER SEQUESTERING HIMSELF IN THE LIGHTHOUSE, Joseph K., a lonely cosmologist, gazed down at the blue and pellucid waters of the gulf, where the parrotfish nipped at the yellow coral, and the white foam suspirated a *sotto voce* syntax on the tops of the passing waves. A fractious gull screamed a cacophonous cadenza as it swept after the refulgent and retreating sun, and the wind split in dichotomous schism on both sides of the lighthouse. It whistled in the interstices of the windows and howled lugubriously at the amorphous congeries of rocks at the base, but the superfluous stability of the lighthouse was manifest. The lighthouse stood on *terra firma*. It had been built in 1932, and Joseph knew that nothing short of a typhoon could extirpate it from its foundation.

Despite the wind, he looked without apprehension over the ranks of waves that marched in a concatenation of crests to the horizon. Fate, he knew, could be proscribed by no human interdiction. Crimes must be expiated. And the truth must receive credence, whether it is manifestly credible or not. Across the water, he knew, belligerent civilizations were slouching toward each other; and their hour would come round, and he feared that the next chapter of the history books was waiting insidiously for its sanguinary and inexorable conclusion, which nothing could intervene to prevent. Pugnacious belligerence was antediluvian, superannuated, even anachronistic, but it was still human nature.

Even so, these incipient intramural altercations meant little in his broader cosmological view. With stoic sagacity, he was cognizant that the incorporeal principles of nature, *mirabile dictu*, had their own schedules of gravitation and electromagnetism, of strong force and weak force, and that this ineluctable geometry made egomania or megalomania condign only to the pusillanimous.

At the horizon's edge, purple clouds cracked with white fulgurations of lightning, but the sententious tautology of thunder was inaudible, like the subliminal forces that quietly powered Joseph K.'s passive idealism.

Reading Comprehension

1. In Translation 55, the author does all of the following EXCEPT:
    A. describe the structural stability of the lighthouse
    B. indicate that the cosmologist has resigned himself to nature's forces
    C. indicate that the cosmologist is a chronically apprehensive person
    D. indicate that global affairs in this story are not optimistic

2. It can be inferred from the passage that:
    A. Joseph intends to find a solution to the world's diplomatic problems.
    B. Joseph thinks, like Homer, that even Zeus can't overrule the Fates.
    C. Joseph has retreated to the lighthouse because of a personal failure or disgrace.
    D. Joseph is optimistic about the immediate future of civilization.

Analogies

3. **PELLUCID : DIAMOND ::**
    A. diamond : crystal
    B. lugubrious : farewell
    C. opaque : sanguine
    D. manifest : belligerent

4. **EXPIATE : SAGACIOUS ::**
    A. proscribe : efficacious
    B. intervene : vacuous
    C. sequester : feckless
    D. extirpate : belligerent

Antonyms

5. **PELLUCID :**
    A. opaque
    B. tenebrous
    C. oblique
    D. nebulous

pellucid

6. **APPREHENSION :**
    A. optimism
    B. equanimity
    C. stoicism
    D. sagacity

synthesis

Use any five words from List 55 in a single sentence. If that is too easy, then use any five different words from List 55 in a sentence that contradicts the first sentence! If that is too easy, rewrite the two sentences so that the same words are used in reverse order and the sentences are no longer contradictory! Surely that's not too easy.

intuition and imagination

In the **pellucid** waters of the Bahamas, take your outboard boat out over the reef, where the warm salt waters are replete with schools of fish. In the refulgent sunlight, you anchor the boat, put on your mask, fins, and aqualung (thank you, J. Cousteau), and drop into the water, swimming down through the gregarious marine life in search of sunken galleons and Spanish doubloons. But what you discover on the sandy bottom is a complete surprise; it is even better than a galleon; it is something you would never have expected to find underwater at all! Continue . . .

analysis

Using a dictionary, carefully explain the differences between the etymology, the grammar, and the best usage of the words **proscribe** and **interdict**.

interdict

Neologist's Lexicon

Use the stems in this list to create a new word (neologism). Give the word, the pronunciation, the part of speech, the etymology, and the definition(s).

surhension (sir hen' shun) n. [sur (over), hend (grasp) tion (act)] 1. the ability to grasp what is presently over one's head, resulting in intellectual growth 2. fascination with what one is unable to understand. syn.: hyperplussed

Sesquipedalian Mystery Theater

Use the words from List 55 and previous lists to write a scene from a detective story, using a favorite character, such as Sherlock Holmes, as a paradigm if you like.

Cadenzo, the Solo Detective

Cadenzo, the solo homicide detective, is called in to investigate when the body of a millionaire is found in a luxury apartment. Cadenzo arrives in his ratty trench coat, peering obliquely out of one eye, and finds the millionaire's curly-haired nephew, Larry Moe, standing in the room as the police conduct their incipient inductive investigation. As Cadenzo enters, the other officers leave.

Cadenzo: (with manifest solicitude), Scuse me, sir, I'm Lieutenant Cadenzo. I'm sorry to intervene at a lugubrious time like this, when you've just lost your wealthy uncle, thereby inheriting millions of dollars, but I just have to ask you a few questions. Just a few questions, it's all routine. I just have to expedite the paperwork for the department; you understand. We have to extirpate the iniquitous and find etiologies.

Moe: Not at all, Mr. . . . I'm sorry officer, but what was your name? This is a difficult time for me. (then querulously) If you don't mind, let's make this brief.

Cadenzo: (ingenuously) Oh, I completely understand, Mr. Moe. I'm Lieutenant Cadenzo. I'll try to be as brief as I can. But Mr. Moe, what is this on your uncle's desk? It looks like a curly wig. (vociferously) Wowww. Wait 'til I tell Mrs. Cadenzo about this. If you were to wear this, you would be a curly Larry Moe. That's really some wig.

Moe: (Apprehensively) I've never seen this wig before. Lieutenant Cadenzo, please be germane. If you have no further sagacious questions, I really need to be leaving.

Cadenzo: Oh, I certainly understand, Mr. Moe. In fact, I have to be going myself. (Cadenzo exits, and Moe surreptitiously slips the wig into his pocket. Suddenly Cadenzo reenters the room, pointing his finger in the air.)

Cadenzo: Oh, one more thing, Mr. Moe, why do you think your uncle would have a curly wig in his office? I mean what would he want with a wig? Elucidate that anomaly for me.

Moe: I'm sure I don't know, Lieutenant Cadenzo. He wore it or he didn't; I don't mean to equivocate. My antediluvian uncle had idiosyncrasies.

Cadenzo: (dissembling) As a detective, I'm just an autodidact and a neophyte. Don't expostulate. We just can't be too circumspect in filling out paperwork. Well, goodbye, Mr. Moe. (Exits, returns) Oh, one more thing. Why would a supercilious plutocrat like your uncle sequester himself in this twentieth floor apartment if he had acrophobia? Can you explain that? (temporizes) Yeah, I guess not. (Exits)

Moe: (Takes out the wig, rubbing it, speaking in soliloquy) Obsequious, prolix fool. Out, sanguinary spot, out, I say. Will nothing make this blood less manifest?

(Exeunt omnes.)

pathogen

renascent

emollient

melancholy

admonitory

metamorphosis

recumbent

excrescence

• **nasc**	(born)	renascent		• **flect**	(bend)	deflect
• re	(again)	renascent		• in	(not)	infirmity
• re	(back)	recumbent		• tempor	(time)	extemporize
• pugn	(fight)	pugilist		• **monit**	(warn)	admonitory
• **casus**	(case)	casuistry		• **firm**	(strong)	infirmity
• *meta*	(change)	metamorphosis		• *morph*	(shape)	metamorphosis
• *patho*	(disease)	pathogen		• *gen*	(origin)	pathogen
• **cumb**	(lie down)	recumbent		• **cresc**	(grow)	excrescence
• sine	(without)	sine qua non		• *mela*	(black)	melancholy
• moll	(soft)	emollient				

renascent (showing new life) There was a renascent interest in the arts after the museum opened.

extemporize (improvise) She began to extemporize a spontaneous response to his complaint.

deflect (turn away, bend) He gracefully deflected embarrassing questions.

pugilist (boxer) The pugilist's pugnacious posturing was comical to the boxing fans.

excrescence (abnormal outgrowth) The fungus caused an ugly excrescence on his nose.

casuistry (specious reasoning) His speech was a masterpiece of casuistry and deception.

infirmity (feebleness) His infirmities prevented him from attending the ceremony.

recumbent (reclining) The tired surgeon was recumbent on her sofa.

admonitory (warning) His message had an admonitory purpose—to warn them away.

incorrigible (not correctable) They could not alter the incorrigible child's behavior.

• • •

metamorphosis (change of shape) Dr. Jekyll's metamorphosis was startling to behold.

pathogen (disease-causer) Dr. Stockman, the people's friend, found pathogens in the water.

sine qua non (essential element) Courage is the *sine qua non* for success in espionage.

emollient (softener) The creamy emollient softened his chapped skin.

melancholy (dark sadness) He felt a brooding melancholy on rainy days.

As Used by John Gardner in *Grendel*

	Simple	facts	in	isolation	are	the	**sine qua non.**
Parts of Speech:	adj.	n.	prep.	n.	v.	adj.	**n.**
Parts of Sentence:		subject			LVP		subject complement
Phrases:			---prep. phrase---				
Clauses:	-----------------------------------independent clause--------------------------------- one independent clause, a simple declarative sentence						

Here Gardner uses *sine qua non* as a noun and subject complement. Notice that *sine qua non* is modified by an adjective, the definite article *the*.

Pronunciation

renascent	re NASS ent	**admonitory**	ad MON ih tory
extemporize	ex TEM por ize	**incorrigible**	in KOR ih ji bel
deflect	de FLEKT	**metamorphosis**	meta MOR fo siss
pugilist	PYOO jil ist	**pathogen**	PATH o jen
excrescence	ex KRESS ence	*sine qua non*	sin eh kwah NON
casuistry	KAZ yoo iss tree	**emollient**	ee MOLL yent
infirmity	in FIRM ih tee	**melancholy**	MEL an kol lee
recumbent	re COME bent		

Spanish Cognates

renascence	renacimiento	**deflection**	deflección
pugilist	pugilista	**excrescence**	excrecencia
casuistry	casuística	**infirmity**	enfermedad
admonitory	admonitivo	**incorrigible**	incorregible
metamorphosis	metamorfosis	**pathogen**	patógeno
emollient	emoliente	**melancholy**	melancólico

1. A **Classic Word**: The noun or adjective **melancholy** comes from the Greek word for black bile, believed to make one gloomy, depressed, pensive, mournful, or sad. As you might expect from such an emotional word, **melancholy** is frequently encountered in the classics and can be found from Shakespeare's *Romeo and Juliet* (1596) to Edith Wharton's *Ethan Frome* (1911). Daniel Defoe used it, as did Swift, Cooper, Stowe, Twain, Hardy, Stevenson, Crane, Wells, London, Barrie, and Grahame. In the adjective form of **melancholy**, we find melancholy bells, a melancholy disposition, melancholy solicitude, a wild and melancholy dirge, a soft and melancholy movement with Aetolian accompaniment, melancholy conviction, a melancholy mummer, grey melancholy woods, a melancholy fatality in the voice, a melancholy march, a melancholy pilgrimage, and the melancholy rippling of waves on lonely beaches. The last one is from London's *The Call of the Wild*. In the noun form of **melancholy**, we find a dumb melancholy, a gentle melancholy, a profound melancholy, and a deep melancholy. My favorite sentence is one from Barrie's *Peter Pan* that describes the villainous Captain Hook, James Hook, who signed his name Jas: "His eyes were of the blue of the forget-me-not, and of a profound melancholy, save when he was plunging his hook into you, at which time two red spots appeared in them and lit them up horribly."

2. **Casuistry**, in its negative connotation, is specious reasoning, oversubtle reasoning, disingenuous reasoning, fallacious reasoning, dishonest reasoning. Why? Well, this noun comes from the Latin *casus*, meaning case, and is better understood if you consider its positive connotation: the application of ethics to specific cases or specific situations. It is the MISuse of casuistry (the good kind) that gives casuistry a bad name. The casuist, in other words, is a kind of **sophist**, a **disingenuous** reasoner who uses subtle and **specious** arguments to sound **cogent**, with dishonest disregard for the truth.

3. The adjective **incorrigible** comes from the Latin *incorribibilis*, meaning not (in) correct (*corrigere*) able (*ibilis*). To be incorrigible is to be uncorrectable, so bad that you cannot be reformed. We especially use this adjective to modify the dreaded noun *child*. In the classics we find **incorrigible** modifying Toad in *The Wind in the Willows*: "the incorrigible rogue and hardened ruffian whom we see cowering in the dock before us," and Melville's *Moby Dick* also contains such a rascal: "Bildad, I am sorry to say, had the reputation of being an incorrigible old hunks."

4. **Recumbent** is an adjective that comes from the Latin *recumbere*, lying back, which in turn is made of *re* (back) and *cubare* (to lie down). In *Of Mice and Men* John Steinbeck describes "sycamores with mottled, white, recumbent limbs." Conrad refers to recumbent bodies, Hardy to a recumbent figure, Melville to recumbent elephants (!), and Cooper to the recumbent forms of Hawkeye's companions. I know, I know, you want to know what the Melville sentence about the elephants is. OK. In *Moby Dick* Melville writes that "the stranger at a distance will sometimes pass on the plains recumbent elephants without knowing them to be such." What I wonder is whether the elephants know that people are passing . . . .

In each case below, one of the choices was really the word used by the author in the sentence provided. All of the choices can be found in the example words on the first page of this lesson. Your challenge is to decide which word the author used. This is not a test; it is more like a game, because more than one word choice may work perfectly well.

1.   **From H.G. Wells's** *The War of the Worlds*

It was not time for _____ chivalry, and my brother laid him quiet with a kick.
a. renascent
b. recumbent
c. pugilistic
d. incorrigible

2.   **From Kenneth Grahame's** *The Wind in the Willows*

How can we possibly make it sufficiently hot for the _____ rogue?
a. recumbent
b. incorrigible
c. melancholy
d. admonitory

3.   **From Mary Wollstonecraft's** *Vindication of the Rights of Woman*

It would puzzle a keen _____ to prove the reasonableness of the greater number of wars that have dubbed heroes.
a. emollient
b. pugilist
c. casuist
d. infirmity

4.   **From James Fennimore Cooper's** *The Last of the Mohicans*

He was able to distinguish the _____ forms of his companions as they lay stretched on the grass.
a. recumbent
b. melancholy
c. admonitory
d. renascent

5.   **From Charles Dickens's** *A Tale of Two Cities*

[There were] _____ strong-rooms made of kitchens and sculleries.
a. renascent
b. extemporized
c. recumbent
d. incorrigible

Though it is good to have a rich vocabulary, it is not good to abuse that vocabulary by writing verbose, abstruse, sesquipedalian sentences (such as this one). Those who overuse their vocabularies often do so at the expense of clarity. Translate the following showy, ponderous passage into graceful, direct English. Do not use slang, but do use words that seem familiar and comfortable.

AN INSIDIOUS PATHOGEN IN THE EMOLLIENT HAD CAUSED A STRANGE METAMORPHOSIS, and now the surgeon lay recumbent in a melancholy infirmity, like an incorrigible pugilist who'd been unable to deflect the opponent's blows and whose ears had been pounded into amorphous excrescences. No admonitory prescience had warned the surgeon not to use the emollient, jekyllhydium, and the instructions on the bottle had argued, in a case of commercial casuistry, that the jekyllhydium was the *sine qua non* for personal renascent vigor. In the past, the surgeon had attempted to extemporize other healthful remedies, to no avail, and had procured the jekyllhydium only as a last resort.

But now this unexpected transmogrification had left the surgeon in a saturnine and nonplussed incredulity, uttering suspirated maledictions and longing for some chemical legerdemain to reverse the damage. At least the morphological alterations had been mild, leaving the surgeon's body in its normal anthropomorphic form, but the surgeon was cognizant that the etiology of this condition was cryptic, and the prognosis for recovery and restoration was dismal, since no amount of rhinoplasty would likely restore the distended anomaly on the front of the surgeon's face to the aquiline nose that she had previously possessed.

With apprehension, she looked again lugubriously at the bottle of jekyllhydium and suddenly noticed a sentence in small print: "Caution: use of this emollient may, in some cases, result in irreversible *bergeracus cyranosis*." And yet, had she read the admonitory label in time, would she have been circumspect or sagacious enough to give it credence? Who could tell? "Well," she stoically soliloquized, "at least I now have a proboscis to preclude the egocentric perils of narcissism. My days as a paragon of patrician physiognomy are done. All proboscis monkeys have a proboscis; I have a proboscis; therefore, I am a proboscis monkey." This specious pseudosyllogism, we must interpolate, was hardly perspicuous.

Reading Comprehension

1. In Translation 56 it can be inferred that:
     A. The surgeon possesses a sanguine equanimity.
     B. The surgeon possesses a supercilious sangfroid.
     C. The surgeon is a narcissistic hedonist.
     D. The surgeon lacks the perspicacity to accept herself.

2. The author's attitude in Translation 56 is best described as:
     A. giving a high value to the importance of physical appearance
     B. not giving a high value to the importance of physical appearance
     C. communicating no attitude toward the importance of physical appearance
     D. accepting the surgeon's attitude toward the importance of physical appearance

Analogies

3. INCORRIGIBLE : TRACTABLE ::
     A. pathogen : vitamin
     B. metamorphosis : metempsychosis
     C. corrugated : traction
     D. pugilist : philosopher

4. INFIRMITY : MELANCHOLY ::
     A. contretemps : jocose
     B. admonition : incorrigible
     C. casuistry : incredulous
     D. cholera : sickness

Antonyms

5. RENASCENT :
     A. renaissance
     B. concatenated
     C. moribund
     D. exogenous

6. SINE QUA NON :
     A. dichotomy
     B. superfluity
     C. reiteration
     D. tautology

tractable

synthesis

An **incorrigible** character is one who, like Huckleberry Finn, is incapable of being reformed, even through punishment. Huck, who resisted stiff clothes, stiff weekly schedules, stiff manners, and other forms of *rigor culturus*, was incorrigible, though lovably so. What other incorrigible characters in history or fiction can you think of?

analysis

By breaking the words into their component stems, explain the difference between **incorrigible**, **intractable**, and **intransigent**, or between **metamorphosis**, **metempsychosis**, and **transmogrification**. You may use a dictionary to look up the etymologies, if you would like more information than the stems we have studied provide.

intuition and imagination

First, let me do some synthesis: **Metamorphosis** is for lycanthropes, for the subjects of entomology, for frog-princes, and for doctors named Jekyll. **Metamorphosis** is for the lonely novelist Franz Kafka, in his story of Gregor Samsa, who woke up as an insignificant and neglected bug, the symbol of that anonymous nonentity, *Homo bureaucraticus*. **Metamorphosis** is for vampires named *Dracula* who turn into wolves, bats, and sharp-toothed creatures of the night. **Metamorphosis** is for Ovid, the Roman poet, who wrote magical and lovely story-poems of the great myths, such as Daphne and Apollo, Phoebus and Phaeton, and Echo and Narcissus (read the Rolfe Humphries translation of Ovid's *Metamorphoses*, and then look up a photograph of Bernini's AMAZING sculpture of Daphne changing into a laurel tree just as Apollo catches up with her). **Metamorphosis** is for tadpoles. **Metamorphosis** is for the malefic monsters of science fiction who insidiously adopt the morphology of whatever species they encounter. **Metamorphosis** is not for the birds, though it is a *sine qua non* in the life of butterflies. **Metamorphosis** is for the Incredible Hulk, whom you would not like when he is angry.

Now for the intuition and imagination: If you were to write a creative story involving a new form of metamorphosis, which you are the first person to imagine (if Narcissus dwindled away to become a narcissus flower, pining narcissistically for his own image in the water, does that mean that I might pine away until I have become a quarter-pounder with cheese?) (does it drive you crazy when I **interpolate** these comments?), what would your new form of metamorphosis be? Think of a fun or funny form of metamorphosis, and, if you would like to, write a short story in which your metamorphosis plays a part.

ethics

After thinking carefully about what **casuistry** is (disingenuous and specious ethical ratiocination, is what it is), see if you can think of an actual example of casuistry that you have encountered in the world. Remember that the casuist is a *case-ist who* makes the wrong thing sound like the right thing through the unprincipled use of specific cases. If you want a paradigm for casuistry, think of a character such as Archie Bunker from television's *All in the Family*, who used casuistry and sophistry to try to make his chauvinism and xenophobia sound American.

Neologist's Lexicon

Use the stems in this list to create a new word (neologism). Give the word, the pronunciation, the part of speech, the etymology, and the definition(s). Keep a record of the neologisms you create from list to list. Here is an example:

sinecrescence (sin uh kress' ence) n. [sine (without), cresc (grow)] 1. avoiding epiphanies or profound reflections on experience, so as to avoid the need for changing one's ideas 2. interpreting all experiences as a concatenation of verifications of one's prior beliefs.

Sesquipedalian Bete Noire

Using the words from List 56 and previous lists, write a sesquipedalian version of your *bete noir* (something that drives you crazy, that you dread, that is your personal pet peeve). An example:

Burgers 'n' Pies at the Drive Thru

Machine:	Welcome to MaDoodle's. May I take your order please!!!!!!!!!!!
Human:	Cheeseburger n fries n a large DietSipp.
Machine:	Would you like a HOT APPLE PIE WITH THAT???
Human:	Cheeseburger' n fries' n a large DietSipp, to reiterate.
Machine:	Would YOU LIKE A HOT APPLE PIE WITH THAT?????
Human:	Cheeseburger, fries, sipp. Are you incorrigible?
Machine:	Would you like a HOT APPLE PIE WITH THAT???
Human:	What retort is this? I want a cheeseburger and fries and a DietSipp.
Machine:	Would YOU LIKE TO HAVE A NICE HOT APPLE PIE WITH THAT???
Human:	What?? Is pie a *sine qua non* of the cheeseburger meal? Are you intractable?
Machine:	Sir, WOULD YOU LIKE A HOT APPLE PIE WITH THAT??
Human:	I wasn't cognizant I'd mentioned a pie. What casuistry is this? What *idée fixe*?
Machine:	HOW 'BOUT A NICE HOT APPLE PIE WITH THAT???
Human:	Is there no subterfuge I can use to deflect your assiduous question?
Machine:	D'JA like a HOT APPLE PIE WITH THAT??
Human:	Take my admonitory expostulation, before I metamorphose into a pugilistic and belligerent gastronome: offer your pathogenic pie to someone else! Extemporize. You can do it.
Machine:	HOW 'BOUT A HOT APPLE PIE WITH THAT??
Human:	(soliloquizing) Oh, lyssophobia, vex not me. (aloud) GIMME A CHEESEBURGER!
Machine:	LIKE A HOT APPLE PIE WITH THAT??
Human:	You're trying to mollify me, right? The pie is an emollient for my acerbity?
Machine:	WOULD YOU LIKE A HOT APPLE PIE WITH THAT??
Human:	Oh, melancholy. Oh, excrescence on the body of life. Oh, failed renascence.
Machine:	HOW'D'JA LIKE A HOT APPLE PIE WITH THAT?????!!!!!!
Human:	Keep the cheeseburger. Keep the fries. KEEP THE DIETSIPP! (drives away)
Machine:	LIKE A PIE?? HOW 'BOUT A PIE?? HAVE A PIE WITH THAT? SOME PIE???

finis

• **flect**	(bend)	inflection	• patri	(father)	expatriate
• punct	(point)	compunction	• *archy*	(government)	anarchist
• sta	(stop)	stasis, status quo	• *an-*	(not or without)	anarchist
• **sens**	(feel)	sentient	• bon	(good)	bonhomie
• mur	(wall)	immure	• **sap**	(taste or know)	insipid
• *muta*	(change)	mutable	• in	(not or without)	insipid
• **im**	(in or not)	immure	• **nod**	(knot)	denouement
• *eco*	(house)	ecumenical			

denouement (outcome, unraveling) The class read the amateurish novel's tedious denouement.

solecism (substandard speech) Athenians laughed at the solecisms spoken by colonists in Soloi.

compunction (feeling of remorse) The egotistical sociopath acted without compunction.

inflection (change of vocal tone) She signaled her question by vocal inflection.

stasis (state of equilibrium) Is the universe in flux or in stasis?

immure (to wall in) Having never traveled, he was immured within his own provincialism.

sentient (conscious) The exobiologist believed in sentient extraterrestrial life.

ecumenical (universal) We have an ecumenical, general view of the event.

ex officio (by virtue of office) The disgruntled mayor became the *ex officio* dogcatcher.

insipid (without flavor, boring) His insipid conversation bored even the dog.

• • •

expatriate (banish) The intractable dissident was expatriated from the fatherland.

anarchist (one opposed to government) The sullen anarchist refused to vote at all.

bonhomie (good-naturedness) The good fellow charmed us with his amiable bonhomie.

status quo (the present state) The daring new policy disrupted the political *status quo*.

mutable (changeable) He chased the mutable laws of high fashion.

As Used by Edith Wharton in *Ethan Frome*

	Her	look	smote	him	with	compunction.
Parts of Speech:	adj.	n.	v.	pron.	prep.	n.
Parts of Sentence:		subject	AVP	direct object		
Phrases:						--prepositional phrase--
Clauses:	----------------------------------independent clause---------------------------------					
	one independent clause, a simple declarative sentence					

Here Wharton uses the noun *compunction* as the object of a preposition. The prepositional phrase modifies the verb. *Her* is a possessive adjective; the possessive pronoun is *hers*.

Pronunciation

denouement	de NOO ay MAHN	*ex officio*	EX o FISS ee o
solecism	SOLL e sizm	**insipid**	in SIP id
compunction	com PUNKT shun	**expatriate**	ex PAY tree ate
inflection	in FLECK shun	**anarchist**	AN ar kist
stasis	STAY siss	**bonhomie**	bon o MEE
immure	im MYOOR	*status quo*	sta tus KWO
sentient	SEN tee ent	**mutable**	MYOO ta bel
ecumenical	ek yoo MEN ik al		

Spanish Cognates

solecism	solecismo	**compunction**	compunción
inflection	inflexión	**ecumenical**	ecuménico
insipid	insípido	**expatriate**	expatriado
anarchist	anarquista	**mutable**	mudable

1. The adjective **ecumenical** means universal, global, or in a specific sense, it means of the whole Christian church. The word comes from the Latin *oecumenicus*, belonging to the whole inhabited world, and this comes from the Greek *oikein*, to inhabit. The stem with which we are familiar is *eco*, house or habitation.

2. A **solecism** is an error of grammar or etiquette, an impropriety. The noun comes from the idea of the ancient Greeks that the Greek spoken in Soloi was ungrammatical and crude. A Solecism is a Soloi-ism. Charlotte Brontë refers to the embarrassment of being made conspicuous by some solecism or blunder, and Melville notes, "by a solecism of terms there are birds called grey albatrosses."

3. The verb **immure** is a relative of the words **mural**, **intramural**, and **intermural**. To immure is to imprison, to wall in. In Grahame's 1908 classic *The Wind in the Willows*, the incorrigible Toad "found himself immured in a dank and noisome dungeon."

4. A **Classic Word**: The noun **compunction** refers to the feeling of remorse we have when we have done something wrong or when we are about to do something wrong. The word comes from the Latin *compungere*, to prick (punct) severely. You might not expect this word to have much play in the classics, but in fact we see **compunction** in steady use for hundreds of years. Shakespeare used it in 1606 in *Macbeth*: "Stop up th'access and passage to remorse, / That no compunctious visitings of nature / Shake my fell purpose." Walter Scott used it, as did Emily Brontë, Herman Melville, Charles Dickens, Thomas Hardy, Stephen Crane, and Edith Wharton. In 1851 Melville referred to men "who still have left in them some interior compunctions against suicide," and in *The Red Badge of Courage*, Henry Fleming "of course felt no compunctions for proposing a general as a sacrifice."

5. The adjective **insipid** means not (in) sapid; **sapid** means tasty and comes from the Latin *sapidus*, flavored. So to be insipid is to be boring, flavorless, lacking interesting qualities. Gulliver refers to a very insipid diet. Scott describes the insipidity of mind that sometimes attaches to fair beauties. Charlotte Brontë describes an interesting dichotomy: "their presence was pungent, but their absence would be felt as comparatively insipid." In Kipling's *Kim*, we read that "This was not insipid, single-word talk of drummer-boys." And in Twain's *Tom Sawyer* the boys are made to talk so properly that speech has become insipid in their mouths.

6. The verb **expatriate** always reminds me, and a million other people, of the writer Ernest Hemingway, who spent much of his time abroad and who wrote about expatriates, victims of wounding wars who found it impossible to go home and who spent their lives drifting from hotel to hotel, insulating themselves from their own care with alcohol. It is no surprise, therefore, to find that Hemingway himself used this word in *The Sun Also Rises* to describe an "expatriated newspaper man." In addition to Hemingway's novels, you might enjoy his book *Death in the Afternoon*, which is a description and explanation of bullfighting.

In each case below, one of the choices was really the word used by the author in the sentence provided. All of the choices can be found in the example words on the first page of this lesson. Your challenge is to decide which word the author used. This is not a test; it is more like a game, because more than one word choice may work perfectly well.

1.   **From Aldous Huxley's** *Brave New World*

"I beg your pardon," said the reporter, with genuine _____.
a. inflection
b. bonhomie
c. denouement
d. compunction

2.   **From Herman Melville's** *Moby Dick*

By a _____ of terms there are birds called gray albatrosses.
a. *status quo*
b. solecism
c. denouement
d. inflection

3.   **From Herman Melville's** *Moby Dick*

_____ professors of Sabbath-breaking are all whalemen.
a. *ex officio*
b. sentient
c. mutable
d. insipid

4.   **From Rudyard Kipling's** *Kim*

This was not _____, single-word talk of drummer-boys.
a. ecumenical
b. *ex officio*
c. solecism
d. insipid

5.   **From Henry James's** *The American*

And then she looked at the undusted nymph, as if she possibly had _____ ears.
a. insipid
b. sentient
c. mutable
d. ecumenical

Though is is a good thing to have a rich vocabulary, it is not good to abuse that vocabulary by writing verbose, abstruse, sesquipedalian sentences (such as this one). Those who overuse their vocabularies often do so at the expense both of clarity and of others' patience. Translate the following ostentatious, ponderous passage into graceful, direct English. Do not use slang, but do use words that seem familiar and comfortable.

THE COMPUNCTION HE FELT was like an immutable melancholy prison, a remorse within which he was immured and for which there was no postlude. He had reached a plateau of lugubrious stasis. Behaving like a vociferous anarchist in a plutocracy, he had insensitively accused his best friend of solecisms, of circumlocutions, of tautologies, of malapropisms, of effusive inflections, and—worst of all—of insipid conversation, wounding his friend with this acerbic obloquy and disrupting the bonhomie and equanimity that were the friend's typical *status quo*.

And he was no vacuous inanimate object; he was a sentient being, with an ecumenical world view; he was ordinarily a sensitive friend who never pronounced objurgations. But now he had egocentrically contravened his own best instincts, and he felt like sequestering himself like a troglodyte in a cave, or like becoming an expatriated apostate, who as a perfidious villain was entitled to become an *ex officio* member of the supercilious cosmopolitan cognoscenti. But this reaction was a *non sequitur*.

There was only one condign thing to do: to abjure narcissism, to abase himself in a posture of obsequious humility, and to go ask for exculpation through the euphony of forgiveness to transmogrify himself into a penitent. But this was an ethical funambulism to which he was unaccustomed, and he was soon lost in casuistry, asking himself, "Why should I apologize? In some cases, apologies are rebuffed. In some cases, we apologize to those even less punctilious than ourselves. Is what I have done so ignominious, when in many cases people do far worse and are still lionized?"

Slowly, however, he began to feel contrite again, and he went to find his friend, unequivocally gave his *mea culpa*, averred that he was cognizant of his error, expressed commiseration, execrated himself for his effusion of invective, and announced that all his epithets had been misnomers in which he had failed to discern his friend's manifest excellence.

As you might imagine, the denouement of this story was a mutual panegyric of solicitude.

Reading Comprehension

1. For Translation 57, which of the following does the passage suggest:
    A. Normally, people are reluctant to forgive those who wrong them.
    B. You should describe things as you see them, even if this is hurtful.
    C. Apologize for your errors, and you will probably be forgiven.
    D. There's no sense crying over spilt milk.

2. The character's thinking could be best described as:
    A. an introspective *Odyssey*
    B. an introspective *Iliad*
    C. an introspective *Inferno*
    D. an introspective *Moby Dick*

Analogies

3. **STASIS : MUTABLE ::**
    A. stop : car
    B. system : fuel
    C. stable : status quo
    D. equipoise : metamorphic

4. **EXPATRIATE : ANARCHIST ::**
    A. father : governor
    B. evict : tenant
    C. *ex officio* : officer
    D. convict : criminal

Antonyms

5. **SENTIENT :**
    A. inanimate
    B. insipid
    C. acrimonious
    D. compunctious

expatriate

6. **ECUMENICAL :**
    A. clerical
    B. *ex officio*
    C. provincial
    D. dogmatic

emotion and ethics

As emotions go, **compunction** is one of the least pleasant. As we saw in the Notes on page 225, a compunction is a severe sense of remorse that one feels before or after doing something regrettable or immoral. For my money (to use a dreaded cliché), the most piercing expression of this emotion is Macbeth's compunctious agony after he has killed the good king, Duncan: "Full of scorpions," Macbeth says grimly, "is my mind, dear wife." Full of scorpions is my mind. . . . Imagine that.

A less poetic but equally poignant example of compunction is King Lear's grievous realization of what he has done to his truest daughter, Cordelia, whom he has banished and disinherited because she told the simple truth, which is that when she weds, she will give half of her love to her husband, rather than continuing to love her father all, as her wicked and dissembling sisters claim they will do. Lear at last realizes the tragedy that he has brought upon himself and gasps to his fool, in a heart-breaking *non sequitur* to what the fool has just said, "I did her wrong,—" (Act I, Scene 5).

Huckleberry Finn feels compunctions about taking food from farmers' fields, about helping Jim escape, about leaving a gang of murderers to die on a house floating down the river, and about how the Duke and the Dauphin are duping and conning the crowds.

Frankenstein's monster—the sensitive sentient being of Mary Shelley's lovely book, not the lumbering ignoramus of the film—feels frequent compunction about the harm he causes. In this book, it is really the monster who is the person, and the people who are monsters to him.

Another way to think about compunction is to perceive the chill of its absence. We expect compunction to be present as an essential emotional aspect of our humanity, and when we do not see it, we become dramatically cognizant of the tenebrous gap it leaves. It is, for example, the hideous absence of compunction that gives the truculent Mr. Hyde his peculiar power over our emotions. Hyde tramples a little girl and cudgels an old gentleman, and not only does Hyde not manifest compunction, but he even enjoys a sadistic hedonism in his barbarity.

One aspect of the Nazi holocaust that gives it such profound horror is the absence of compunction in those who created and who obeyed the command to murder. Compunction is a kind of alarm, a signal of the conscience to itself that something immoral is happening. The complete absence of compunction is synonymous with monstrosity.

Do you remember the word **sociopath** from our discussion of egotism? Well, a sociopath is a person, usually very bright, who ruthlessly manipulates others to achieve his or her own ends, having no scruples and feeling no compunctions about the injuries caused to the lives or emotions of the people who get sacrificed to his or her egotism. The sociopath is a moral vacuum. The mythical paradigm for the sociopath is the vampire. You might think a sociopath would be despised by everyone, but it is characteristic of the sociopath to be so talented at manipulation that the victims are charmed, impressed, and incredulous that the sociopath has intentionally harmed them. They may even regard the sociopath as their heroic ally in the struggle against whomever the sociopath is blaming for their misfortunes. When they finally begin to suspect the sociopath, they first doubt their own perspicacity. Only later do they realize what the sociopath has done to them. For an overpowering literary example of the sociopath, read Shakespeare's *Othello*, and watch closely, if you can stand the horror, Iago's brilliant, systematic destruction of Othello and Desdemona, done with such malefic skill that Othello actually cherishes Iago as a trusted friend until it is too late. Iago is evil genius incarnate, a sociopath utterly without compunction.

What would you like to do with this idea of **compunction**? Would you like to discuss other examples you can think of, or write a short story, or analyze the internal human phenomena that cause us to feel compunction? Well, either do one of these, or design a compunction exercise of your own. (It's ok, we're in this together. You don't need to be always following directions; you can be creating directions sometimes. The world needs that, too.)

Neologist's Lexicon

Use the stems in this list to create a new word (neologism). Give the word, the pronunciation, the part of speech, the etymology, and the definition(s). Keep a record of the neologisms you create from list to list. Here are some examples:

sapiarchy (say' pi arkee) n. [sap (taste), archy (government)] 1. the government of those who profess to have sublime taste 2. the dictatorship of the cognoscenti

sensiflection (sens' ih flek shun) n. [sens (feel), flect (bend), tion (act) 1. having one's feelings manipulated by emotional influences, such as television advertisements that associate poignant experiences with the possession of industrial products

Sesquipedalian Walden

Have you read Thoreau's *Walden*? Thoreau describes going to the woods, building his own cabin, and living in connectedness with the creatures and manifest life of the forest. He has entire chapters on food, on sounds, on sights. He rows on the lake and plays games with a diving loon. It is peaceful reading . . . a relief from the plot-filled stories we normally read. Here is a spoof:

Walden

I sequestered myself in the woods six hours ago, and I just finished extemporizing my own clever cabin with my own clever hands and will enjoy the *status quo* in a spirit of ecumenical bonhomie with all woodland creatures, unless doing so costs me more than a dollar and sixty-seven cents, which is all I have budgeted for my expenses this year. I do not expect to need half so much money, as all my entertainment and sustenance will be provided by the woodland creatures for free. I am so perspicaciously stoic. And so very very clever.

Men are born free, but everywhere they obsequiously immure themselves in insipid towns, hypothecating their freedom for profits, when they could live sentiently and harmoniously with the great stasis of Nature—like me—cleverly delighting in the cacophonous anarchy of squirrels, rather than the solecisms of tax collectors! Men could be impecunious and still enjoy the mutable seasons, but they have expatriated themselves from their natural homes to live as xenophobic strangers in the neophilia of what is by misnomer called civilization. Instead, they should extirpate themselves—like me—from this insidious hebetude and participate in the isocracy of living things. Why do men contravene their nature and choose manumission to the omnibus demands of society?

My clever house is snug, a wooden quadrilateral four feet by four feet, and provides every need. It is as manifest as a bird's nest, and the inflections of a robin's euphonic cadenza come through the window with the evening breeze. And from the pellucid lake the lugubrious loon shatters the tranquility without compunction, exhorting me to enjoy the nick of time. But I must be out the door, for I am the clever self-appointed *ex officio* inspector of paths and mud puddles, and I record the denouement of rain storms as I listen to the suspiration of the wind in the trees.

When they write my hagiography, let them record that I marched cleverly to the beat of a *sui generis* axiology, omnisciently abjuring the specious, the superfluous, and the supererogatory; and let them tell all readers that—like me—they can be cleverly less anthropocentric and more cosmological, which is a beatifically different drum.

• **ment**	(mind)	demented	• *terato*	(monster)	teratology	
• vert	(turn)	tergiversate	• sap	(know)	sapient	
• **ten**	(hold)	tenacious	• rogat	(ask)	prerogative	
• *antho*	(flower)	anthology	• fract	(break)	infraction	
• **quis**	(ask)	inquisition	• *gen*	(origin)	indigenous	
• *meta*	(beyond)	metaphysics	• corp	(body)	esprit de corps	
• *idio*	(peculiar)	idiosyncrasy	• reg	(rule)	interregnum	
• *platy*	(flat)	platitude	• inter	(between)	interregnum	

sapient (wise) *Homo sapiens* is the most sapient primate, according to itself.

indigenous (native) The aborigines are the indigenous people of Australia.

demented (insane) In the silent film, the demented villain tied the heroine to the railroad track.

metaphysics (speculative philosophy) Ontology, the study of being, is a branch of metaphysics.

inquisition (punitive investigation) The Spanish Inquisition was feared by thinking people.

prerogative (exclusive privilege) Her noble prerogatives were abolished when she was deposed.

tenacious (holding firmly) The suspect tenaciously held to his story during the interrogation.

teratology (science of monstrosities) The teratologist was studying congenital birth defects.

tergiversate (to desert) The tergiversator turned his back on the cause; he was an apostate.

esprit de corps (group pride) The troops' *esprit de corps* helped them survive the grim retreat.

• • •

anthology (a literary collection) The editor picked the best poems for the anthology.

platitude (a flat trite remark) We need fresh new ideas—not tired, empty platitudes.

interregnum (time between rulers) There was an ephemeral peace in the interregnum.

infraction (violation) There should be no infraction of these ten edicts.

idiosyncrasy (peculiar behavior) Over the years, the hermit developed odd idiosyncrasies.

As Used by William Shakespeare in *King Lear*

	Thou,	**sapient**	sir,	sit	here.
Parts of Speech:	pron.	**adj.**	n.	v.	adv.
Parts of Sentence:	subject		AVP		

Phrases: --appositive phrase--

Clauses: ------------------------independent clause------------------------
one independent clause, a simple imperative sentence

Here Shakespeare uses the adjective *sapient* to modify a noun, and the two words form an appositive phrase. The appositive phrase is enclosed in commas.

Pronunciation

sapient	SAY pient	**tergiversate**	TURJ i ver sate
indigenous	in DIJ en us	*esprit de corps*	eh SPREE de COR
demented	de MEN ted	**anthology**	an THOH lo jee
metaphysics	MET a fiz iks	**platitude**	PLAT i tood
inquisition	in kwiz ISH un	**interregnum**	inter REG num
prerogative	pre ROG a tiv	**infraction**	in FRAK shun
tenacious	ten AY shus	**idiosyncrasy**	id ee o SIN kra see
teratology	ter a TOLL o jee		

Spanish Cognates

sapient	sapiente	**indigenous**	indígena
demented	demente	**metaphysics**	metafísica
inquisition	inquisición	**prerogative**	prerrogativa
tenacious	tenaz	**tergiversation**	tergiversación
anthology	antología	**interregnum**	interregno
infraction	infracción	**idiosyncrasy**	idiosincrasia

1. The noun **prerogative** refers to an exclusive right or privilege, but it contains the stems that mean ask (rogat) before (pre). Why? Well, **prerogative** comes from the Latin *praerogativus*, voting first. In the Roman empire it was sometimes the prerogative, the exclusive right, of a tribe to vote first! Consider the honor implied by having the right to be asked first what your opinion is of something. Harper Lee refers to the royal prerogative, Charlotte Brontë refers to the prerogatives of the crown, and Walter Scott to the prerogatives of a jovial friar.

2. A **Micropoem**: The intransitive verb **tergiversate** means to desert, to turn renegade, to repeatedly change one's position toward something. The basis for this meaning is found in the imagery contained in the stems. **Tergiversate** contains our old friend, *vert* (turn), and the Latin *tergum* (back); to tergiversate is to turn one's back. Someone who tergiversates could become an apostate. In *A Tale of Two Cities* Dickens refers to "the utmost tergiversation and treachery."

3. An **idiosyncrasy** is a peculiar behavior, such as a habit or mannerism that one associates only with a certain individual. Stand-up comedians and impressionists make careers out of imitating the idiosyncrasies of famous individuals. You might imagine that this word has something to do with the idea of government (cracy), but actually the noun comes from the Greek stems *idio* (peculiar), *syn* (together) and *krasis* (blending). An idiosyncrasy is a peculiar blending together! This explains why **idiosyncrasy** is not spelled *idiosyncracy*. In John Knowles's *A Separate Peace*, Gene says that the students "had been an idiosyncratic, leaderless band" and that there was "nothing idiosyncratic about Brinker unless you saw him from behind." Poor Brinker. Robert Louis Stevenson, in *Dr. Jekyll and Mr. Hyde*, refers to "some idiosyncratic, personal distaste." And Thomas Hardy, in *The Return of the Native*, describes the human face this way: "But the mind within was beginning to use it as a mere waste tablet whereon to trace its idiosyncrasies as they developed themselves."

4. The noun **teratology** refers to the study of monstrosities, such as abnormally formed plants and animals. We see this word used in child development texts, where it describes the study of congenital birth defects. Agents involved in the etiology of birth defects are called **teratogens**, and we have learned that most fetuses are exposed to some teratogens. These teratogens are most dangerous at the time organs are being formed, about three weeks after conception. Teratologists indicate that the fetus's brain, eyes, heart, and legs are each especially vulnerable at certain stages of development.

5. A **Classic Word**: The adjective **indigenous** means native-born; you would not really expect such a scientific-sounding term in the classics, but it's there. It was used by Thoreau, Stowe, and Melville. In *To Kill a Mockingbird* Harper Lee used **indigenous** to note "peculiarities indigenous to the region" and "diseases indigenous to filthy surroundings."

metaphysics

When Kipling, in his novel *Kim*, describes "occasional gatherings of long-coated theatrical natives who discussed metaphysics in English and Bengali," he is referring to one of the primary branches of philosophy, named after its position, after the Physics, in Aristotle's writings, which are the *locus classicus* for many of our ideas. **Metaphysics** is the question, What is real? In asking this question, philosophers ask about the reality of God and human immortality, about whether the universe really has a purpose, about whether everything is just atoms, and so forth. Metaphysics asks about being. The branch of metaphysics that examines being in its most abstract form, *Being as such*, is known as **ontology**. There are several main branches of metaphysical inquiry, including:

Materialism. To the metaphysical materialist, what is real is **matter**. Atoms. Stuff. In this view, the universe is a vast collections of atoms and forces, and everything can be ultimately explained as a manifestation of these material phenomena. The mind itself, in this view, is a manifestation of material phenomena, including atoms, cells, and organs. The universe has no purpose, though it may have processes and directions, as dictated by the Big Bang or by the process of evolution. Obviously, many thinkers have difficulty accepting a merely materialistic view of what is metaphysically real.

Idealism. To the metaphysical idealist, what is real is **ideas**, and matter itself is only an idea. **Subjective idealists**, such as Bishop Berkeley, do not believe that objects as things-in-themselves really exist "out there." This may seem like a frivolous view, but try to prove the separate existence of a solid object without depending on your sense perceptions, each of which is known to be variable and ultimately unreliable. For example, when we "see," we are not really directly viewing the supposed object; we are actually only perceiving the stimulation of our own brain neurons that we assume are activated by the cells in the backs of our eyes which we assume are stimulated by light hitting the eyes after being reflected off of the object which we assume is "out there." But as we know from changing light and numerous examples of optical illusions, things are not always accurately represented by visual appearances. To make matters worse, even the materialist would admit that human eyes only respond to a portion of the available light, while other animals often have far more acute vision. So how does an object REALLY look? Hmmm. What is real? How does something really feel? Really smell? Really sound? Careful thought reveals that these ideas are relative, at best. Once you start vigorously and rigorously doubting what you actually KNOW about the reality of an object, the seeming obviousness of **naive materialism** comes rapidly unglued! To make it even worse, the scientists (those rascally materialists) tell us that there is actually far more empty space in the interstices between the atoms of seemingly solid objects than there is matter. Even to the materialists, in other words, stuff is mostly not stuff, and the appearance of solidity is an illusion! In idealism, you lose the reality of matter, but you get to have such non-material things as souls, selfs (I don't mean selves), and divine Spirits. In most forms of idealism, **teleology** is important; teleology is the idea that an ultimate purpose is a fundamental reality in the nature of things.

Dualism. Are you confused enough? I hope so. You probably find yourself partly attracted to materialism and partly attracted to idealism. Well, maybe you are a Cartesian. Descartes is famous for his metaphysical dualism, the **mind/body dichotomy**. The ghost in the machine. An ideal self living in a physical body. The physical body may die, but the ideal self can pass on to eternity. This solves some problems, but then you have a new one: how does the non-physical self affect the physical body? If I think, "I will now type a question mark at the end of this sentence," how does my ideal mind make my material body do that? ?? ??? ???? . . . . . ? Philosophy is fun.

234

In each case below, one of the choices was really the word used by the author in the sentence provided. All of the choices can be found in the example words on the first page of this lesson. Your challenge is to decide which word the author used. This is not a test; it is more like a guessing game, because more than one word choice may work perfectly well.

1.   **From Charles Dickens's** *A Tale of Two Cities*

        [He succeeded] in spite of his utmost _____ and treachery.
        a. infraction
        b. *esprit de corps*
        c. tergiversation
        d. idiosyncrasy

2.   **From Henry James's** *The American*

        He was gazing away, absently, at some _____ image of his implacability.
        a. tenacious
        b. metaphysical
        c. indigenous
        d. sapient

3.   **From Geoffrey Chaucer's** *The Canterbury Tales* **(Written in 1385!)**

        A greet amender eek of _____ to him that taketh it in pacience.
        a. sapience
        b. platitude
        c. idiosyncrasy
        d. metaphysics

4.   **From Harper Lee's** *To Kill a Mockingbird*

        She would exercise her royal _____.
        a. prerogative
        b. interregnum
        c. platitude
        d. inquisition

5.   **From Herman Melville's** *Moby Dick*

        Strictly this word is not _____ to the whale's vocabulary.
        a. sapient
        b. indigenous
        c. tenacious
        d. idiosyncratic

Though it is good to have a rich vocabulary, it is not good to abuse that vocabulary by writing verbose, sesquipedalian sentences (such as this one). Those who overuse their vocabularies often do so at the expense both of clarity and of others' patience. Translate the following ostentatious, ponderous passage into graceful, direct English.

IN THE TENEBROUS AND VIOLENT INTERREGNUM that followed the *coup d'état*, the deposed King—deprived of all royal prerogatives—slowly transmogrified from the sapient and incisive leader he had been into a demented patriarch uttering platitudes and manifesting idiosyncrasies. Lugubriously perambulating through the mist, he picked pink-purple nosegays of indigenous heather and in soliloquy decried the tergiversators and apostates whose infractions of royal interdictions and whose lack of *esprit de corps* had brought his lovely kingdom to such a pass. Aiming his inquisitions at the gray-faced fogs, he tenaciously repeated his metaphysical question: "Does Heaven protect the sanity of old men, or is my fate the ineluctable denouement of material nature?"

Suddenly, up from the damp heather popped the King's obsequious toady. "Oh Nuncle, Nuncle," the toady explained, "I have searched everywhere for you, and here you are, lost in the fog, collecting your wits."

"Wits?" replied the doddering King, "I am gathering poems, which I find concealed in the flowers of the heather. See, here is a poem now." He reached his hand out to a teratological anomaly of a plant with long, sharp thorns and flowers as translucent as glass. Picking a flower, he added it to his nosegay. "Take this anthology," said the King, handing the nosegay to the toady, "and read it."

"Oh Nuncle, Nuncle," replied the incredulous toady, "thou hast plucked the sacrosanct flower of thine own mind and given it to a fool."

Slowly, the two figures wandered into the melancholy mist, which closed softly around them.

apostate

Reading Comprehension

1. In Translation 58, the toady's attitude is best described as:
    A. acerbic
    B. nonplussed
    C. supercilious
    D. compassionate

2. With which statement would the author likely agree:
    A. The vicissitudes of fate strike everyone equally.
    B. Metaphysical questions are unanswerable.
    C. The value of a friend is not measured by social status.
    D. There is a thin line between sapience and dementia.

Analogies

3. ANTHOLOGY : SELECTION ::
    A. poem : story
    B. book : literature
    C. nosegay : flower
    D. editor : author

4. INDIGENOUS : AUTOCHTHONOUS ::
    A. sapient : perspicacious
    B. tenacious : tenuous
    C. *esprit de corps* : hebetude
    D. metaphysics : metamorphosis

Antonyms

5. SAPIENT :
    A. platitudinous
    B. vacuous
    C. demented
    D. insipid

anthology

6. METAPHYSICS :
    A. physics
    B. mythology
    C. poetry
    D. magic
    E. fiction
    F. non-fiction
    G. astrology
    H. faith
    I. perplexity
    This question is open-ended!

synthesis

In List 58 there are nine nouns and four adjectives. Which adjective/noun pairs work? Could, for example, there be a **sapient platitude**? Or would that be a logical contradiction, a paradox, or an oxymoron? [An oxymoron is a figure of speech that is self-contradictory, as in the 'cruel kindness' of Hamlet, who must be cruel, only to be kind. The oxymoron is a kind of witticism that makes its point (oxy) thorough seeming foolishness (moron)]. See which adjective/noun pairs can be effectively connected and which can not. For an interesting task of **analysis**, you could take the thirty-six pairs that result, and sort them into the categories that seem to exist. You will have to decide how many categories of pairs you have and to give them names.

emotion

If any emotion could be said to be primary, perhaps it would be care. It is the feeling of care that underlies our most positive acts, whether they are personal or interpersonal. It is the feeling of care that is the profound foundation of all learning and teaching. In Robert Ruark's book, *The Old Man and the Boy*, Ruark describes his boyhood relationship with his **sapient** grandfather, the Old Man, who taught him to hunt and fish, to clean his boat before leaving it, to avoid shooting more than a small fraction of any quail covey, to leave a campsite looking clean and wild as though no one had ever been there, to value conservation, and many other things. The Old Man was as likely to discuss Shakespeare or ancient history as to discuss duck hunting, and the fundamental message communicated was not one of outdoor life but one of care for life itself, of willingness to expend effort on the details that make experiences excellent and worthwhile, and of the deep personal regard that the Old Man had for the boy and that gave the boy a sense of worth.

Who have you known that manifested this humane **sapience** and who cared about you enough to teach you things that are important to know? Think about a sapient person in your life, and write a short description of this person and his or her sapience.

convergence

Considering the sound, meaning, and stem sense that each word contains, which word on List 58 do you like best?

analysis

Pick four words from List 58, and break them down into their stem components, explaining in each case why the word means what it means, based on the stems it contains.

Neologist's Lexicon

Use the stems in this list to create a new word (neologism). Give the word, the pronunciation, the part of speech, the etymology, and the definition(s). Keep a record of the neologisms you create from list to list. Here are some examples:

metaquisical (meh tah kwizz' ih kal) adj. [meta (beyond), quis (ask)]   1. wanting to know more about everything, regardless of how much one already knows   2. the compulsively reiterated response of "Why?" to every declarative sentence

menttenacity (men ten a city) n. [ment (mind), ten (hold)]   1. absolute and undistractable concentration of mind   2. the philosophical belief that being in perspicacious control of one's intellectual faculties is of paramount importance

Sesquipedalian Mythology

Use words from List 58 and previous lists to paraphrase the story of one of the great Greek or Roman myths, such as those in Ovid's *Metamorphoses* or Edith Hamilton's *Mythology*. For example, Ovid tells the story of the god Apollo and the demigod Daphne, daughter of the river god Peneus:

One day Apollo, anthropomorphic Lord of Delphi, sage of metaphysics, was walking in the woods where he suddenly came upon the beautiful and ingenuous Daphne, perambulating in idiosyncratic happiness in the forest among the indigenous plants and sentient forest creatures. In the presence of such beauty, Apollo lost all sapience and, effusively uttering amorous platitudes, ran without temporizing toward Daphne, who fled in fear. "Do not run," exhorted Apollo, whose shadow fell on the swift Daphne's shoulder, "I mean you no infraction. I am the Lord of Delphi, a nonpareil." But Daphne ran on, as though fleeing a teratological anomaly. "I know that the immortals of Olympus have a confident *esprit de corps*," Daphne expostulated as she fled, "but to love any mortal you choose is not one of your divine prerogatives. To me you are a narcissistic nonentity." But the gregarious and incredulous Apollo was incorrigible.

At last the race was ending, for the diffident Daphne could not outrun the swift god, ineluctable. His shadow fell on her hair, and his breath was on her shoulder, and he reached out for her, thinking to hold on tenaciously and not let her go. But the forest cleared in front of them as they fled, and Daphne suddenly saw her father's river, and she cried out to Peneus to intervene. He was no tergiversator. From his tenebrous current, he flung his spell down the forest path, and even as Daphne spoke, her toes grew long and plunged into the soft forest earth. From her fingers and hair came an effusion of limbs and green leaves, and bark shot up from her feet, covering her body. She had metamorphosed into a laurel tree. At last, too late, Apollo caught her, just in time to discern a heart beating beneath the bark. His perspicuous prognosis was that the syndrome was irreversible. Apollo glanced fiercely at the river, but Peneus was submerged, unavailable for inquisition, and the translucent river ran euphonic beneath the trees.

With fulgurating eyes, the sad and sedate Apollo spoke a panegyric for Daphne. "*Mea culpa, mea culpa*," he said in valediction. "If I had shown more solicitude, this transmogrification would not have happened. From today, the laurel tree shall be my tree, and your shining leaves shall be joined with my name and crown the heads of winners."

• **dur**	(hard)	obdurate	• pugn	(fight)	oppugn
• **dol**	(grief)	dolorous	• **tens**	(stretch)	ostensible
• **de**	(god)	deify	• ob	(toward)	ostensible
• fy	(make)	deify	• oss	(bone)	ossify
• quis	(ask, search)	exquisite	• *ostra*	(shell)	ostracism
• vita	(life)	viable	• lent	(full of)	opulent
• vid	(look)	invidious	• *geron*	(old man)	gerontocracy
• omni	(all)	omnifarious			

obdurate (hardhearted) His stubbornly obdurate bigotry infuriated her sense of justice.

exquisite (of rare quality) The exquisite designs gave her exquisite pangs of memory.

dolorous (full of grief) We heard the pathetic widower's dolorous cries all through the night.

deify (make into a god) The Martians had deified the dunespider, and built temples to it.

oppugn (argue against) It is risky for a politician to oppugn the popular viewpoint.

innocuous (not harmful) Her diplomatic comments were innocuous enough.

ostensible (apparent)   The ostensible reason for his sudden levity seemed insufficient.

ossify (turn to bone) The "boneheads'" minds were rigid and ossified.

ostracize (totally reject) He was ostracized by those who resented his outspoken viewpoint.

opulent (rich) The opulent antique furnishings of the mansion intrigued the historian.

• • •

invidious (causing envy) The invidious compliment made the friend jealous.

gerontocracy (government of the old) The Soviet gerontocracy needed new faces.

viable (able to live) The fetus was not mature enough to be viable on its own.

kleptomaniac (pathological thief) The manager arrested the kleptomaniac with the big coat.

omnifarious (of all kinds) His omnifarious exploits were in all the papers.

As Used by Kenneth Grahame in *The Wind in the Willows*

	"No	bread!"	groaned	the	Mole	**dolorously.**
Parts of Speech:	adj.	n.	v.	adj.	n.	**adv.**
Parts of Sentence:		direct object	AVP		subject	
Phrases:	--no prepositional, appositive, or verbal phrase--					
Clauses:	-------------------------------independent clause---------------------------- one independent clause, a simple declarative sentence					

Here Grahame uses the adverb *dolorously* to modify the action verb *groaned*. Note that the usual order of terms is reversed: D.O.- AVP-SUBJ.

Pronunciation

obdurate	OB dur at	**ostracize**	OSS tra size
exquisite	EX kwiz it	**opulent**	OP yoo lent
dolorous	DOLE or us	**invidious**	in VID ee us
deify	DEE ih fy	**gerontocracy**	jer on TOCK ra see
oppugn	o PYOON	**viable**	VI a bel
innocuous	in NOCK yoo us	**kleptomaniac**	KLEP to MAY nee ack
ostensible	os TEN si bel	**omnifarious**	OM ni FAIR ee us
ossify	OSS if fy		

Spanish Cognates

exquisite	exquisito	**dolorous**	doloroso
deification	deificación	**innocuous**	innocuo
ostensible	ostensible	**ossification**	osificación
ostracism	ostracismo	**opulent**	opulento
viable	viable	**kleptomaniac**	cleptómano

1. The adjective **obdurate** is a relative of **durable**, **indurate**, and **endure**. It is composed of the Latin *ob* (against) and *dur* (hard). The obdurate person is stony and unmoved, hardened against persuasion or feeling. In Crane's brilliant *The Red Badge of Courage*, a grim and obdurate group of soldiers makes no movement, and Cooper's Hawkeye is obdurate as he exclaims, "Not a karnel!"

2. The adjective **dolorous** means full of grief, such as the complete disappointment felt by Kenneth Grahame's Mole in his 1908 classic, *The Wind in the Willows*: "'No bread!' groaned the Mole dolorously." Grahame's riverside creatures are sensible animals (except for Toad, who is not sensible at all), and fully appreciate the importance of a tasty meal.

3. To **deify** is to make (fy) into a god (de). Melville, in *Moby Dick*, reports that the Egyptians "deified the crocodile of the Nile, because the crocodile is tongueless." He adds that if the great Sperm Whale had been known to the Orient World, it would have been deified, too.

4. The adjective **innocuous** comes from the Latin *innocuus* and means harmless, not offensive, or even insipid. In Jack London's *The Call of the Wild*, Hal swears innocuously. In Kipling's *Kim*, the explosion of dynamite is said to be milky and innocuous when compared to the report of the C. 25. And in Sylvia Plath's *The Bell Jar*, Sylvia's autobiographical alter ego, Esther Greenwood, says that the "only other address I had was the innocuous box number which people used who didn't want to advertise the fact they lived in an asylum."

5. The adjective **ostensible** means apparent, displayed, or even pretended. The idea is that in displaying something to someone, you stretch (tens) your arms out toward (ob) the person as you offer what you are displaying for him or her to see. Notice that in this word we encounter a new meaning of *ob*, which often means against, but in this word really means toward. Kipling refers to natives whose ostensible business was the repair of broken necklaces. Hardy refers to a person who is ostensibly frank as to his purpose while really concealing it. Melville mentions the ostensible reason why Ahab did not go on board the whaler. Dickens mentions a man's ostensible calling. And so we see that sometimes the ostensible truth is the truth, but sometimes the ostensible truth is not the truth.

6. A **Classic Word**: The adjective **opulent** means rich, full of (lent) wealth (opes) and comes from the Latin *opulentus*, wealthy. It can also refer to richness as abundance, as in the opulent refulgence of the sun. This word has a distinguished history in English letters. Shakespeare used it in Lear's fatal question to his lovely and loyal daughter, Cordelia. Intending to divide his kingdom into three parts among his three daughters, Lear asked each daughter to profess her love for him, that he might divide his kingdom according to the degree he was loved. "What can you say," Lear asked Cordelia, "to draw a third more opulent than your sisters?" Cordelia's unforgettable answer: "Nothing."

7. A **Micropoem**: In the verb **ostracize**, we can see the ancient Greeks casting the shells (*óstreion*) in a vote to banish some undesirable person from a glittering Greek island.

exquisite

The adjective **exquisite** can be elusive. It is one of those words that is frequently encountered and yet that has a subtle series of meanings that defy simple articulation. We say that **exquisite** means elaborate, or lovely, or keen. We say that something is exquisite if it is rare or appealing, excellent, refined, or elegant. We use it to describe something carefully made, or to describe something that shows a sensitive touch, as music. We use **exquisite** to describe weather, charm, a face, pleasure or even pain, workmanship, taste—it seems to have no limit in its application. Only when we look at the etymology of the word do we begin to understand: **exquisite** comes from the stems *ex* (out) and *quis* (search). It comes from the Latin word *exquisitus*, sought after. Something is exquisite if it is sought out, prized, searched for, the object of a quest.

Writers from Shakespeare to Cooper to Hawthorne to Barrie to Wilder have used **exquisite** to describe phenomena that are prized. Cooper described a character's exquisitely molded head, exquisite simplicity, an exquisite countenance, and the exquisite proportions of a character's person. Hawthorne noted exquisite suffering and exquisite pain. Stowe referred to exquisite paintings of children and exquisite delight. In Stevenson's *Dr. Jekyll and Mr. Hyde*, we find the chilling sentence: "My blood was changed into something exquisitely thin and icy." Crane refers to an exquisite drowsiness that spreads through Henry Fleming. In *The Time Machine*, Wells describes the Eloi as exquisite creatures. Conrad notes exquisite sensibilities and uses the phrase several times. Jack London describes exquisite agony and the exquisite pitch to which every fiber of Buck's body was keyed. In *Peter Pan* Barrie presents "a girl called Tinker Bell exquisitely gowned in a skeleton leaf," and notes exquisite tortures to take place at the break of day. In Wharton's *Ethan Frome* Ethan and Mattie are drawn together by "other sensations, less definable but more exquisite, which drew them together with a shock of silent joy."

One author who loved **exquisite** was Thornton Wilder. In *The Bridge of San Luis Rey*, Wilder uses the adjective over and over. Wilder notes that an exquisite daughter was born, refers to the exquisite sensibility of some letters, and says: "It is true that the Limeans were given to interpolating trivial songs into the most exquisite comedies." A lovely insight into the charming power of Spanish is provided by Wilder's sentence: "But what divine Spanish he speaks and what exquisite things he says in it!"

But wait. We said that **exquisite** means sought after and then talked about exquisite pain, exquisite agony, exquisite torture. What? Well, the idea of being sought after is the concept from which we begin, but the idea leads immediately to the idea of something being rare. We seek after what is rare. In describing pain or agony, the adjective has taken on a new dimension. It now does not indicate desirability; it indicates that the suffering is of a rare purity and intensity, one rarely found.

In each case below, one of the choices was really the word used by the author in the sentence provided. All of the choices can be found in the example words on the first page of this lesson. Your challenge is to decide which word the author used. This is not a test; it is more like a game, because more than one word choice may work perfectly well.

1.   **From George Orwell's** *1984*

All past oligarchies have fallen from power either because they _____ or because they grew soft.
a. ossified
b. ostracized
c. deified
d. oppugned

2.   **From Eudora Welty's** *One Writer's Beginnings*

An _____ of story books covered my bed.
a. gerontocracy
b. obdurate
c. ostracize
d. opulence

3.   **From Frederick Douglass's** *Narrative*

He was artful, cruel, and _____.
a. obdurate
b. ostensible
c. ostracized
d. dolorous

4.   **From Joseph Heller's** *Catch-22*

Doc Daneeka roosted _____ like a shivering turkey buzzard beside the closed door.
a. opulently
b. innocuously
c. dolorously
d. exquisitely

5.   **From Maya Angelou's** *I Know Why the Caged Bird Sings*

[They were] snubbed by their friends and _____ from every society.
a. ossified
b. oppugned
c. ostracized
d. deified

Though it is good to have a rich vocabulary, it is not good to abuse that vocabulary by writing verbose, sesquipedalian sentences (such as this one). Those who overuse their vocabularies often do so at the expense both of clarity and of others' patience. Translate the following ostentatious, ponderous passage into graceful, direct English.

FAR, FAR AWAY IN THE TENEBROUS VACUUM OF SPACE, in a seldom visited corner of the cosmos, was the littlest galaxy, NGC2BR2B. It was far smaller than all of the other galaxies; the big galaxies all had omnifarious millions or even opulent billions of stars, but the little one had only eighteen stars. It had five red giant stars, two fulgurating yellow stars, six hot blue stars, and five new stars that were sparkly white. Once, the littlest galaxy had swirled in a great cluster, joining the symphonic euphony of the galaxies in their radiant festival.

But the obdurate big galaxies, those execrating megalomaniacs, had ostracized NGC2BR2B from their gerontocracy of ancient galaxies, the hierarchy of the superannuated Old Ones, and had chosen every ostensible infraction to superciliously criticize it, to oppugn its best ideas, and to turn its every innocuous effort into an exquisitely dolorous experience. "You are not a true galaxy," they said. "A galaxy of only eighteen stars is not viable," they said. "You are a kleptomaniac," they said, "for you must have stolen your stars from one of us." And every effort that NGC2BR2B made to mollify the other galaxies was rebuffed with acerbic maledictions and obloquy. The ingenuous NGC2BR2B could not dissemble; it whirled softly away and gradually passed out of sight into the cosmic distance.

And then, a miracle. The eighteen stars of NGC2BR2B began to whirl introspectively and spin around. Faster and faster they raced, until BOOM, they collapsed together with a *fortissimo* implosion, transmogrifying into a black hole! And soon this black hole began to attract every solitary star that perambulated by, and every dark cloud of nebulous matter, every congeries of lost asteroids, and every unattached molecule that had no good place to be. And in no time at all, mere millions of years, NGC2BR2B became a great galaxy of 300 billion stars, the recipient of the glittering remnants of the cosmos, the tired and poor and huddled stars, yearning to join gregariously with others in a *sui generis* symphony of gravitational interaction.

And on starwheel galaxies throughout the cosmos, astronomers and cosmologists peered assiduously through huge lenses at the effulgent new galaxy, watched it whirl and spiral, lionized it, and wondered where it had come from. But only NGC2BR2B, deep in the center of its strong black hole, was cognizant how a great galactic system had been made from such a small precursor.

Reading Comprehension

1. For Translation 59, which of the following does the passage suggest:
   A. Black holes are the source of all galactic structures.
   B. The universe is stable, in a condition of unchanging stasis.
   C. The powerful overpower the powerless.
   D. Condescension and ostracism are illogical and immoral.

2. Which of the following is the best title for Translation 59:
   A. The Littlest Galaxy's Bright Idea
   B. Galaxy Wars in the Whirling Universe
   C. The Loneliness of the Long Distance Galaxy
   D. A Neoeffulgence in the O'erhanging Firmament

Analogies

3. **INNOCUOUS : INVIDIOUS ::**
   A. harmful : harmless
   B. harmless : harmful
   C. dolorous : viable
   D. opulent : exquisite

4. **OPPUGN : OSTRACIZE ::**
   A. obdurate : stony
   B. kleptomaniac : megalomaniac
   C. A : not A
   D. various : omnifarious

Antonyms

ostracize

5. **OPULENT :**
   A. gaudy
   B. impecunious
   C. stoic
   D. exquisite

6. **OBDURATE :**
   A. dolorous
   B. callous
   C. durable
   D. compassionate

evaluation

Which is more **innocuous**: to be **obdurate** or to be **invidious**? Explain the criteria by which you make this evaluation. Notice that in this case you are really trying to determine the least harmful of two harmfuls. I know, *harmfuls* is not a noun, or even a word. I used an adjective as though it were a noun, and even committed the **egregious** error of making it pseudoplural by adding an *s*. Ah, the perils of the ineffable.

analysis

Explain why the noun **kleptomaniac** means what it means, based on its etymology or stem construction. Similarly, explain the meaning of **oppugn** and of **gerontocracy**. You may use a dictionary for extra information.

synthesis

For any one of the words in List 59, connect the word to various works of literature or historical events with which you are familiar. For example, the word **obdurate** reminds me of Iago in Shakespeare's *Othello*, of Lady Macbeth in *Macbeth*, of Goneril and Regan in *King Lear*, and of historical events such as the Inquisition, the holocaust, Ghengis Khan's total destruction of villages that resisted his advance, Rome's final annihilation of Carthage, the destruction of autochthonous tribes and their environment in the rain forest, and American slavery. Pick one of the words and see how many synthetic connections you can make.

application

For three of the words in List 59, write both a literal sentence and a metaphorical sentence. For example, the word **ossify** means to turn to bone. We could therefore use the word either in a literal sense, describing a physical process such as the ossification of the skeletal structure that takes place as a child matures, or we could describe the hardening of attitudes that characterizes those whose minds are no longer flexible:

> **Literal:**   The injury would not have resulted in a broken bone in a younger person, whose bones had not **ossified** and become less flexible.

> **Metaphorical:**   In Paris, the crowd's feelings had **ossified** into an obdurate pitilessness, and it cheered as the hunchback shook his fist in rage and terror from the top of the cathedral.

imagination

Your ship slowly descends into the atmosphere of a newly discovered planet, Omnifaria. It is characterized by **omnifarious** forms of life, millions of species never before seen by *Homo sapiens sapiens*. Imagine what you see as you explore Omnifaria. Now imagine the emotions that Marco Polo must have felt as he explored the Orient, or the excitement that Christopher Columbus must have felt as he approached the New World.

Neologist's Lexicon

Use the stems in this list to create a new word (neologism). Give the word, the pronunciation, the part of speech, the etymology, and the definition(s). Keep a record of the neologisms you create from list to list. Here is an example:

ostralence (oss' trah lent) n. [ostra (shell), lent (full of)] 1. chronic shyness, characterized by retreating mollusk-like into one's shell 2. chronic timid reluctance to interact with others

Sesquipedalian Hamlet, or Something

One form of creative writing you might enjoy is to combine completely dissimilar things. For example, Shakespeare's *Hamlet* has been one of the crown jewels of English theater for centuries, with many actors playing the title role. Each actor has brought a unique perspective to the part. What if we were to imagine Hamlet being acted by someone who has never done so, and what if that actor was another fictional character, such as Long John Silver, or Dracula, or Tweety Bird? If Tweety Bird played the part of Hamlet, the result might be something like this:

Good Night, Tweet Prince, or
I Tought I Taw a Ghostwy Puddytat!
Enter Tweety (I mean, Hamlet) and Horatio.

"To bewieve a ghostwy puddytat, or not to bewieve a ghostwy puddytat,"
That is the question. (I DID! I DID bewieve the incorporeal admonitory puddytat!)
Whether 'tis more innocuous in the mind
To suffer the omnifarious arrows of egregious fortune,
Or to oppugn a sea of somnambulating puddytats, and by opposing, end them.
For who would bear the obdurate execrations of puddytats,
The ostracisms of puddytats, the exquisite pains inflicted by puddytats,
The invidious condescensions of opulent puddytats,
The public deifications of cartoon puddytats, the regicides of pusiwanimous puddytats,
When he could his quietus make, with a bare bodkin? To die, to sleep, to dream, but
O, Horatio, I could be immured in a nutshell and count myself a king of infinite space,
Were it not that I dream of regicidal puddytats!
But soft, what puddytat skull from yonder grave outsticks?
It IS, it IS a puddytat skull!
Alas, it is the skull of York, the King's truculent jester.
Alas, poor York. I knew him, I knew York, knew York, knew York, Horatio.
A kleptomaniac puddytat of infinite jest.
He hath belligerently chased me from my cage a thousand times.
Where be your teeth now? Your refractory mewlings? All quite ossified. Quite feckless.
Here hung those fangs that bit I know not how oft, and now how innocuous they are.
Now get you to my ladies chamber, and drink milk an inch thick, poor York.
Alas, there's more to heaven and earth, Horatio, than puddytats,
If eschatology could find it out.

• **plic**	(fold)	explicit		• tang	(touch)	noli me tangere
• non	(not)	persona non grata		• ped	(foot)	pied-a-terre
• terr	(land)	pied-a-terre		• carn	(flesh)	incarnadine
• lent	(full of)	somnolent		• somn	(sleep)	somnolent
• pro	(for)	prorogue		• rogat	(ask)	prorogue
• **cliv**	(slope)	proclivity		• vid	(look)	improvident
• fic	(make)	prolific		• *gen*	(origin)	disingenuous

persona non grata (unwelcome person) She is *persona non grata* in Japan.

pied-a-terre (part-time dwelling) They have a charming *pied-a-terre* at the shore.

explicit (openly stated) The agreement was explicit, not merely implicit.

noli-me-tangere (touch me not) We saw the *noli-me-tangere* in his anxious eyes.

incarnadine (flesh-colored) Could blood turn the multitudinous seas incarnadine?

insouciant (not bothered, carefree) Her insouciant vivacity charmed us.

sub rosa (secretly) The conspirators operated *sub rosa*, unknown to the government.

prorogue (end a session) The long session of Parliament was finally prorogued.

somnolent (sleepy) The quiet town had shady trees and somnolent dogs.

proclivity (discreditable tendency) He slid down into his unfortunate proclivity for gambling.

• • •

improvident (without foresight) The improvident spendthrift went broke in two years.

prolific (productive) The prolific writer produced two novels each year.

disingenuous (lacking frankness) The disingenuous story convinced no one.

hagiocracy (government of saints) The conservative Iranian hagiocracy ruled stringently.

inexorable (inescapable) She could not escape her inexorable fate.

As Used by James Hilton in *Lost Horizon*

	We	have	no	rigidities,	no	**inexorable**	rules.
Parts of Speech:	pron.	v.	adj.	n.	adj.	**adj.**	n.
Parts of Sentence:	subject	AVP		direct object			direct object

Phrases: --no prepositional, appositive, or verbal phrase--

Clauses: -----------------------------------independent clause---------------------------------
one independent clause, a simple declarative sentence

Here Hilton uses the adjective *inexorable* to modify the plural noun *rules*, which is the second term in a compound direct object.

Pronunciation

persona non grata	per SO na non GRA ta	**somnolent**	SOM no lent
pied-a-terre	pee AY da TAIR	**proclivity**	pro KLIV ih tee
explicit	ex PLISS it	**improvident**	im PROV ih dent
noli-me-tangere	NO lee me tan JER ay	**prolific**	pro LIF ik
incarnadine	in KARN a dine	**disingenuous**	dis in JEN yoo us
insouciant	in SOO shant	**hagiocracy**	hay jee OCK ra see
sub rosa	sub RO sa	**inexorable**	in EX or ah bel
prorogue	pro ROG		

Spanish Cognates

explicit	explícito	**incarnadine**	encarnado
somnolent	soñoliento	**proclivity**	proclividad
improvident	impróvido	**prolific**	prolífico
inexorable	inexorable		

1. The phrase **persona non grata** is Latin for unwelcome person and is used especially in diplomatic speech to describe a diplomatic representative who is unacceptable to the government to which he or she is assigned.

2. In ancient times the rose was used as a symbol of secrecy, of sworn confidence, at meetings. Participants at these secret meetings held under the rose were expected to keep these **sub rosa** communications private and confidential.

3. A **Micropoem**: The noun **proclivity** refers to a discreditable tendency or inclination, such as gambling. Oscar Wilde's character Dorian Gray succumbed to his proclivities. But the word comes from the Latin *proclivitas*, a steep descent, a forward (pro) slope (cliv)! In order to indulge in one of your proclivities, you must descend the steep forward slope.

4. A **Classic Word**: The adjective **inexorable** comes from the Latin *inexorabilis*, and means inescapable, unrelenting, merciless. If something is inexorable, you can not (in) get out (ex) of it. There is no exit. Shakespeare, Cooper, Charlotte Brontë, Harriet Beecher Stowe, Herman Melville, Charles Dickens, Thomas Hardy, Jack London, and Edith Wharton all used **inexorable** to describe such inescapable things as disease (Stowe), truth (Wharton), a murderer (Cooper), and the soul (Brontë). In Cooper's *The Last of the Mohicans*, a victim "looks steadily on the keen glittering knife that was already upheld by his inexorable judge." Jack London described the lightning of an overburdened sled: "And so it went, the inexorable elimination of the superfluous." Perhaps the most poignant use of **inexorable** is from Shakespeare's 1596 tragedy, *Romeo and Juliet*. In Act V, Scene 3, Romeo and Balthazar enter the tomb where Juliet lies, and Romeo, knowing he is going to kill himself, sends Balthazar away:

> Therefore hence, be gone.
> But if thou jealous dost return to pry
> In what I farther shall intend to do,
> By Heaven I will tear thee joint by joint
> And strew this hungry churchyard with thy limbs.
> The time and my intents are savage-wild,
> More fierce and more inexorable far
> Than empty tigers or the roaring sea.

Notice that Shakespeare's lines are poetry, written in iambic pentameter:

> But IF thou JEA lous DOST reTURN to PRY
> In WHAT I FAR ther SHALL inTEND to DO
> By HEA ven I will TEAR thee JOINT by JOINT
> And STREW this HUN gry CHURCH yard WITH thy LIMBS
> The TIME and MY inTENTS are SAV age-WILD
> More FIERCE and MORE inEX orAB le FAR
> Than EMP ty TIG ers OR the ROAR ing SEA.

In each case below, one of the choices was really the word used by the author in the sentence provided. All of the choices can be found in the example words on the first page of this lesson. Your challenge is to decide which word the author used. This is not a test; it is more like a game, because more than one word choice may work perfectly well.

1. **From Upton Sinclair's** *The Jungle*

   He smiled...and then started talking again, with his blissful _____.
   a. somnolence
   b. proclivity
   c. improvidence
   d. insouciance

2. **From Kenneth Grahame's** *The Wind in the Willows*

   ...when you live a life of intense activity for six months a year, and of comparative or actual _____ for the other six...
   a. improvidence
   b. insouciance
   c. somnolence
   d. hagiocracy

3. **From Herman Melville's** *Billy Budd*

   [He was] a sailor of distinction even in a time _____ of renowned seamen.
   a. prolific
   b. improvident
   c. explicit
   d. inexorable

4. **From Marjorie Kinnan Rawlings's** *The Yearling*

   In a straight line... the track of Old Slewfoot stretched _____.
   a. prolifically
   b. inexorably
   c. improvidently
   d. somnolently

5. **From Jane Austen's** *Emma*

   _____ and double dealing seemed to meet him at every turn.
   a. insouciance
   b. improvidence
   c. disingenuousness
   d. somnolence

Though it is good to have a rich vocabulary, it is not good to abuse that vocabulary by writing verbose, sesquipedalian sentences (such as this one). Those who overuse their vocabularies often do so at the expense both of clarity and of others' patience. Translate the following ostentatious, ponderous passage into graceful, direct English.

THE DAYS OF INSOUCIANT, SOMNOLENT, AND IMPROVIDENT HAPPINESS at her sunny *pied-a-terre* on the Riviera were over. Her prolific work for the State Department, at least on this assignment, was over. She had been pronounced *persona non grata* by the host government who disingenuously accused her of proclivities to espionage, and her diplomatic duties were abruptly terminated. Why?

And then she had received the cryptic telephone call: "The grotto, sunset," the voice had said. But now as she descended the cool steps into the grotto, she sensed that there was more to this meeting than had been made explicit. Ahead, glowing from the tenebrous shadows above the transom, she saw a candle-lit rose, incarnadine against the gray and black of the ancient stones, and with a chill she realized that she was entering into something beyond her understanding, some *sub rosa* secrecy, and she felt a sudden foreboding of inexorable fate bearing down upon her. Beside the rose, scrawled in red on a strip of white paper, she discerned the Latin words, *noli-me-tangere*, touch me not—the warning of the 13th century hagiocracy believed to have mysterious followers even today, followers believed dangerous to those they considered miscreants or apostates. To the diplomat's mind, the warning seemed to be an eerie anachronism.

And then, a sedate figure emerged from the shadows. Hooded, physiognomy concealed in darkness, it raised its hand in a sort of benediction and then gesticulated, as if beckoning her to follow him. Her sangfroid flagged, but she stepped forward with as much fortitude as she could summon.

Suddenly the hooded figure turned and faced her. She stopped. "We know who you are," he said, *sotto voce*. "We know that you are *persona non grata*. You are in danger. There is a schism in the Intelligence Division, and you are being linked to subversive activities. You are being watched by people with xenophobic and paranoid ideas. Their antipathy is inexorable. You must leave the country at once." He paused, and she could see the light of the candle behind her sparkling surrealistically in the hooded figure's eyes. "Leave the country at once," he reiterated in valediction, and then he was gone. There was something about his voice. . . . But it was too late to remonstrate, and she turned without temporizing, ascended the steps, and two hours later, with a suspiration of relief, she boarded a plane for Paris.

Reading Comprehension

1. In Translation 60, it can be inferred that:
    A. The hooded figure is a government employee.
    B. The hooded figure is lying to scare the diplomat out of the country.
    C. The diplomat is a spy.
    D. The diplomat would recognize the figure if she could see him.

2. The author does all of the following EXCEPT:
    A. suggest the identity of the hooded figure
    B. suggest that the diplomat is innocent of intrigue
    C. suggest that the diplomat is afraid
    D. suggest that the hooded figure wishes not to be identified

Analogies

3. **INCARNADINE : CARNATION ::**
    A. rose : thorn
    B. azure : blue
    C. green : grass
    D. blood : vein

4. **SUB ROSA : EXPLICIT ::**
    A. insouciant : somnolent
    B. prolific : hebetude
    C. cryptic : manifest
    D. arcane : overt

im*provid*ent

Antonyms

5. **IMPROVIDENT :**
    A. economical
    B. squandering
    C. dissipated
    D. proved

6. **PROROGUE :**
    A. *pro rata*
    B. prolific
    C. prologue
    D. prohibit

imagination and aesthetics

Imagine a scene in which you feel completely **insouciant**. It could be a happy time that you create in your own imagination, or it could be a memory of a day at the beach, or a hike on a mountain path, or a trip to a foreign city, or a happy time that you have spent with a friend or a pet. Any insouciant time will do. Imagine this insouciant time vividly and concretely. Try to see the colors, smell the smells, feel the breeze on your face, and so forth. Write a one-page description that captures this insouciant mood.

intuition and imagination

You walk out the front door of your **pied-a-terre** in Athens on an expedition to find and purchase something you have been thinking about for a long time. You have the money now, and as the breezy Mediterranean sun strikes your face, you detect the scent of olive oil in the air and **insouciantly** hurry off down the sidewalk to find the **exquisite** object you imagine. What is it that you are looking for?

convergence

Which two words in List 60 do you think are the most interesting? Why? Which two would you most like to use frequently in conversation? Why?

analysis

Using a dictionary, study the etymology of **improvident**, **prolific**, and **disingenuous**, and see if you can explain why each word means what it means.

ethics and evaluation

Think of a **disingenuous** literary character with whom you are familiar, such as Long John Silver in Robert Louis Stevenson's *Treasure Island*, or Iago in Shakespeare's *Othello*, or Captain Hook in Barrie's *Peter Pan*. Long John pretended to be Jim Hawkins's friend but was not. Iago pretended to be Othello's friend but actually schemed to destroy Othello and Desdemona. Captain Hook was a treacherous dissembler who had nothing but malevolent intentions toward Peter Pan, Wendy, and the boys. On the other hand, Hamlet is also disingenuous but is not a villain. Polonius's foolish words, "To thine own self be true, and it must follow as the night the day, thou canst not then be false to any man," do not apply to Hamlet, who is true to himself but false to others as he stealthily attempts to observe his murdering uncle. It would appear that Hamlet is disingenuous in the cause of righteousness. What do you think? Are there times when it is acceptable or moral to be disingenuous if the reasons have merit, or is it inherently wrong to be disingenuous, regardless of the cause? Explain your thinking about disingenuousness, including the criteria by which you come to a decision.

Neologist's Lexicon

Use the stems in this list to create a new word (neologism). Give the word, the pronunciation, the part of speech, the etymology, and the definition(s). Keep a record of the neologisms you create from list to list. Here are some examples:

carnorogation (karn oh row gay' shun) n. [carn (flesh), rogat (ask), tion (act)]   1. the cheeky habit of asking others how much they weigh 2. the obsessive need to read all of the dietary information on every item of packaged food in the supermarket before adding it to the shopping cart

vidotangence (vid' oh tanj ence) n. [vid (look), tang (touch)] 1. eye contact   2. the initial indication of romantic attraction, as seen in the eye

Sesquipedalian Mud Pies

It goes without saying that one of life's great pleasures is making mud pies. And sand castles, of course, but sand castles are disturbingly clean and have none of the complete relish of the correctly made mud pie, which results in the happiest sort of mess in which the discriminating playful person can find himself, or herself. The question is, can you write sesquipedalian instructions for the prolific production of exquisite mud pies and their subsequent use? See if you can write mud pie instructions, using words from List 60 and previous lists.

Sesquipedalian Fair

Another of life's great events is going to the fair. There are rides and games and haunted houses. There are snow cones, cotton candy, and hot dogs. There are the smells of sawdust and ponies and the mechanical smell of grease on the machinery. There are the sounds of the crowd and the music of the rides, and the calls of the employees drumming up business. Pick a scene or experience from the fair, and write a short sesquipedalian description of it, using words from as many lists as you can.